Words in the Mind

We thought a day and night of steady rain
was plenty, but it's falling again, downright tireless . . .
. . . Much like words
But words don't fall exactly; they hang in there
In the heaven of language, immune to gravity
If not to time, entering your mind
From no direction, travelling no distance at all,
And with rainy persistence tease from the spread earth
So many wonderful scents . . .

Robert Mezey, 'Words'

Words in the Mind

— An Introduction to the Mental Lexicon —

JEAN AITCHISON

Basil Blackwell

Copyright © Jean Aitchison 1987

First published 1987

Basil Blackwell Ltd
108 Cowley Road, Oxford, OX4 1JF, UK

Basil Blackwell Inc.
432 Park Avenue South, Suite 1503
New York, NY 10016, USA

British Library Cataloguing in Publication Data

Aitchison, Jean
 Words in the mind: an introduction to
 the mental lexicon.
 1. Psycholinguistics
 I. Title
 401'.9 BF455
 ISBN 0-631-14441-2
 ISBN 0-631-14442-0 Pbk

Library of Congress Cataloging in Publication Data

Aitchison, Jean, 1938–
 Words in the mind.
 Bibliography: p.
 Includes index.
 1. Lexicology. 2. Psycholinguistics. I. Title.
P326.A4 1987   401'.9   86–26443
ISBN 0-631-14441-2
ISBN 0-631-14442-0 (pbk.)

Typeset in 10 on 12 Ehrhardt
by Joshua Associates Limited, Oxford
Printed in Great Britain by
T.J. Press Ltd, Padstow

Contents

Preface

This book deals with words. It sets out to answer the questions: how do humans manage to store so many words, and how do they find the ones they want? In brief, it discusses the nature of the human word-store, or 'mental lexicon'.

This is a topic which has recently attracted the attention of a large number of researchers. Unfortunately, most of the work is tucked away in scholarly journals and conference proceedings. It is also excessively fragmented, since many of those working on the subject have concerned themselves only with a small section of it. This book is an attempt to make recent findings on the mental lexicon available to a wide range of people, and to provide a coherent overall picture of the way it might work. Hopefully, it will prove of interest to anyone concerned with words: students of linguistics and psychology, speech therapists, language teachers, educationalists, lexicographers, and the general reader who would just like to know how humans remember words and how children learn them. It could also be regarded as a general introduction to linguistics from a novel angle.

The book does not presuppose any previous knowledge of linguistics or psychology. It contains a minimum of jargon and all technical terms are fully explained. For those interested in pursuing any topic further, there are copious references and suggestions for further reading in the course of the text.

I am grateful to friends and colleagues who made helpful suggestions concerning the book. I would particularly like to thank John Ayto (freelance lexicographer) and Paul Meara (Birkbeck College, London) who read through the whole manuscript and made a number of useful comments. Valuable suggestions on various chunks of the book were made by Andy Ellis (Lancaster University), John Morton (MRC Cognitive Development Unit, London) and Hilary Wise (Queen Mary College, London). In addition, there were numerous people who helped me to track down references, made occasional useful suggestions, approved of sections of the text, or reported slips of the tongue which I included in the book: Christine Allen, Michael Banks, Edward Black, Sylvia Chalker, Raymond Chapman, Shula Chiat, Stefanie Cookson, Carla

Garapedian, Eugenie Henderson, Sara Lodge, Sara Rule, Elaine Simmonds are names which spring to mind – though I have probably forgotten to mention many more than I have included. My thanks – and apologies – to those I have inadvertently omitted.

In addition, I would like to thank numerous other colleagues and friends with whom over the past few years I have had stimulating discussions which have helped to clarify my thoughts on the topics in this book. The following, at least, deserve mention: Bernie Baars, Martyn Barrett, Maria Black, Cathy Browman, Keith Brown, Brian Butterworth, Anne Cutler, Irene Fairley, Harold Goodglass, David Green, Nigel Harvey, Norman Hotopf, Jim Hurford, John Lyons, William Marslen-Wilson, John McShane, Marlys Macken, Lise Menn, Howard Pollio, Marilyn Pollio, Steve Pulman, Janet Randall, Peter Reich, Anjani Kumar Sinha, Miron Straf, Lorraine Tyler, Marilyn May Vihmann. Once again, my thanks and apologies to those I have forgotten to mention.

Of course, the views expressed in this book are my own and do not necessarily reflect the opinions of those listed above, who sometimes helped me to formulate my ideas more precisely by disagreeing with me. And I alone am responsible for any errors which may remain.

Finally, a stylistic point. I have used two devices to combat the sexism which is widespread in the English language. In some places, I have used *she* as well as *he* when a neutral between-sexes pronoun is required. In other places, I have followed the increasingly common practice of using *they* and *their* as singular forms after a neutral noun.

Jean Aitchison

Acknowledgements

The author and publishers are grateful to the following for permission to reproduce extracts:

to Collins and The Sterling Lord Agency Inc. for lines from Norton Juster, *The Phantom Tollbooth* (London: Collins, 1962) copyright © 1961 by Norton Juster;

to Roald Dahl for lines from *My Uncle Oswald* (London: Michael Joseph Ltd and Penguin Books Ltd, 1979) copyright © 1979, 1980 by Roald Dahl, and reprinted by permission of Alfred A. Knopf, Inc.;

to André Deutsch and Little, Brown and Company for lines from Ogden Nash, 'Who Called that Pied-Billed Grebe a Podilymbus Podiceps Podiceps?' copyright © 1968 by Ogden Nash. First appeared in the *New Yorker*, and 'The Joyous Malingerer . . .' copyright © 1967 by Ogden Nash, in *There's Always Another Windmill* (London: André Deutsch, 1969); and for lines from Ogden Nash, '. . . Any Millenniums Today, Lady . . .?' copyright © 1948 by Ogden Nash. First appeared in the *New Yorker*, 'Are You a Snodgrass?' copyright © 1934 by Ogden Nash. First appeared in the *Saturday Evening Post*, 'Thunder over the Nursery . . .' copyright © 1936 by Ogden Nash, 'Away From It All' copyright © renewed 1975 by Frances Nash, Isobel Eberstadt Nash and Linnell Nash Smith, in *I Wouldn't Have Missed It* (London: André Deutsch, 1983);

to Faber and Faber Ltd and Grove Press Inc. for lines from Samuel Beckett, *All That Fall*, in *The Complete Dramatic Works* by Samuel Beckett (London: Faber, 1986);

to Faber and Faber Ltd and Harcourt Brace Jovanovich Inc. for lines from T. S. Eliot, 'Macavity the Mystery Cat', in *Old Possum's Book of Practical Cats* (London: Faber, 1939) copyright © 1939 by T. S. Eliot, renewed 1967 by Esme Valerie Eliot. Reprinted by permission of Harcourt Brace Jovanovich Inc., and for lines from 'Little Gidding' and 'Burnt Norton', from 'Four

Quartets', *The Collected Poems 1909–1962* by T. S. Eliot (London: Faber, 1969) copyright © 1943 by T. S. Eliot, renewed 1971 by Esme Valerie Eliot. Reprinted by permission of Harcourt Brace Jovanovich Inc.;

to Harmony Music Ltd and Sanga Music Inc. for lines from 'Words, Words, Words' by Pete Seeger. Copyright © 1967 Harmony Music Ltd, 19/20 Poland Street, London W1V 3DD. International copyright secured. All rights reserved. Used by permission. Copyright © 1967, 1968 by Sanga Music Inc. All rights reserved. Used by permission;

to Laurence Lerner and Secker and Warburg for lines from 'Meanings', in Laurence Lerner's *Rembrandt's Mirror* (London: Secker and Warburg, in press);

to Ira Levin for lines from *The Stepford Wives* (London: Michael Joseph Ltd, 1972);

to James MacGibbon for lines from Stevie Smith, 'In the Park', from *The Collected Poems of Stevie Smith* (London: Allen Lane, Penguin, 1975);

to Robert Mezey for lines from 'Words', in *The State of the Language* ed. Leonard Michaels and Christopher Ricks (Berkeley: University of California Press, 1980). The poem will also be appearing in *Evening Wind* (Wesleyan University Press, forthcoming);

to Spike Milligan for lines from 'The Bongaloo', in *Silly Verse for Kids* (London: Puffin Books, 1959);

to Pan Books and The Crown Publishing Group for lines from Douglas Adams, *So Long and Thanks for All the Fish* (London: Pan, 1982).

Part 1

Aims and Evidence

1

Welcome to Dictionopolis
— *The human word-store* —

Before long they saw in the distance the towers and flags of Dictionopolis sparkling in the sunshine, and in a few moments they reached the great wall and stood at the gateway to the city.

'A-H-H-H-R-R-E-M-M-', roared the sentry, clearing his throat and snapping smartly to attention. 'This is Dictionopolis, a happy kingdom, advantageously located in the Foothills of Confusion and caressed by gentle breezes from the Sea of Knowledge . . . Dictionopolis is the place where all the words in the world come from. They're grown right here in our orchards.'

Norton Juster, The Phantom Tollbooth

'Words glisten. Words irradiate exquisite splendour. Words carry magic and keep us spell-bound . . . Words are like glamorous bricks that constitute the fabric of any language . . . Words are like roses that make the environment fragrant', asserts the writer of a textbook urging people to improve their vocabulary (Chand, n.d.: 3–4).

Few people regard words with the awe and reverence of this author. Most of us use them all the time without thinking. Yet words are supremely important. Everyone needs them, and a normal person probably comes into contact with thousands in the course of a normal day. We would be quite lost without them: 'I wanted to utter a word, but that word I cannot remember; and the bodiless thought will now return to the palace of shadows', said the Russian poet Mandelstam (quoted by Vygotsky, 1934, in Saporta, 1961: 509).

The frustration of being without words is vividly expressed in Stevie Smith's poem 'In the Park':

'Pray for the Mute who have no word to say.'
Cried the one old gentleman, 'Not because they are dumb,
But they are weak. And the weak thoughts beating in the brain
Generate a sort of heat, yet cannot speak.

Thoughts that are bound without sound
In the tomb of the brain's room, wound. Pray for the Mute.'

On a less poetic level, someone who has had a stroke can illustrate clearly the handicap suffered by those who just cannot think of the words they want. For example, K.C., a highly intelligent solicitor, was quite unable to remember the name of a box of matches: 'Waitresses. Waitrixies. A backland and another bank. For bandicks er bandiks I think they are, I believe they're zandicks, I'm sorry, but they're called flitters landocks.' He had equal difficulty when shown a telephone: 'Ooh that, that sir. I can show you then what is a zapricks for the elencom, the elencom, with the pidland thing to the ... and then each of the pidlands has an eye in, one, two, three, and so on' (Butterworth, 1979).

Most people are convinced that they need to know a lot of words, and become worried if they cannot recall a word they want. Yet most of the time they will have relatively little difficulty in remembering the thousands of words needed for everyday conversation. This is a considerable feat.

However, speakers of a language are unlikely to have given much thought to this remarkable skill. Even those who deal with language professionally, such as speech therapists and teachers, know relatively little about how humans cope with all these words. Their lack of knowledge is not surprising since there is little information readily available about key issues, such as 'How are words stored in the mind?' 'How do people find the words they want when they speak?' 'Do children remember words in the same way as adults?', and so on.

This is the topic of this book. It will primarily consider how we store words in our mind, and how we retrieve them from this store when we need them. Our overall aim is to produce outline specifications, as it were, for a working model of the word-store in the human mind. This turns out to be a huge subject. In order to narrow it down somewhat, the book will focus on the spoken words of people whose native language is English. English has been selected because, up till now, more work has been done on it than on any other language. And spoken speech has been chosen because native speakers of English talk it before they learn to read or write it. Reading, writing and other languages will therefore be mentioned only intermittently, when work on them illuminates the topic under discussion. The decision to concentrate on spoken English means that bilingualism and multilingualism are not directly discussed – though hopefully the findings will shed light on how people cope with the vocabulary of more than one language.

Mazes intricate

Mazes intricate,
Eccentric, intervolved, yet regular
Then most, when most irregular they seem.

Milton's description of the planets in *Paradise Lost* (v, 622–4) could apply equally well to the human word-store. Planets might appear to the untrained observer to wander randomly round the night sky, yet in fact their movements are under the control of natural laws which are not obvious to the naked eye. Similarly, words are not just stacked higgledy-piggledy in our minds, like leaves on an autumn bonfire. Instead, they are organized into an intricate, interlocking system whose underlying principles can be discovered.

Words cannot be heaped up randomly in the mind for two reasons. First, there are so many of them. Second, they can be found so fast. Psychologists have shown that human memory is both flexible and extendable, provided that the information is structured (for useful summaries of work on memory see Baddeley, 1976, 1983; Gregg, 1986). Random facts and figures are extremely difficult to remember, but enormous quantities of data can be remembered and utilized, as long as they are well organized.

However, to say that humans know 'so many' words and find them 'so fast' is somewhat vague. What number are we talking about? And what speed are we referring to? Let us briefly consider these two points.

Native speakers of a language almost certainly know more words than they imagine. Educated adults generally estimate their own vocabulary at only one to ten per cent of the real level, it has been claimed (Seashore and Eckerson, 1940: 14). Most people behave somewhat like the rustics in Oliver Goldsmith's poem 'The Deserted Village'. The villagers gather round to listen in awe to their parson, whose verbal knowledge amazes them:

> Words of learned length and thund'ring sound
> Amazed the gazing rustics rang'd around,
> And still they gaz'd, and still the wonder grew,
> That one small head could carry all he knew.

While admiring the word power of their local clergyman, the rustics did not realize that the word-store within each person's head was probably almost as great as that of the parson. Even highly educated people can make ludicrously low guesses. In the middle of the last century Dean Farrar, a respected intellectual, pronounced on the vocabulary of some peasants after eavesdropping on them as they chatted: 'I once listened for a long time together to the conversation of three peasants who were gathering apples among the boughs of an orchard, and as far as I could conjecture, the whole number of words they used did not exceed a hundred' (Farrar, 1865: 59). They managed with this small number, he surmised, because 'the same word was made to serve a multitude of purposes, and the same coarse expletives recurred with a horrible frequency in the place of every single part of speech'.

More recently, the French writer Georges Simenon was reported as saying that he tried to make his style as simple as possible because he had read somewhere that over half the people in France used no more than a total of 600 words (Bresler, 1983). Simenon's figure is perhaps as much the product of wishful thinking as his claim to have slept with 10,000 women in his life. At the very least one should probably exchange the numbers of words and women, though 10,000 words is still likely to be an underestimate.

An educated adult might well know more than 150,000 words and be able to actively use 90 per cent of these, according to one calculation (Seashore and Eckerson, 1940). This figure is controversial, because of the problems of defining the notion 'word' and the difficulty of finding a reliable procedure for assessing vocabulary knowledge. However, Seashore and Eckerson's figure is still sometimes quoted, so it might be useful to consider how they reached their conclusions.

Seashore and Eckerson defined a 'word' as an item listed in the 1937 edition of Funk and Wagnall's *New Standard Dictionary of the English Language*, which contains approximately 450,000 entries. Of these, they reckoned that just under half, about 166,000, were 'basic words' such as *loyal*, and the remaining 204,000 or so were derivatives and compounds, such as *loyalism*, *loyalize*, *loyally* and *Loyal Legion*. Obviously it is impractical to test anyone on all the words in the dictionary, so a representative sample of the total needs to be obtained. The researchers did this by taking the third word down in the first column of every left-hand page. This gave a list of 1,320 words, which they divided into four. Several hundreds of college students were tested on their ability to define the words on each list and to use them in illustrative sentences.

Seashore and Eckerson found that their subjects were surprisingly knowledgeable. On average, the students knew 35 per cent of the common 'basic words' on the list, 1 per cent of the rare 'basic words' and 47 per cent of the derivatives and compounds. When these proportions were applied to the overall number of words in the whole dictionary, the average college student turned out to know approximately 58,000 common 'basic words', 1,700 rare 'basic words' and 96,000 derivatives and compounds. The overall total comes to over 150,000. The highest student score was almost 200,000, while even the lowest was over 100,000.

Later researchers have pointed out a number of flaws in Seashore and Eckerson's methodology. For example, the students might have been able to guess the meaning and use of derivatives from a knowledge of the 'basic words' to which they are related. There was no need to 'know' them in advance. And the unreliability of this type of study is shown by the 'big dictionary' effect: the bigger the dictionary used, the more words people are found to know. (For further problems see Diack, 1975; Anderson and Freebody, 1981.) But even if we assume that Seashore and Eckerson's claim that the average college student knows over 150,000 words is a threefold exaggeration, a knowledge of 50,000 words is still very considerable. Compare this with the vocabulary of any of the 'talking apes', animals who have been taught a language-like system in which signs stand for words. The chimps Washoe and Nim actively used around 200 signs after several years' training, while Koko the gorilla supposedly uses around 400 (Aitchison,

1983). None of these animals approaches the thousand mark, something which is normally achieved by children soon after the age of two.

Moreover, we should not automatically assume that Seashore and Eckerson's estimate is exaggerated. A similar test carried out by an applied linguist some 30 years later put the average total of words 'definitely known' by college students at just under 250,000, almost a hundred thousand more than Seashore and Eckerson's figure (Diller, 1978).

[The number of words known by an educated adult, then, is unlikely to be less than 50,000 and may be as high as 250,000. These high figures suggest that the mental lexicon is arranged on a systematic basis.]

The second reason why words are likely to be well organized in the mind is that they can be located so fast, literally in a split second. This is apparent above all from the speed of normal speech, in which six syllables a second, making three or more words, is fairly standard (Lenneberg, 1967). And experiments have confirmed this figure, showing that native speakers can recognize a word of their language in 200 ms (milliseconds) or less from its onset, that is, approximately one-fifth of a second from its beginning (Marslen-Wilson and Tyler, 1980, 1981). In many cases this is well before all the word has been heard. Indeed, the average duration of words used by Marslen-Wilson and Tyler in their experiments was around 375 ms – almost twice as long as the recognition time. One way in which the researchers demonstrated this was by pointing to the behaviour of subjects in a 'speech shadowing' task. Shadowing is a fairly common technique in psycholinguistic experiments, and is reminiscent of simultaneous interpretation. The experimenter asks the subjects to wear headphones into which a stream of speech is played. Subjects are then asked to repeat what they hear as they hear it. People who are good at shadowing can repeat back speech with a delay of little more than 250–275 ms – around one-quarter of a second. If we assume that 50–75 ms is taken up with the actual response, and deduct this from the overall time taken, then we get the figure of 200 ms (one-fifth of a second) quoted above. These good shadowers are not just parroting back what they hear. They are genuinely 'processing' the words since they correct mistakes, such as changing *tomorrance* to 'tomorrow'.

The detection of non-words provides further evidence of fast and efficient word-searching ability. Subjects are able to reject a sound sequence which is a non-word in around half a second. This has been shown by means of a lexical decision task, an experiment in which subjects are asked to decide whether a sequence of sounds is a word of the language or not (Marslen-Wilson and Tyler, 1980, 1981). Some of the sequences presented were real words, others non-words, such as *vleesidence*, *grankiment*, *swollite*. Subjects were asked to press a button as soon as they heard a non-word. They did this surprisingly fast, in just under half a second (450 ms) from the point at which the sound sequence diverged from being a possible real word. Once again, this suggests that speakers are able to conduct an orderly search through their mental word-store in a surprisingly short length of time.

Of course, the fact that speakers are usually able to distinguish fast between real words and non-words is something which we can also sometimes see happening for ourselves, as in the following extract from a short story, 'De Bilbow' by Brigid Brophy. Barney is questioned by his foreign girlfriend about the meaning of a word:

'There is an English word I am not knowing. I am not finding it in the dictionary . . . "Bilbow".'
'Bilbow?'
'Yes.'
'There's no such word. It's a surname, not an ordinary word.'
'Please? You are not knowing this English word?'
'I AM knowing', Barney said. 'I'm knowing damn well the word doesn't exist.'

Note that Barney responded without hesitation. This is quite a feat. Suppose he knew 60,000 words. If he had checked through these one by one at the rate of 100 per second, it would have taken him ten minutes to discover that *bilbow* didn't exist. The problem sequence *bilbow*, incidentally, came from Shakespeare's *Henry V* (III, iv), in a passage in which the French-speaking Katherine mispronounces the English word 'elbow'.

Native speakers, then, seem able to carry out a thorough search of their word-store in well under a second when they need to recognize a real word or reject a non-word. These figures relate to words that are clearly words and non-words that are unlike actual words, since most of us have a grey area of sequences such as *concision* which sound as if they might be 'real' words, but we are not quite sure.

Most humans are also impressively fast at finding the words they need when they produce speech. Unfortunately, we cannot time the production process as easily as we can measure recognition speed. Some researchers have made attempts in this direction by arguing that pauses in speech, which are measurable, often occur before major lexical items. They may therefore have been caused by word searching (Butterworth, 1980a). However, the pauses vary in length and their interpretation is controversial: we cannot easily tell whether a speaker is pausing to choose the words themselves or the order in which they will occur. So we cannot produce convincing figures for selection times, especially as some words seem to be easier to find than others.

Indeed, some words seem to be particularly hard to seek out. Almost everybody has had the annoying experience of not being able to think of the particular word they want, even though they are sure they know it. Yet such problems probably seem more frequent than they really are. Even when struggling to find a particular word, normal speakers have plenty of others at their disposal in order to carry on a reasonable conversation. This can be illustrated by a fictional but not unrealistic dialogue from Douglas Adams's science fiction satire *Life, the Universe and Everything*:

Arthur shook his head in a sudden access of emotion and bewilderment.
'I haven't seen anyone for years,' he said, 'not anyone. I can hardly even remember

how to speak. I keep forgetting words. I practise you see. I practise by talking to . . . talking to . . . what are those things people think you're mad if you talk to? Like George the Third.'

'Kings?' suggested Ford.

'No, no', said Arthur. 'The things he used to talk to. We're surrounded by them for heaven's sake. I've planted hundreds myself. They all died. Trees! I practise by talking to trees.'

Arthur cannot remember the word *trees*. Yet while he struggles to retrieve it he uses approximately 50 other different words seemingly effortlessly, with no conscious searching. Such fast and efficient retrieval must be based on a structured system, not on random rummages around the mind.

Our conclusions so far, then, are as follows: the large number of words known by humans, and the speed with which they can be located, point to the existence of a highly organized mental lexicon.

However, the requirements of massive storage capacity and fast retrieval are not necessarily the same. This can be illustrated by an analogy. Suppose the words in the mental lexicon were like books. If we wanted to store thousands of books, how would we do this? The simplest method would be to find a large room and to stack them up in heaps which go from floor to ceiling. We would start at the side of the room opposite the door and carry on heaping them up until the room was quite full. Then we would shut the door. In this way we could store the maximum possible number of books. But suppose we then needed to consult one of them. How would we find it? We might never locate the book we wanted, unless it happened to be one of the few stored near the door.

In brief, the system which allowed the greatest storage capacity might not be compatible with efficient retrieval. And there might be further discrepancies between storage requirements and speedy retrieval. To continue with the book analogy, libraries often keep all really big and heavy books near the floor. But this means that they cannot be kept in strict sequence. Similarly, in the human mind, extra long words might need a specialized storage system which could separate them from shorter words, and which might cause some delay when it came to retrieving them.

In dealing with words in the mind, therefore, we must treat storage and retrieval as interlinked problems but not identical ones. Although common sense suggests that the human word-store is primarily organized to ensure fast and accurate retrieval, we cannot assume that this is inevitable. Humans might have adopted a compromise solution which is ideal neither for storage nor for retrieval.

Words in the mind and words in books

The human word-store is often referred to as the 'mental dictionary' or, perhaps more commonly, as the *mental lexicon*, to use the Greek word for 'dictionary'. There is, however, relatively little similarity between the words in our minds and words in book dictionaries, even though the information will sometimes overlap. Let us therefore look at some of the differences between a human's mental dictionary and a book dictionary. The dissimilarities involve both organization and content.

With regard to organization, book dictionaries standardly list words in alphabetical order. As a first guess, one might suggest that the mental lexicon of someone who can read and write could also be organized in this way. After all, many of us spend a considerable amount of time looking things up alphabetically in telephone directories and indexes. So, one might assume that educated English speakers had set up their mental lexicons to fit in with their alphabetical expectations.

This is an easy hypothesis to test. People occasionally make mistakes when they speak, selecting one word in error for another. If the mental lexicon was organized in alphabetical order, one might expect speakers to accidentally pick an adjacent entry when making errors of this type. So, in place of the musical instrument 'zither' one would predict, perhaps, the wrong selection of *zircon* (a mineral), or *zloty* (a Polish monetary unit), which precede and follow *zither* in the *Concise Oxford Dictionary* (*COD*). Similarly, in error for the word 'guitar' one might expect someone to accidentally pick *guinea*, or *guipure*, or *guiser*, or perhaps *Gujerati*, *gulch*, *gulden*, *gules*, *gulf*, all words which immediately surround it in *COD*.

But mistakes of this type are quite unlikely, as becomes clear when we look at a few 'slips of the tongue', such as 'He told a funny antidote', with *antidote* instead of 'anecdote', or 'The doctor listened to her chest with his periscope', with *periscope* replacing 'stethoscope'. These errors suggest that even if the mental lexicon turns out to be partially organized in terms of initial sounds, the order will certainly not be straightforwardly alphabetical. Other aspects of the word's sound structure, such as its ending, its stress pattern and the stressed vowel, are all likely to play a role in the arrangement of words in the mind.

Furthermore, consider a speech error such as 'The inhabitants of the car were unhurt', where the speaker presumably meant to say *occupants* rather than 'inhabitants'. Such mistakes show that, unlike book dictionaries, human mental dictionaries cannot be organized solely on the basis of sounds or spelling. Meaning must be taken into consideration as well, since humans fairly often confuse words with similar meanings, as in 'Please hand me the tin-opener' when the speaker wanted to crack a nut, so must have meant 'nut-crackers'.

Arrangement in terms of meaning is found in some collections of synonyms, such as *Roget's Thesaurus*, but not generally in book dictionaries where a desire to be neat and tidy in an alphabetical fashion may outweigh other considerations. For example, the word *horsefly* occurs soon after *horse* in *Collins Concise English Dictionary* (*CCED*), but there is no mention of it near the entry *fly*. Similarly, *workhorse* occurs soon after the entry for *work*, but does not appear with *horse*. In brief, the organization of the mental lexicon is likely to be considerably more complex than that of book dictionaries, for whom orderliness is a prime requirement.

As for content, a book dictionary contains a fixed number of words which can be counted. Book dictionaries are therefore inescapably outdated because language is constantly changing, and vocabulary fastest of all. As the eighteenth-century lexicographer Samuel Johnson pointed out in the preface to his famous *Dictionary of the English Language* (1755): 'No dictionary of a living tongue can ever be perfect, since while it is hastening to publication, some words are budding, and some fading away.' Everyone must at times have been frustrated to find occasions when a book dictionary concentrates on an archaic meaning of a word, or omits a moderately common item. *COD*, for example, defines *buzz* only in terms of sound. It does not mention its more recent and perhaps equally frequent meaning of 'pleasant stimulus'. Or take the word *wimp*, meaning 'a weak ineffectual person', as in the 'lonely hearts' ad: 'Wimp needs bossy lady' (*Time Out*, July 1984), or the comment by a singing group that 'the trying-hard wimps' were an easy target for humour (*The Guardian*, July 1984), or the magazine column which noted that 'your cad, pale-faced wimp, Byron with malnutrition, Little Boy Lost . . . have a great appeal for women since they are vulnerable' (*Cosmpolitan*, July 1984). This word occurs fairly often these days, and so does its adjective *wimpy*: a women's magazine called attention to a calendar which features 'six most decidedly wimpy males in varying states of undress' (*Over 21*, August 1984). But neither *wimp* nor *wimpy* has yet made its way into most British book dictionaries.

The way written dictionaries dodder along behind language is amusingly satirized in Douglas Adams's book *Life, the Universe and Everything*:

> The mattress globbered. This is the noise made by a live, swamp-dwelling mattress that is deeply moved by a story of human tragedy. The word can also, according to 'The Ultra-Complete Maximegalon Dictionary of Every Language Ever', mean the noise that is made by the Lord High Sanvalvwag of Hollop on discovering that he has forgotten his wife's birthday for the second year running. Since there was only ever one Lord High Sanvalvwag of Hollop, and he never married, the word is only ever used in a negative or speculative sense, and there is an ever-increasing body of opinion which holds that 'The Ultra-Complete Maximegalon Dictionary' is not worth the fleet of lorries it takes to cart its microstored edition around in. Strangely enough, the dictionary omits the word 'floopily', which simply means 'in the manner of something which is floopy'.

Turning to the mental lexicon, its content is by no means fixed. People add new words all the time, as well as altering the pronunciation and meaning of existing ones. Humans, however, do not just add on words from time to time, in between utterances. They often create new words and new meanings for words from moment to moment, while speech is in progress. A caller asking an American telephone operator about long-distance charges was told: 'You'll have to ask a zero.' The caller had no difficulty in interpreting this as 'a person you can reach on the telephone by dialling zero'. Similarly, it was not difficult

for native speakers to guess that 'The newsboy porched the newspaper yesterday' meant 'The newsboy left the newspaper in the porch', or that the instruction 'Please do a Napoleon for the camera' meant posing with one hand tucked
inside the jacket, as in most pictures of Napoleon, even though they had probably never come across these usages before (Clark and Gerrig, 1983).

In the examples above, the speakers and hearers were already familiar with
other uses of the word *zero* and *porch*, and with the characteristics of a famous
character such as Napoleon. They simply reapplied this knowledge in a new
way. But human creativity goes beyond this. Quite often, totally new lexical
items can be created and interpreted on the spur of the moment. This skill has
been tested experimentally (Clark and Gerrig, 1983). The researchers gave a
short description of a somewhat eccentric imaginary character to a number of
students: 'Imagine that a friend of yours has told you about his neighbour, Elvis
Edmunds. Elvis loves to entertain his children in the evenings with several
magic tricks that he knows. He often surprises them by pulling dollar bills out
of his ear. During the day, Elvis is employed as a professional skywriter. He
likes to work best on days when there is not a cloud in the sky. To supplement
his income, Elvis carves fruit into exotic shapes for the delicatessen down the
road.' The students were then quizzed about the meaning of the phrase 'doing
an Elvis' in various contexts, a task they found easy. They were confident, for
example, that a sentence they could not possibly have heard before, such as 'I
have often thought about doing an Elvis Edmunds to some apples I bought',
meant 'carving apples into exotic shapes'. The fluidity and flexibility of the
mental lexicon, then, contrasts strongly with the fixed vocabulary of any book
dictionary.

But the biggest difference between a book dictionary and the mental lexicon
is that the latter contains far, far more information about each entry. All book
dictionaries are inevitably limited in the amount they contain, just because it
would be quite impracticable to include all possible data about each word. In
any case it is unlikely that anyone has ever assembled the total range of knowledge which could be brought together about any one dictionary entry. As one
linguist notes: 'There is no known limit to the amount of detailed information
. . . which may be associated with a lexical item. Existing dictionaries, even
large ones, specify lexical items only incompletely' (Hudson, 1984: 74).

For example, one popular dictionary (*COD*) suggests that the verb *paint*
means 'cover surface of (object) with paint'. But 'If you knock over the paint
bucket, thereby covering the surface of the floor with paint, you have not
thereby painted the floor' (Fodor, 1981: 287). Nor can one patch up the *COD*
definition by suggesting that one must intentionally cover something with
paint: 'For consider that when Michelangelo dipped his brush into Cerulian
Blue, he thereby covered the surface of his brush with paint and did so with the
primary intention that his brush should be covered with paint in consequence
of his having so dipped it. But MICHELANGELO WAS NOT, FOR ALL
THAT, PAINTING HIS PAINTBRUSH' (Fodor, 1981: 288). All this

suggests that people have a much more detailed knowledge of the meaning of words than any book dictionary would have the space to specify.

Furthermore, why don't people wear rancid socks? Or eat rank eggs? There is nothing to suggest that this is abnormal in the *Longman Concise English Dictionary* (*LCED*). It defines the word *rancid* as '(smelling or tasting) rank', with *rank* in turn defined as 'offensive in odour or flavour'. This suggests that one ought to be able to attach both words to dirty socks, or cow dung, or bad eggs. Yet it would sound very odd to say 'Alphonse was ashamed of his rancid socks', or 'Mary's egg was rank'. Written dictionaries list only a small selection of the range of words with which a lexical item can occur. As one lexicographer comments: 'The world's largest data bank of examples in context is dwarfed by the collection we all carry around subconsciously in our heads' (Ayto, 1980: 45).

Moreover, in book dictionaries, words are mostly dealt with in isolation. A *child* is defined by *COD* as a 'young human being'. But this fails to inform us us how the word *child* relates to all the other words for young human beings, such as *baby*, *infant*, *toddler*, *youngster*. Similarly, *LCED* tells us that *warm* means 'having or giving out heat to a moderate or adequate degree' Yet in order to fully understand *warm*, one needs to know how it slots into the range of temperature words such as *cold*, *tepid*, *hot*. This type of information seems to be an intrinsic part of one's mental lexicon.

To continue this list of differences between words in the mind and words in books, a book dictionary tends to give information that is spuriously cut and dried. It is likely to tell you that *pelicans*, *sparrows*, *parrots* and *flamingos* are all birds but will not rank them in any way. Humans seems able to judge that a sparrow is a more 'birdy' bird than a pelican or a flamingo. Or more likely, a human would say that a pelican is a 'funny' kind of bird. In addition, book dictionaries do not often spare the space to comment on frequency of usage. There is no indication in *COD* that *abode* is less usual than *house*, or that *coney* is uncommon beside *rabbit*. People, on the other hand, seem well aware which words are rare and which not.

Or, to take another facet of words, book dictionaries contain only a very small amount of data about the syntactic patterns into which each word can slot. *Wide* and *main* are both classified as adjectives in *COD*. But it does not tell us that you can say 'The road is wide' but not 'The road is main'. Both *eat* and *resemble* are classified as transitive verbs (verbs which take an object), but it does not tell us that whereas 'A cow was eaten by my aunt' is possible, 'A cow was resembled by my aunt' is not.

If we move on to consider how book dictionaries cope with sounds, we note that they normally specify only one pronunciation for each word. Yet native speakers of a language are likely to be able to understand quite different pronunciations by different speakers. In addition, they are likely to have more than one pronunciation in their own repertoire, depending on the formality of the occasion and how fast they are speaking. Sometimes, for example, one might pronounce a word such as *handbag* with all the sounds found in the conventional spelling, and at other times it might sound like 'hambag'.

The examples listed above could be multiplied. They show that the mental lexicon is indeed a mammoth structure (for attempts to list its outline contents see Fillmore, 1971; Butterworth, 1983a). The relationship between a book dictionary and the human mental lexicon may be somewhat like the link between a tourist pamphlet advertising a seaside resort and the resort itself. A tourist pamphlet gives us a small, partial glimpse of a place as it was at some point in the past, with no real idea of how the different parts of the resort fit together to form a whole, living town. Similarly, a book dictionary gives us a spuriously neat, static and incomplete view of the mental lexicon.

The differences between words in the mind and words in books are therefore profound. The point of this section, however, was not to point out the short-comings of book dictionaries, which serve a useful, though limited, purpose. They enable one to to check on the conventional spelling of a word and to find out its approximate meaning. Indeed, if we did expect a book dictionary to include the same information as the mental lexicon, then we would un-doubtedly require a fleet of lorries to cart its microstored edition around in, like the 'Ultra-Complete Maximegalon Dictionary' mentioned earlier. The comparison between mental dictionaries and book dictionaries was made in order to show that we cannot deduce much about our mental lexicons from studying the way words are dealt with in books. In the next two chapters, therefore, we shall consider how we can build up a more adequate picture of the human word-store.

Summary

In this chapter we have noted that humans know tens of thousands of words, most of which they can locate in a fraction of a second. Such huge numbers, and such efficiency in finding those required, suggest that these words are carefully organized, not just stacked in random heaps. This book will discuss the storage and retrieval of words by both adults and children, bearing in mind that a system which is ideal for storage might not necessarily be the best for fast retrieval. Its overall aim is to provide outline specifications for a working model of the human word-store.

We further noted that ordinary dictionaries are limited in scope in comparison with the mental lexicon. Their organization is oversimple, their content is fixed and outdated, and they contain only a relatively small amount of information about each item.

The mental lexicon, then, is both large and complex. In the next two chapters we shall consider how we should set about studying this mammoth structure.

2

Links in the Chain
— *Assessing the evidence* —

I picked up a magazine from the table . . . One of the articles attempted
to show how much an observant man might learn by an accurate and
systematic examination of all that came in his way . . .

'From a drop of water', said the writer, 'a logician could infer the
possibility of an Atlantic or a Niagara without having seen or heard of one
or the other. So all life is a great chain, the nature of which is known
whenever we are shown a single link of it.'

Arthur Conan Doyle, A Study in Scarlet

The writer who made the grandiose claims in the article quoted above was the
fictional detective Sherlock Holmes. And psycholinguists investigating the
human word-store have been likened to Sherlock Holmes in pursuit of the
master-criminal Professor Moriarty, the elusive director of a vast criminal
organization (Ohala, 1981). The detective had to work out what the master-
mind was like with the aid of limited resources: his knowledge of the world, his
deductive powers, his imagination, and a simple magnifying glass, with which
he examined the isolated clues left by Moriarty's crimes. Psycholinguists
similarly have few powerful tools with which to build up a model of the mental
lexicon – mainly their own intelligence and a heterogeneous collection of
different types of clue.

These clues are the topic of this chapter. They are of four main types (figure
2.1): first, word searches and 'slips of the tongue' of normal speakers; second,
the word-finding efforts of people with speech disorders; third, psycholinguistic experiments; fourth, the findings of theoretical linguistics. In this
chapter we shall consider what these sources of evidence have to offer, and
discuss some of the problems associated with them.

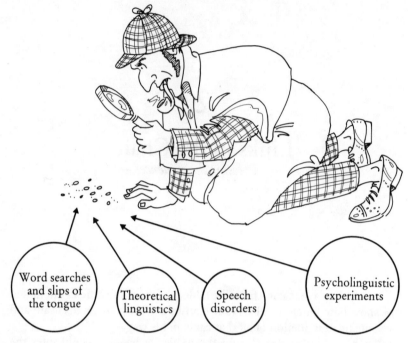

Figure 2.1   Clues to the mental lexicon

Word searches: black holes and oysters

'The name of those fabulous animals (pagan, I regret to say) who used to sing on the water, has quite escaped me.'
Mr. George Chuzzlewit suggested 'Swans'.
'No', said Mr. Pecksniff, 'Not swans. Very like swans, too. Thankyou.'
The nephew . . . propounded 'Oysters'.
'No', said Mr. Pecksniff . . . 'nor oysters. But by no means unlike oysters; a very excellent idea, thankyou my dear sir, very much. Wait! Sirens, of course.'

In the passage above, Mr Pecksniff, a character in Charles Dickens's novel *Martin Chuzzlewit*, has difficulty in retrieving a word which ordinarily he knows quite well. When such word searches occur in real life they may provide valuable information about the mental lexicon if we assume, as did the psychologist William James at the end of the last century, that 'We make search in our memory for a forgotten idea, just as we rummage our house for a lost object. In both cases we visit what seems to be the probable neighbourhood of that which we miss' (1890/1981: 615). The intermediate stages through which a person passes in the struggle to locate a missing item may give us clues to the general organization of a whole area – though the notion of 'neighbourhood' should not be taken too literally: words which seem to be closely related may be stored close together, or they may be more distant but have strong links binding them.

Of course, sometimes the searcher feels completely blocked, unable to remember anything about the word required, like George, a character in Iris Murdoch's novel *The Philosopher's Pupil*, who likens his inability to remember his wife's whereabouts to the 'black hole' left by an elusive word: 'He thought, I know, but I've forgotten . . . she's there in the form of a black hole, like not being able to find a word. I can't remember anything about her . . .'.

Quite often, however, the hole left by the missing word is far from empty. As William James noted: 'There is a gap . . . but no mere gap. It is a gap that is intensely active. A sort of wraith of the name is in it, beckoning us in a given direction, making us at moments tingle with the sense of our closeness . . .' (1890/1981: 243). This wraith can sometimes lead us to the required word, as shown by Sigmund Freud's insightful account of a successful word search. 'One day I found it impossible to recall the name of the small country of which Monte Carlo is the chief town. The substitute names for it ran: Piedmont, Albania, Montevideo, Colico. Albania was soon replaced in my mind by Montenegro; and it then occurred to me that the syllable "Mont" (pronounced "Mon") was found in all the substitute names except the last. Thus it was easy for me, starting from the name of Prince Albert [the ruling prince], to find the forgotten name Monaco. Colico gives a pretty close imitation of the sequence of syllables and the rhythm of the forgotten name' (Freud, 1901/1975: 96–7). The same type of rooting around can be observed quite often today. For example: 'He took a . . . er . . . something interest in it. What's the word I want? It's something like *salient*, but I may be confusing it with *prurient*. I know it begins with an *s*. Ah, yes, SALACIOUS.' These intermediate guesses may indicate groups of words which the mental lexicon treats as closely related.

Word searches, then, can provide useful evidence. But they also have certain drawbacks. First, the words mislaid tend to be relatively uncommon ones, so the method of finding them may not be the same as for frequently used ones. Second, perhaps the speakers were taking a roundabout and unnatural route to the target, because the straightforward way was blocked (Goodglass *et al.*, 1984). Therefore evidence from word searches needs to be supplemented by other types of information.

Looking in on the cogs

Minor malfunctions can often reveal more about underlying mechanisms than a perfectly working system. If we turn on a tap (fawcet), and pure water runs out, we may have no idea where this water was stored before it splashed down into the sink. If, however, some pigeon feathers arrive with the water (as reputedly happened in an old hospital), then we might surmise that the water supply came from a tank on the roof to which pigeons had access. Similarly, 'slips of the tongue' – errors which occur involuntarily in spontaneous speech – can give us clues about speech mechanisms which are normally hidden. In the words of two researchers at the end of the last century, 'the cover is lifted from the clockwork and we can look in on the cogs' (Meringer and Mayer, 1895/1978: vii).

Speech error evidence is valuable for several reasons. First, when speakers pick a wrong word in error they often think, perhaps only momentarily, that they have grabbed the right one. Therefore they are unlikely to have approached the target by a roundabout route, so we are witnessing the results of a normal retrieval process. Second, everybody makes slips of the tongue, no matter how well educated they may be: so they reflect the working of normal brains, not diseased or senile ones. But the major reason why tongue-slips are useful is that they are 'rule-governed' in the sense that they follow predictable patterns, a fact expressed in the title of a well-known paper on the topic: 'The non-anomalous nature of anomalous utterances' (Fromkin, 1971). This means that we can build up a data bank of recurring types of error from which we can investigate the nature of the normal processes involved. (There is a useful appendix of speech errors in Fromkin, 1973, from which some of the examples used in this book have beeen taken.)

Tongue-slips fall into two major categories, *assemblage errors* and *selection errors*. In the first, we find errors such as *patter-killer* for 'caterpillar', or *par cark* for 'car park', in which the right items have been chosen but assembled in the wrong order. Such errors probably have relatively little to do with the mental lexicon. In this book, therefore, we shall concentrate mainly on the second type of error.

In this second type, a wrong item appears to have been selected from the mental word-store. For example, in a television interview about his old school, Prince Edward of England noted: 'Corporal punishment is a last resort. It is difficult to use capital punishment in any institution. A beating is very valuable: it shows people you have come to the end of your tether.' In the second sentence, he appears to have mistakenly substituted the word *capital* for 'corporal'. Such selection errors can shed light on the mental lexicon if we assume that anyone who accidentally produces a wrong word is likely to have picked one closely related to the intended word or 'target'.

It is popularly assumed that selection errors are 'Freudian slips', based on Freud's claim that slips of the tongue often reveal suppressed thoughts which have involuntarily pushed their way to the surface. This does happen occasionally. However, if one looks objectively at the examples Freud quotes, they give us more information about the mental lexicon and less about secret thoughts than he would have us believe (Ellis, 1980). For example, one of his patients made a fairly common slip, saying *week* when she meant 'day'. Freud recounts the incident as follows: 'A woman patient who was acting entirely against my wishes in planning a short trip to Budapest, but who was determined to have her own way, justified herself by telling me that she was going only for three days, but she made a slip of the tongue and actually said "only three WEEKS". She was betraying the fact that, to spite me, she would rather spend three weeks than three days there in the company which I considered unsuitable for her' (Freud, 1901/1975: 146–7). An alternative interpretation is that Freud's obvious disapproval distracted the patient from what she was saying, and led her to pick the wrong word out of several closely related words. But it is unnecessary to assume that the word *week* had any special significance in the conversation.

Selection errors may be based on meaning similarity, sound similarity, or both. For example:

MEANING:
I wonder who invented *crosswords* (jigsaws)?
He came *tomorrow* (yesterday).
SOUND:
The emperor had several *porcupines* (concubines).
There were lots of little *orgasms* (organisms) floating in the water.
MEANING AND SOUND:
You can hear the *clarinets* (castanets) clicking.
I don't have much sympathy with rich-looking *burglars* (beggars).

The examples above are all single words which replaced the target, the word intended. However, each of the types of error mentioned above can also occur as 'blends', cases in which two words have been combined into one. For example:

MEANING BLEND:
I don't *expose* (expect/suppose) anyone will eat that.
SOUND BLEND:
Akbar Khan was a *lustrious* (lustful/illustrious) and passionate man.
SOUND AND MEANING BLEND:
My *tummach* (tummy/stomach) feels funny.

These types are summarized in figure 2.2.

	SINGLE ERRORS	BLENDS
MEANING	*crosswords* (jigsaws)	*expose* (expect/suppose)
SOUND	*orgasms* (organisms)	*lustrious* (lustful/illustrious)
MEANING/SOUND	*burglars* (beggars)	*tummach* (tummy/stomach)

Figure 2.2   Types of selection errors

Such tongue-slips can provide valuable clues to the way the human word-store works. But the evidence must be used with care, for several reasons. There can be slip-ups in the collection of data, and in its interpretation. Let us consider these problems.

In order to gather data, many tongue-slip collectors carry round a small notebook in which they write down errors whenever they hear them – on a bus, at parties, or at mealtimes. This can produce a lot of interesting data – but even trained researchers sometimes hear inaccurately, or fail to note the surrounding context properly. The obvious alternative is to use only tape-recorded data. But since one cannot keep a tape-recorder running all the time, many errors would be missed. Moreover, the number of errors produced in any one hour of spoken speech is fairly small, and we would need hundreds of hours of tape-recordings in order to write a single paper. In brief, the notebook type of data may be unreliable, and tape-recorded data produces too few errors to be regarded as a representative sample.

The interpretation of the evidence can also be tricky. Not all slips fit neatly into one or other of the categories suggested earlier. For example, is *conversation* for 'conservation' a selection error, in which one similar sounding word has been picked instead of another? Or an assemblage error, in which the [s] and [v] were reversed? Or what about the student who, describing her new boy-friend, said: 'He's such a lovely *huskuline* man.' Was this a genuine blend, in which the similar meaning words *husky* and *masculine* had been bundled together, when she meant to say only one? Or was it simply a 'telescopic' blend, in which two adjacent words had been telescoped together in a hurry, so that she had really meant to say 'husky AND masculine'? Or what went wrong in the slip *peach seduction* for 'speech production' (Fromkin, 1973: 248)? This one is especially hard to categorize .

A further problem is that it is often difficult to know whether we are dealing with a momentary selection error or an error of ignorance, in which the speaker was simply unaware of the correct word, like the fictional Mrs Malaprop in Sheridan's play *The Rivals*, who repeatedly confused similar-sounding words such as *alligator* and *allegory*: 'She was as headstrong as an allegory on the banks of the Nile.' Sometimes the strangeness of the mistake indicates that the hearer had no idea of the appropriate word, as with *blue bonnet plague* instead of 'bubonic plague' (Zwicky, 1982), but at other times the distinction is quite unclear.

We also need to be careful about the conclusions we draw. Suppose we find many more tongue-slips involving nouns than verbs. This does not automatically mean that humans find nouns harder to cope with than verbs: our evidence may just reflect the fact that the English language contains more nouns than any other part of speech (Cutler, 1982a).

In brief, the spontaneous word selection errors of normal speakers provide useful evidence. But they are not without problems and one needs to be aware of the possible ways in which they could be misleading. Let us now move on to the somewhat more bizarre errors produced by people with speech disorders.

Lost for words

'I often had the impression that I had the ... word within my power but through a tempestuous cleavage another element would come and take its place and this would give to my speech a quality often incomprehensible and fantastic ...' (quoted by Critchley, 1970/1973: 60). This is a description by a recovered patient of what it was like to suffer from aphasia – severe speech difficulties, which are most commonly caused by a stroke or head injury.

Word-finding difficulties are the commonest aphasic symptom, and are present in almost all types of aphasia. A typical example is the case of Mr Philip Gorgan, a 72-year-old retired butcher (Gardner, 1974). When asked to name objects, his responses were hardly ever wholly wrong: he said *chair* for 'table', *knee* for 'elbow' and *hair* for 'comb'. 'Clip' came out as *plick*, 'butter' was renamed *tubber* and 'ceiling' became *leasing*. For 'ankle' he said 'ankely, no mankel, no kankle', 'paper' was named 'piece of handkerchief, pauper, hand pepper, piece of hand paper', 'fork' was called *tonsil, teller, tongue, fung*. As these examples show, 'Sometimes ... he would manage to hit, or at least circle in upon, the sought-for target; sometimes not ... Like a soldier in a strange country, who knows there is an enemy somewhere but is unfamiliar with the terrain and type of warfare, he searches about, periodically lunging in various directions, sometimes coming close to, or even to grips with, the enemy; but he is just as likely to shoot completely wide of the mark or get caught in a booby trap' (Gardner, 1974: 70).

Mr Gorgan is not mad. He does not try to sit on the table, nor spear food with his tongue, though obviously it is important to distinguish people like Mr Gorgan from someone who is truly confused, such as the 53-year old painter who insisted that a bedpan was a paint pot (Benson, 1979: 313). When asked what a paint pot was doing in his hospital bed, he replied that his job was to paint automobiles so he always worked with a paint pot. At this stage of his illness the patient genuinely believed that he had a paint pot beside him.

Researchers study aphasics because they assume that 'certain symptom patterns would not be possible if the normal intact cognitive system were not organized in a particular way' (Ellis, 1985: 108). Those who carry out this type of work hope above all to find patients whose mental lexicon is selectively impaired, in that some parts may be damaged but others not. This might indicate possible subsystems within the mental lexicon. Suppose, for example, we found a patient who could remember nouns but not verbs. This would suggest that these were organized differently from one another in the mind.

Another justification for studying speech disorders is that, in a number of cases, the problems of aphasic patients are simply an exaggeration of the difficulties which normal speakers may experience. Freud observed in 1891 that the errors of aphasics do 'not differ from the incorrect use and the distortion of words which the healthy person can observe in himself in states of fatigue or divided attention or under the influence of disturbing affects' (Freud, 1891, in Ellis, 1985: 111). And similarities between the the the errors of aphasics and the slips of the tongue of normal speakers have been found in more recent work (Ellis, 1985).

The lexicon of aphasics can be studied either by analysing their spontaneous speech, or by attempting to elicit words through showing pictures or pointing. A really thorough investigation tests the ability to name not only objects the patient can see but also things he or she can touch or smell or hear, such as identifying handclapping, or the smell of lavender. It also tests different categories of objects, such as body parts, countries of the world, colours, as well as the ability to list members of these categories: 'How many types of fruit can you think of?' It would also see if the patient could name an item from a description of its use, such as 'What type of a machine would you use to clean carpets?', and would see if cues, such as hearing the initial sound, could jog their memory (Benson, 1979).

There are, however, two major problems in dealing with aphasics. The first and most obvious is that damaged brains may not always be representative of normal ones. Strange effects may occur not only as a result of the original injury, as when patients use bizarre nonsense words such as *rugabize* for 'TV set', *lungfab* for 'window' and *dop* for 'nose' (Benson, 1979: 302), but also because patients may develop strange and idiosyncratic strategies to deal with their speech problems. One helpless patient whom I met objected to being treated as a baby by the hospital staff. In her speech she sometimes gave the impression that long, strange words were easier to access than short common ones. For example, when shown a picture of someone knitting, she said: 'My dear, she's reticulating.' This may have been a genuine symptom of her illness. On the other hand, it may have been a conscious attempt to sound 'grown-up'.

A second problem is that the same output might be due to a variety of underlying causes, and only careful probing can reveal the difference. At the very least, one needs to distinguish between patients who have totally lost the word and those who just cannot locate it temporarily. One patient failed utterly to name a comb. When told it was a comb, he commented: 'You may call it a comb, but that's not the word I would use' (Benson, 1979: 303). The word seemed to have been obliterated from his mental lexicon. Another also failed to remember the name *comb*, but when reminded said: 'Yes, of course, a comb.' In the latter case, to quote a nineteenth-century researcher: 'The words representing his ideas were preserved in the treasury of his memory, but the mere origination of the idea was not sufficient to effect the verbal expression of them' (Bateman, 1892, quoted in Ellis, 1985: 116). And there are a few patients who may be perfectly aware of the word *comb* in their mind but may be quite unable to 'spit it out'.

These examples suggest that, as in the case of normal slips of the tongue, the errors and word-finding attempts of dysphasics can provide valuable evidence, provided they are treated with caution and compared with information from other sources. Let us now go on to consider another of these sources, the results of psycholinguistic experiments.

Controlling the situation

One day towards the end of the nineteenth century the pioneering British psychologist Francis Galton wrote down 75 words on slips of paper, then put them aside until he had forgotten the particular words selected. After a few days he glanced at a word at a time and, taking a pen in one hand, quickly wrote down the first two ideas which came into his head. In his other hand he held a watch, so that he could time his reactions. He notes: 'The records lay bare the foundations of a man's thoughts with curious distinctness and exhibit his mental anatomy with more vividness and truth than he himself would probably care to publish to the world' (1883: 145). This is the first recorded experiment on the organization of words in the mind.

Galton's idea was immediately seized on by a number of other psychologists. This basic word association experiment, slightly modified, is still in use today. The experimenter presents the subject with a series of words and for each item asks her to name the first word which comes to mind: 'Give me the first word you think of when I say *day*.' The subject will say, perhaps, 'Night' or 'Light' or anything else which pops into her mind in response to *day*. The advantage of this type of experiment is that it is extremely simple. Furthermore, it is likely to be useful, since different people tend to give rather similar responses, so much so that one can talk about 'norms of word association' – the title of a well-known book on the topic (Postman and Keppel, 1970). An analysis of these responses may therefore give useful information about how words might be linked together in a person's mind.

Another famous though more recent experiment involves the 'tip of the tongue' (TOT) phenomenon. In the mid-1960s two American psychologists tried to artificially induce the state in which people feel that a word is 'on the tip of their tongue' but cannot quite remember it (Brown and McNeill, 1966). Subjects in a 'TOT state' are left with 'a disembodied presence, like the grin without the Cheshire cat' (Brown, 1970: 234). The experimenters evoked this state by reading out definitions of relatively uncommon words, such as 'navigational instrument used in measuring angular distances, esp. the altitude of sun, moon and stars at sea'. Some people didn't know the word *sextant* at all, but a few went into a 'TOT state'. The experimenters then quizzed them about the word they could almost remember. Could they name words with similar meaning? Or suggest similar sounding words? Could they guess the initial consonant or the number of syllables? Some of them managed to do all these things. Brown and McNeill's findings, and the findings of others who have replicated this experiment, provide a useful supplement to the information gleaned from spontaneous word searches.

These days, experimental psychology has become highly sophisticated, utilizing expensive and accurate equipment. However, in any one area of enquiry a few basic techniques tend to recur. Lexical decision tasks, 'priming' and 'phoneme monitoring' are particularly common in investigations of the mental lexicon. Let us briefly outline what these involve.

A lexical decision task has already been mentioned in chapter 1. In its simplest form, the experimenters present subjects with a number of sound or letter sequences, asking them to say whether each is a word or not. Their reaction times are measured in milliseconds (thousandths of a second). This is likely to provide information as to which words are the most easily available in a person's mental lexicon – though care must be taken to distinguish between word-finding time and various processes which might be happening in the mind after the word has been found and before the response has been given (Balota and Chumbley,1984).

The basic lexical decision task can be varied in several ways, most obviously by altering the type of word being tested. Reaction time to common words might be compared with responses to uncommon ones. Or the rejection speed for nonsense words which are similar to real ones might be checked against that for non-words which are quite different from actual words.

Another way of varying this task is to see whether a subject's response to a word is altered by the words presented before it. For example, suppose you had measured the recognition time for a word such as *game* when the previous word was another common word, such as *level*. You might then check whether this recognition time was significantly altered if you put a less common word in front of it, such as *tithe* (Gordon, 1983).

Preactivating a listener's attention, as in the example above, is known as 'priming', the assumption being that if a word 'primes' another (i.e. facilitates the processing of another) the two are likely to be closely connected. A variety of possibilities can be tested in this way. Suppose one found that the subjects responded faster to the words *spider* or *bug* after hearing the word *insect*. One might then check whether the word *insect* still primed *bug* even when the bug in question was clearly an electronic bug (Swinney, 1979).

If a person is having trouble in dealing with a word, then he will have less attention for handling other tasks. This is the rationale behind another technique known as 'phoneme monitoring', which means listening for the presence of a particular sound: 'Press the button when you hear a [b].' If the required sound comes immediately after a complicated word, then the listener's response is likely to be slower. For example, one might want to check whether a word such as *yellow* was harder or easier or the same as *empty*, and ask subjects to listen for a [b] in a sentence such as:

The dog sniffing round the yard stuck its nose into the empty bucket.

The time taken to find [b] would be measured. Then, some time later, the sentence would be presented again, but with *yellow* in place of 'empty' (Cutler and Norris, 1979).

In addition to lexical decision tasks, priming and phoneme monitoring, there are a number of other psycholinguistic experiments which can be used to find out about the mental lexicon. For example, word-learning experiments seem to be particularly useful with children (e.g. Carey, 1978; Aitchison and Chiat, 1981). The experimenters teach children new words and then, some time later, check how well they have been remembered. Misremembered words, such as *puss-puss* for 'cuscus', *gandigoose* for 'bandicoot', can show which parts of the word children find easiest to recall (Aitchison and Chiat, 1981).

The advantage of experiments is that the experimenter can simplify the situation and manipulate one variable at a time, instead of being faced with the tens or even hundreds of uncontrollable factors found in ordinary speech. But this creates a problem. In order to be fully in control, it is necessary to create a quite artificial situation. This sometimes leads people to devise abnormal strategies for coping, which they would never use in a normal conversation. Another problem is that a psychologist may not always be aware of all the variables which exist and so may unwittingly have falsified the experiment (Whaley, 1978). So it is important to be aware of this possibility and not place too much reliance on any one experiment.

Experiments, then, can give interesting insights into the mental lexicon but cannot be trusted blindly, since quite misleading conclusions may be drawn from unnatural or badly designed experiments.

The messiness of minds

'Linguists like any other speakers of a language cannot help focusing their attention on the word, which is the most central element in the social system of communication' (Labov, 1973: 340). As the above quotation suggests, those involved in the study of linguistics have treated words as important for a long time, and there are countless discussions of their sounds, their meaning and their syntax. Anyone working on the mental lexicon needs to become acquainted with the enormous and often valuable literature on the topic of words.

There are, however, some problems with the conclusions reached. Theoretical linguists are primarily trying to describe the facts of language in as simple a way as possible. But there is no guarantee that human minds work in this neat and economical fashion. It has been claimed that 'A linguist who could not devise a better system than is present in any speaker's brain ought to try another trade' (Householder, 1966: 100).

A second problem with the writings of theoretical linguists is that in recent years they have regarded syntax, which involves combinations of words, as more important than the words themselves: 'The principal task of linguistics is to investigate and describe the ways in which words can be combined and manipulated to convey meanings' (Brown, 1984: 10). This has led many of them to underestimate the complexities of the lexicon, and to characterize it as a finite list which concentrates on irregularities and idiosyncracies: 'A list of lexical items as provided in the lexicon . . . is unquestionably finite. That is to say, the lexical items of a language can indeed be presented as a mere list' (Kempson, 1977: 102). 'The lexicon is really an appendix of the grammar, a list of basic irregularities' (Bloomfield, 1933: 274). 'Regular variations are not matters for the lexicon, which should contain only idiosyncratic items' (Chomsky and Halle, 1968: 12). Only recently has this viewpoint been challenged, and much that was ignored or placed elsewhere in a grammar is now being shifted back into the lexicon (for a summary of this change of emphasis see Brown, 1984).

The findings of theoretical linguists, then, like the other types of evidence discussed in this chapter, provide useful clues to the mental lexicon but need to be treated with caution.

Summary

In this chapter we have discussed the four main ways in which we can gather clues about the mental lexicon from the way speakers behave: word searches and slips of the tongue of normal people, the word-finding problems of aphasics, psycholinguistic experiments and the work of theoretical linguists. We have shown that each of these can provide valuable information, though each has its own inbuilt problems. We therefore need to combine all these sources, but with some degree of caution.

In the next chapter we shall consider how these clues can be used in relation to our long-term aim, that of providing outline specifications for a working model of the mental lexicon.

3

Programming Dumbella
— *Modelling the mental lexicon* —

'I've got this project I've been working on in my spare time', he said
...'Maybe you've heard about it. I've been getting people to tape-record
lists of words and syllables for me.' ...
He gave her eight yellow-boxed cartridges and a black looseleaf binder.
'My gosh, there's a lot', she said, leafing through curled and mended
pages typed in triple columns.
'It goes quickly', Claude said. 'You just say each word clearly in your
regular voice and take a little stop before the next one.' ...
She went to the desk ... and switched the recorder on. With a finger to
the page, she leaned towards the microphone ... 'Taker. Takes. Taking',
she said. 'Talcum. Talent. Talented. Talk. Talkative. Talked. Talker.
Talking. Talks.'

Ira Levin, *The Stepford Wives*

The best way of finding out about something is to try to make it oneself. If we
were trying to discover the principles underlying, say, a sewing machine, a
working replica would be proof that we had understood the basic mechanisms
involved.

Often, however, it is too expensive or impractical to build a complete replica.
If one was trying to find out how a spacecraft was likely to respond to different
temperatures, it might be better to start by building a scale model of the
original and check its performance in different freezer and furnace heats. In
this case, and in many others, models are likely to be more practical than replicas, so 'model building' is the name given to this type of activity.

In this book, our overall aim is to provide the outline specifications for a
'model' of the mental lexicon. This covers both the way it is organized and how
it works. We shall behave as if we were trying to program a robot to behave like
a human being as far as its word-storage and word-finding abilities are concerned, a situation proposed by Ira Levin in his novel *The Stepford Wives*. In this
work of science fiction, the women of a small town in America are killed by

their menfolk and replaced by smiling robots who do everything the men want. These dummies are programmed to speak just like normal humans. The basis of this ability is a long list of words, since prior to her death every woman has been persuaded to read out the contents of a dictionary on to a tape which is incorporated into the workings of the robot. Let us call the archetype of these dummies 'Dumbella'. In this book we shall try to find out how the words should be organized inside her, so that she may be regarded as a 'model' of a human being as far as the mental lexicon is concerned.

First, however, we need to say more about the nature and limitations of 'models'. After that we shall make suggestions as to how to deal with this task.

Models and maps

The term 'model building' has a fairly modern ring to it, but the activity of building working models in order to understand something is quite old, and is mentioned by the seventeenth-century poet John Milton. In *Paradise Lost* (viii, 76–80) the angel Raphael tells Adam that God has allowed men to argue about the stars and planets, perhaps so he can laugh at their attempts to model the mechanisms underlying them:

> He his Fabric of the Heav'ns
> Hath left to their disputes, perhaps to move
> His laughter at their quaint Opinions wide
> Hereafter, when they come to model Heav'n
> And calculate the Starrs . . .

However, the word 'model' may be misleading, because it gives the impression that we are always dealing with scaled-down copies of originals. In many cases this is false, for two reasons: first, models are often highly simplified, and second, they often represent guesswork rather than copying. Let us discuss these two matters.

Perfect scale models, in which every single detail of the original has been replicated, are time-consuming and expensive to build. It therefore makes sense to leave out insignificant trivia and concentrate on the important characteristics of the 'real thing' that is being simulated: 'Models embody only the essential features of whatever it is they are intended to represent. If a model of an automobile is intended for wind tunnel tests, then the outside shape of the model car is important, but no seats nor any other interior furnishings of the real automobile need be present in the model' (Weizenbaum, 1976/1984: xvii). Sometimes, concentration on only the bare essentials can lead to a model being very far away from the original indeed. When men come to 'model Heav'n', the most important feature may be the 24-hour cycle caused by the rotation of the planet earth. Therefore, one can claim that 'Clocks are fundamentally models of the planetary system' (Weizenbaum, 1976/1984: 24) – and so are digital watches.

The fact that models can be very different from the original, yet still embody some of its essential features, has meant that model building can be used by a wide range of researchers, even people who do not deal with strictly physical things at all, such as economists, psychologists, linguists (Brown, 1984). When economists build a 'model' of the economy, they attempt to encapsulate the crucial features of the present-day economic situation and to show the principles which underlie it. This enterprise helps them to lay plans for the future, since ideally their model will predict what is likely to happen next.

Models, then, are not necessarily scaled-down replicas, but more usually simplified versions of what they represent. But they may be different from the thing they are modelling in another way also: they are likely to be guesses rather than copies. Although it is perfectly possible to unscrew a sewing machine and copy it piece by piece, this approach is just not feasible in a number of situations. For example, scientists studying the hidden thermonuclear reactions in the sun's interior cannot, in the current state of science, place a laboratory inside the sun. They can therefore study only the light emitted at the outermost layers of the sun, and they have to rely on elaborate guesswork when they are trying to construct models which might explain why the sun's light converts into heat (Chomsky, 1978: 202). If they succeed in building a model which produces the same effect as the sun, then they may have guessed right about the underlying principles involved.

However, the fact that some models have to rely on guesses raises a problem. Even if we were successful in simulating some general effect with a model, such as the light and heat emitted by the sun, how do we know we have got its inner workings right? It is sometimes possible to produce the same output by very different mechanisms. For instance, the chemical insulin is produced by the human body, but scientists have also discovered how to manufacture it artificially. But there is no reason to believe that the two processes are the same. Similarly, when dealing with the mental lexicon, two or more models might produce the same output even though their internal mechanisms could be quite different.

Scientists, then, are faced with two similar but related problems. First, they have to build a model which produces the right end result. Second, they have to decide whether the inner mechanism of their model is likely to be a 'real' replica, or simply one which does the same task in a different way. It may happen that two teams of researchers each build a different model which has the same effect. In that case, they will need to decide which is the better one. A number of different models of the mental lexicon have been proposed. In the course of this book we will be discussing why we might want to choose one type of model in preference to another.

Mental maps

Models of the mind built by psycholinguists are somewhere in between the concrete models of spacecraft and the abstract models of economists. Perhaps the best analogy is that of a map, which in some ways fits a 'real life' state of affairs and in other ways is quite different. It is obvious that 'the most useful map is often not an exact representation of the terrain. The well-known map of the London underground . . . provides an elegant way of summarizing essential information . . . It sacrifices realism but given its purpose is a better map for doing so' (Baddeley, 1983: 12). The London Underground map tells one clearly which train-lines connect which stations. There is a line on the map linking Holborn and Covent Garden, and correspondingly there are sets of metal rails linking these two stations. In this way, it presents a true picture of 'reality'. On the other hand, the various lines are represented by different colours on the map. We do not expect either the trains or the railway lines to be painted this colour. Nor do we expect the distances between stations to be accurately represented.

We are trying, then, to produce a diagram of the connections in the mental lexicon which is in some respects comparable to a plan of the London Underground. However, there is one way in which this mental map is quite different. We can go down into the Underground and map the connections between stations. But we cannot view the connections in the mind directly. We are instead in the situation of observers who could watch passengers entering and leaving train stations but could neither enter the system nor communicate directly with the travellers. In this situation, we would probably conclude that it was possible to get from any single station to any other, but would argue about whether one spaghetti-like line linked all the stations or whether there were a number of different lines, so that passengers had to change trains. If a journey took a long time, some observers might propose that the length of time was due to a single train taking a roundabout route. Others might argue that a passenger must have changed trains, and had to wait between them. Similarly, a fast journey between stations might be because they were located near one another or because there was a speedy non-stop train linking them. This is the kind of argument which takes place between psycholinguists when they cannot decide how to interpret evidence on the mental lexicon.

Another way in which a mental map is likely to differ from the London Underground map is that we may be dealing with a system or set of systems which are quite disparate in nature, as if one line involved a train, another a bus, another a camel. Or, to take another analogy, we could be in the same sort of situation as a person trying to reconstruct the processes going on inside the mouth, assuming one could not see inside (Matthei and Roeper, 1983). One might well come to the conclusion that, in order to cope with food, there was some kind of grinder to pulverize it and some kind of wetting mechanism to moisturize it. But what would ever lead us to suggest that in addition there is a tongue that has a strong muscle in it for the manipulation of food? We could equally well have concluded that there was simply a suction mechanism which held the food in place for the grinder and moisturizer, and never discovered the tongue.

The mouth image is useful partly because it reminds us that logical thinking is not necessarily going to lead us to the right conclusions, since the mind may work in a way that is quite counter-intuitive. But the mouth image is useful for another reason also. It suggests that human behaviour is often the end result of the interaction of a number of quite different components, subsystems or 'modules', as they are fashionably called, a term borrowed from computer terminology. The same is likely to be true of the mental lexicon.

Birdcages and libraries

If researchers have to make guesses about the structure of something unknown, where do they get their inspiration from? How does one pull a guess out of thin air, as it were? The mouth and London Underground analogies indicate one fruitful way in which humans are able to contemplate something which is not well understood. They hypothesize that it is like something we already know about, and then test this hypothesis. As one writer notes: 'Since finding out what something is is largely a matter of discovering what it is like, the most impressive contribution to the growth of intelligibility has been made by the application of suggestive metaphors' (Miller, 1978: 9).

Birdcages, treasure-houses, attics, libraries. These are all suggestions which have been put forward for describing human memory (Marshall, 1977). They reflect a recurrent notion that memory is a place of some kind, a metaphor which has persisted for centuries. The ancient Greek philosopher Plato attributes the birdcage analogy to Socrates: 'Let us suppose that every mind contains a kind of large birdcage stocked with all kinds of birds, some in flocks, some in small groups, and some flying around alone . . . When we are babies, we must assume that this container is empty, and suppose that the birds stand for pieces of knowledge. Whenever a person acquires some piece of knowledge, he puts it into the enclosure . . .' (*Theaetetus* 197d–e). The Roman orator Cicero referred to memory as the 'treasure-house of all things' (*De Oratore* 1, 5, 18). A similar metaphor is put into the mouth of Sherlock Holmes by his inventor Conan Doyle: 'I consider that a man's brain originally is like a little empty attic and you have to stock it with such functions as you choose' (Conan Doyle, 1930/1981: 21).

The trouble with birdcages, treasure-houses and attics is that their contents are somewhat varied and difficult to put into order. So the most popular of these place metaphors has involved the notion of a place whose contents could be easily organized – above all, a library. The German philosopher Kant, for example, writing at the end of the eighteenth century, suggested that the material in one's memory was divided into general headings 'as when we arrange the books in a library on shelves with different labels' (quoted in Marshall, 1977: 479). The library is a recurring metaphor not only for memory in general but in particular for the mental lexicon, where words are likened to books on shelves. As a medical writer suggested at the beginning of the century: 'After some brain shock, a person may be able to speak, but the wrong word often vexatiously comes to his lips, just as if . . . shelves had become badly jumbled' (Thomson, 1907, quoted in Marshall, 1977: 479).

But libraries are not at the moment the main source of cerebral metaphors. There is a tendency for the dominant technology of the era to take over, so that almost all modern systems which involve storing information or sending messages have had their turn at providing suggestive metaphors (Marshall, 1977). Earlier in this century the mind was compared to a telephone exchange. More recently, memory traces have been likened to laser holograms. These days, however, computers provide the most powerful suggestive analogies. Computers can sort phenomenally quickly and store huge amounts of data. It is perhaps not surprising that they have taken over as the main metaphor for the mind, including the mental lexicon. Computer notions will pervade our model building throughout, especially as a number of researchers have tried to partially simulate the working of the mental lexicon on computers.

Metaphors, then, can suggest hypotheses for testing and identify questions to ask. For example, libraries normally have a central catalogue which gives outline information about each book and specifies a detailed location for each. This observation might lead one to hypothesize a similar central catalogue for the mental lexicon, where one could check the location of a word. Or, to take another example, libraries often have to decide what to do with popular books. Should they be stored on a shelf just inside the library, so readers can find them easily? And should there be several copies of each? In dealing with the mental lexicon a similar question arises. Are all words to be regarded as equal? Or are frequent words and rare words treated differently? Each analogy, therefore, can provide researchers with a whole range of ideas for testing.

Testing ideas

'I was just thinking that detection must be like science. The detective formulates a theory, then tests it. If the facts he discovers fit, then the theory holds. If they don't, then he has to find another theory, another suspect.'

Dr Howarth said drily: 'It's a reasonable analogy. But the temptation to select the right facts is probably greater.'

These lines, from P. D. James's novel *Death of an Expert Witness*, illustrate a problem faced both by detectives and by psycholinguists. Logically, the idea comes first, then the evidence is examined. Indeed, until one has an outline theory it's difficult to know what kind of evidence to collect. But this means that researchers might subconsciously select speech samples or devise experiments which fit in with their ideas. This is a danger which researchers have to be aware of as they check to see how well facts and theories fit. A theory is likely to be on the right tracks if it can account for a whole range of facts, in particular extra ones which the theorist had not at first taken into consideration. For example, treating the heart as a pump explains not only why blood flows round the body but also why it makes a thumping sound.

In practice, evidence and theory are somewhat more intertwined than the above 'logical order' suggests. Quite often, a chance piece of evidence suggests an idea, which is then checked against further evidence. Aunt Agatha might repeatedly confuse the words *cup* and *saucer*. This could give her nephew the idea that words for crockery were stored near one another in the mind. He could then check this out by devising an experiment which required her to name cups, saucers, plates and jugs. Overall, the situation is somewhat like trying to crack a code. The best way to do this is described by an elderly monk in Umberto Eco's novel *The Name of the Rose*: 'The first rule in deciphering a message is to guess what it means ... Some hypotheses can be formed on the possible first words of the message, and then you see whether the rule you infer from them can apply to the rest of the text.' Similarly, psycholinguists find a piece of evidence, form a hypothesis about it, then check it out on new evidence. In the course of this book we shall be adopting this procedure in relation to the mental lexicon. Of course, we cannot deal with the whole of it straight away, so we shall concentrate at first on finding out about smallish sections of it (Kintsch, 1984). Later we can make hypotheses about how these sections fit together.

What is a word?

We have been calling the mental lexicon 'the human word-store'. Yet so far we have said nothing about one crucial question. What exactly is a word? We need to consider this before we proceed with our investigation.

Everybody thinks they know what a word is, but the matter, which seems so simple, is in fact enormously problematical (see, e.g., Lyons, 1968; Palmer, 1984; Brown, 1984). Consider the rhyme below:

> There once was a fisher named Fisher
> Who fished for a fish in a fissure.
> But the fish with a grin
> Pulled the fisherman in
> Now they all fish the fissure for Fisher.

How many words does this contain? This is easy to answer if one is dealing with a written version of the rhyme, since English conventionally leaves gaps between written words. Therefore one can simply count the overall total, which is 33. But the overall number of words in a passage (word-tokens) does not necessarily correlate with the number of different words (word-types).

How many different words are there in the limerick from the point of view of the mental lexicon? Presumably *fish* (noun) needs to be distinguished from *fish* (verb), since they have different roles in the sentence, even though they sound the same. However, what about *fished* and *fisher*? Do these have entries to themselves? Or is *fished* listed under the verb *fish*? And what about *fisher*?

Surely, some people might say, we could simply consult a dictionary. But, as we saw in chapter 1, book dictionaries are quite unlike the mental lexicon. Moreover, book dictionaries disagree over which words should have entries to themselves and which should not. *Fisher* is given an entry to itself in one well-known dictionary (*CCED*), but is listed under the verb *fish* in another (*LCED*). Both dictionaries give a similar word *runner* a separate entry. In short, 'Dictionaries not only differ from one another as to which words they have the space or inclination to recognize but also tend to be inconsistent within their own covers' (Parlett, 1981: 198). And theoretical linguists show similar disagreements among themselves over what to count as 'words'.

This type of inconsistency shows that, in our discussion of the mental lexicon, we cannot rely on any prior definition of either 'word' or 'lexical entry'. This will have to be determined in the course of the book. Furthermore, how do we know that the mental lexicon is composed of whole words? Perhaps words such as *fisher* are in pieces, with *fish* stored separately from -*er*. This is a question which we need to discuss.

Because of these complications, we shall restrict our discussion in the early stages to items such as *cow*, *tiger*, *square*, *bachelor*, which seem relatively straightforward, at least when compared with *fisher*. Let us assume that these and similar items are 'words' which have their own entries in the mental lexicon. Then, at a later stage, we can move on to the more complicated cases.

Dividing up the work

At the very least, humans must know three things about a word in order to be able to use it: its meaning, its role in a sentence (whether it is a verb or a noun, for example) and what it sounds like. These three facets of words will be discussed in the next few chapters (Part 2: Basic Ingredients, chapters 4–12). We will also consider whether words are stored as wholes or in pieces. After that, we will consider how humans deal with new situations – cases in which no relevant word exists, so they have to extend an old one or create a new one (Part 3: Novelties, chapters 13–14). Finally, we shall discuss how all these various facets combine together (Part 4: The Overall Picture, chapters 15–18).

Summary

The overall aim of this book is to build a 'model' of the mental lexicon. In this chapter, therefore, the notion of models was discussed. We noted that models of the mind are somewhat like plans of the London Underground system: they are simplified diagrams which encapsulate crucial features of something that is in reality considerably more complex.

However, mental maps are unlike real-life maps in that they have to depend on inspired guesswork, since we cannot actually look into the head and see the connections we hypothesize. Our models are therefore often based on metaphors, when we test out the notion that the mind may be like something else we know about, such as a library or a computer.

We then pointed out that we cannot, in advance, decide what we mean by a word: this will have to be determined in the course of the book. So will the question of whether words are stored as wholes or in pieces.

Furthermore, we noted that it was impossible to deal with the whole of the mental lexicon at once. We need to subdivide our enquiry. In the next chapter we will turn to the first of these subdivisions: word meaning.

Part 2

Basic Ingredients

4

Slippery Customers
— *Attempts to pin down the meaning of words* —

'And now we need as it were a tompion to protect the contents of this flask from invading bacteria. I presume you know what a tompion is, Cornelius?'

'I can't say I do, sir', I said.

'Can anyone give me a definition of that common English noun?' A. R. Woresley said.

Nobody could ...

'Oh, come on, sir', someone said. 'Tell us what it means.'

'A tompion', A. R. Woresley said, 'is a small pellet made out of mud and saliva which a bear inserts into his anus before hibernating for the winter, to stop the ants getting in.'

Roald Dahl, My Uncle Oswald

'Words have basic inalienable meanings, departure from which is either conscious metaphor or inexcusable vulgarity', claimed the novelist Evelyn Waugh (quoted in Green, 1982: 254). Words, according to this viewpoint, are precision instruments which should be used with care and accuracy. 'Words matter', asserted the writer A. P. Herbert, 'for words are the tools of thought, and you will often find that you are thinking badly because you are using the wrong tools, trying to bore a hole with a screw-driver, or draw a cork with a coal-hammer' (Herbert, 1935). Supposedly, educated people will know exactly which word to use when because in the course of their education they will have learnt precisely what each word means. If this point of view is correct, then the semantic entries in one's mental lexicon will be fairly cut and dried, and failure to achieve this ideal state will be due either to lack of education or to mental laziness. The overall assumption is that there exists, somewhere, a basic meaning for each word, which individuals should strive to attain. We can label this the 'fixed meaning' assumption.

There is, however, an alternative viewpoint, which argues that words cannot be assigned a firm meaning, and that 'Natural language concepts have vague boundaries and fuzzy edges' (Lakoff, 1972: 183). Word meanings cannot be pinned down, as if they were dead insects. Instead, they flutter around elusively like live butterflies. Or perhaps they should be likened to fish which slither out of one's grasp: 'Words have often been called slippery customers, and many scholars have been distressed by their tendency to shift their meanings and slide out from under any simple definition' (Labov, 1973: 341). Or perhaps word meanings should be likened to birds wheeling in mid-air: 'The proper meaning of a word . . . is never something upon which the word sits perched like a gull on a stone; it is something over which the word hovers like a gull over a ship's stern' (Collingwood, 1938). This alternative viewpoint can be called the 'fuzzy meaning' assumption. If it is correct, then it may be extremely difficult to characterize the entries in a person's mental lexicon.

Why should intelligent people hold such divergent opinions? One possibility is that these are both uninformed, popular viewpoints, which have been put forward solely on the basis of the personality of the proposer. Perhaps the notion of a fixed meaning is promoted mainly by lexicographers and schoolmasters, since their jobs would clearly be simpler if words did have precise definitions. The fictional A. R. Woresley, quoted at the start of the chapter, obviously enjoyed handing over his dogmatic definition of a tompion, which, incidentally, is somewhat narrower than most dictionary definitions of the word. These mostly agree that a tompion or tampion is a plug for stopping an aperture, but the aperture does not have to belong to a bear – it could belong to a wide range of things, such as a cask, a gun, or an organ pipe.

In contrast, we might find that the 'fuzzy meaning' adherents were poets and mystics, such as T. S. Eliot who complained in 'Burnt Norton' that

> Words strain
> Crack and sometimes break, under the burden,
> Under the tension, slip, slide, perish,
> Decay with imprecision, will not stay in place,
> Will not stay still.

Unfortunately, this simple solution will not work. It turns out that there is no simple correlation between the type of person and the viewpoint held. Well-known and respected philosophers, psychologists and linguists are found on each side of the debate – though, on balance, philosophers have tended to favour the fixed meaning viewpoint while psychologists often opt for fuzziness (Johnson-Laird, 1983). As far as the mental lexicon is concerned, we need to know whether it is possible to assign a firm definition to any word or whether words inevitably have fuzzy meanings. The answer will obviously affect our view of how people represent them in their minds. In this chapter, therefore, we will consider the fixed–fuzzy issue. In the next, we will discuss the mental representation of word meaning in more depth (chapter 5). After that we will move on to the organization of words in the mind in relation to one another (chapters 6–7), and then examine how children learn what words mean (chapter 8).

In what follows we shall concentrate on the information which might be in a person's mind rather than on trying to come to grips with the abstract philosophical problems involved in 'the baffling word "meaning"' (Quine, 1961/ 1985: 49). The opinions of philosophers will be mentioned only when these seem likely to illuminate the issues under discussion. (For a useful summary of the differing standpoints of philosophers and psychologists see Johnson-Laird, 1983.)

Similarly, we shall not be particularly concerned with what has been called 'the inscrutability of reference' (Quine, 1971: 142), the complex relationship between a word and the real-world thing it labels. Most people assume that words are linked to things via 'concepts', though exactly how is unclear (see figure 4.1).

Figure 4.1   The word and thing problem

The intermeshing of words and concepts is an area of study which is 'a morass of complexity and ignorance . . . The intricate connection between the labels people use and their conceptions of the things labeled is poorly understood' (Miller and Johnson-Laird, 1976: 212). People argue as to whether there is an abstract layer of concepts which is separate from word meaning or whether the word meanings and the concepts are identical (Aitchison, 1985). In this book we will assume, first, that people translate the real world into 'concepts' which in cases such as *tiger, moon* reflect the external world fairly well, in that there is likely to be considerable agreement over what they are, even between people speaking different languages. Second, we will treat the 'meaning' of a word as overlapping with the concept to a large extent, though not necessarily totally: the overall concept may extend beyond the sections labelled with a word (figure 4.2). This viewpoint will hopefully become clearer as the book progresses.

Let us now consider the fixed–fuzzy issue. We will begin by outlining some ideas put forward by proponents of the fixed meaning viewpoint.

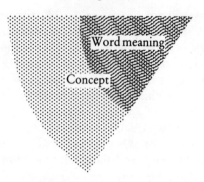

Figure 4.2   The relationship between concepts and word meaning

Snapshots and check-lists

> Yes. I remember Adlestrop –
> The name, because one afternoon
> Of heat the express-train drew up there
> Unwontedly. It was late June.

These lines from Edward Thomas's poem 'Adlestrop' exemplify the simplest possible viewpoint that one could have of fixed word meaning. They suggest that we have words filed as a series of snapshots. The word Adlestrop conjures up a particular photo from the file, in this case a view through a train window.

It seems likely that we all have our Adlestrops: psychologists sometimes talk about 'episodic memory', cases in which a particular episode is remembered with great clarity, sometimes with a word label attached (Tulving, 1972; Baddeley, 1976). However, there are a number of difficulties with the snapshot viewpoint as a general theory of word meaning. One major problem is that we have usually seen any object we are talking about from a number of angles. Take the word *cat*. Are we talking about a cat which is awake and walking about? Or one which is curled up asleep? Or one which is licking milk from a saucer? At the very least we need a number of different snapshots, representing a cat in each of these positions. Furthermore, cats can be different colours and sizes, often with quite personal characteristics, as with T. S. Eliot's mystery cat, Macavity:

> Macavity's a ginger cat, he's very tall and thin;
> You would know him if you saw him, for his eyes are sunken in.
> His brow is deeply lined with thought, his head is highly domed;
> His coat is dusty from neglect, his whiskers are uncombed.

So do people need a whole dossier of photographs for every single cat they have ever seen in every single position? And if so, how could they possibly label a new cat as *cat* if it wasn't in the dossier?

Moreover, the more general a term is, the more difficult it is to specify an associated image. Consider the term *animal*: 'If the generic image is four-footed, how is it that we can identify man as an animal; if it is short-necked how can we identify the giraffe?' (Brown, 1958: 85).

These problems explain why the notion that meaning involves a mental image has generally proved unsatisfactory. It had some popularity at the beginning of the century, when the influential psychologist Edward Bradford Titchenor claimed to have a fixed mental image for every word. For him, *cow* was 'a longish rectangle with a certain facial expression, a sort of exaggerated pout', and the word *meaning* called to mind 'the blue-grey tip of a kind of scoop which has a bit of yellow about it' (Titchenor, 1909, quoted in Brown, 1958: 90). But since then the vast majority of psychologists have abandoned the idea that word meaning involves any straightforward imagery, apart from the occasional Adelstrop-type snapshot.

These observations suggest that a word such as *cat* refers not to the image of a cat but to a somewhat more abstract amalgam. Anyone who understands the word *cat* must have performed some type of analysis which has isolated the essential 'cattiness' involved in being a cat. Perhaps it is these essential characteristics which constitute its basic meaning.

This is the viewpoint of a number of philosophers. They argue that in order to capture the meaning of a word one should establish a set of 'necessary and sufficient conditions', in other words, a list of conditions which are absolutely necessary to the meaning of the word, and which taken together are sufficient or adequate to encapsulate the meaning. Take the word square. This has four necessary conditions (Smith and Medlin, 1981):

1 a closed, flat figure
2 having four sides
3 all sides are equal in length
4 all interior angles are equal.

Each of these conditions is, by itself, necessary in order for something to be a square, and when combined together they are sufficient to define and identify a square, and only a square. Presumably anyone who understands the concept of a square must be aware of these conditions, even if they could not express them in quite this way. These conditions are also called 'conditions of criteriality' or 'criterial attributes' since they are the criteria which one uses to judge whether something is a square or not.

We may refer to this as a 'check-list' theory (Fillmore, 1975). In brief, this theory suggests that for each word we have an internal list of essential characteristics, and we label something as *cat*, or *square*, or *cow* only if it possesses the 'criterial attributes', which we subconsciously check off one by one. This 'check-list' theory is intuitively satisfying to some people, perhaps because it is fairly familiar, as many dictionaries implicitly work on a check-list principle.

However, the check-list theory also involves a number of problems. Let us consider some of these.

A major problem with the check-list theory is deciding which attributes go on to the list. Only a very few words have a straightforward set of necessary conditions, though occasionally officials can decree that words have fixed meanings within a particular context, as in the following bureaucratic definition of a cow: 'A cow is a female bovine animal which has borne a calf, or has, in the opinion of the Minister, been brought into a herd to replace one which has borne a calf' (quoted in a letter to *The Times*).

However, most people's notion of cow would perhaps be more like that of the following ten-year-old: 'A cow is a mammal. It has six sides – right, left, an upper and below. At the back it has a tail on which hangs a brush. With this it sends the flies away so that they do not fall into the milk. The head is for the purpose of growing horns and so that the mouth can be somewhere. The horns are to butt with and the mouth is to moo with. Under the cow hangs the milk. It is arranged for milking. When people milk, the milk comes and there is never an end to the supply' (Gowers, 1986: 43). This child seems to have the word *cow* in its active mental lexicon. But how much of this description involves the actual 'meaning' of *cow* and how much is additional, non-essential information? Is it possible to isolate out from people's overall knowledge a basic hard core of fixed meaning?

A number of linguists and philosophers have claimed that such a distinction is a useful one. Like the Greek philosopher Aristotle, they assume that words have a hard core of essential meaning which it is, in principle, possible to extract and specify. Surrounding this core are a number of fairly accidental facts which can be added or omitted without altering the basic meaning in any important way. The core meaning is assumed to be entered in some kind of linguistic dictionary, whereas the surrounding non-essential facts are stated in an encyclopaedia of general knowledge. Two influential researchers who promoted this viewpoint claimed that they were trying to characterize speakers' internal knowledge of their language, and so seem to be suggesting that there may be a division between a lexicon and an encyclopaedia in the human mind (Katz and Fodor, 1963).

If this is likely to be so, how might one identify the semantic core? Some people propose using the 'That's impossible' test. Suppose you were analysing the meaning of the word *bachelor*. If you say to someone: 'Harry is a bachelor who has been married ten years', you would be likely to get the response: 'That's impossible. Bachelors can't be married, unless you're talking about Harry's first degree or using the word metaphorically.' This suggests that UNMARRIED is a core condition of *bachelor*. You would probably get a similar response of incredulity if you said: 'My aunt Fenella is a bachelor', on the grounds that a *bachelor* has to be male. Similarly, if you stated: 'My baby brother is a bachelor' or 'My tadpole is a bachelor', you would probably be told that bachelors have to be adult and human. So HUMAN, MALE, ADULT,

UNMARRIED might be regarded as components of the 'real meaning' of *bachelor*, in that each of these characteristics seems to be absolutely necessary in order for a person to be labelled *bachelor*. Of course, people might well have additional knowledge or beliefs about bachelors. For example, they might expect bachelors to be childless or to drive fast cars. But this type of information would be a non-necessary extra, which might help in a conversation with a bachelor but would not have anything to do with the meaning of the word.

The idea of sorting out a core meaning which can be distinguished from encyclopaedic knowledge is an enticing one. Unfortunately, however, there are relatively few words which can be sorted out in this apparently useful way. Most words cause considerably more difficulty. Take the word *tiger*. Everybody claims to know what a tiger is but no one is at all clear about exactly what makes a tiger a tiger.

A tiger is a 'large Asian yellow-brown black-striped carnivorous maneless feline' according to one dictionary (*COD*), and 'a very large Asiatic cat having a tawny coat transversely striped with black' according to another (*LCED*). Which of these characteristics are essential? Here the 'That's impossible' test is likely to yield inconclusive results. Most people would accept that ANIMAL is a necessary condition of tigerhood, since if you said 'Harry's tiger's not an animal' you would probably get the reply: 'Then it can't be a tiger.' People might also agree that tigers needn't be carnivorous. If you said: 'Harry's tiger's a vegetarian', it would be quite plausible to receive the reply: 'I'm not surprised, he probably can't afford to feed it on meat.' What about stripiness? 'Of course tigers have to be striped. Whoever heard of an unstriped tiger?' say a few people. But many people are more permissive and make comments such as: 'I read in the paper that you can have white tigers, so stripiness can't be essential' – though white tigers, incidentally, are quite a disappointment: they are in fact honey-coloured, with faint stripes.

The general permissiveness over core characteristics is a problem. 'It's not at all hard to convince the man on the street that there are three legged, lame, toothless, albino tigers, that are tigers all the same . . . What keeps them tigers?' (Armstrong *et al.*, 1983). How does one cope with these apparently 'coreless concepts'?

The check-list viewpoint, therefore, is faced with two critical problems. First, it seems to be extremely difficult to decide what goes on to the check-list, since there appears to be no obvious way to draw a dividing line between essential and non-essential characteristics. Second, for some things the check-list seems to be virtually non-existent, since there appear to be hardly any necessary conditions.

Does this mean that the fixed meaning assumption has to be abandoned if, in practice, it is impossible to fix the meaning for most words? A well-known philosophical viewpoint is that words do indeed have a fixed, correct meaning, but that only a few experts know it (Putnam, 1975). Ordinary people must consult these experts if they need to know about the essential nature of something. Only a specialist, for example, might be able to specify the true nature of gold or arsenic. The problem here is that specialists sometimes disagree, and sometimes change their mind. This leaves us with a quite extraordinary state of affairs: that there might be a 'real meaning' of something which at present nobody can actually specify. But this type of meaning, even if it exists, is not very interesting to someone working on the mental lexicon: 'Either it is in an expert's mind (though no one can know for sure that the right meaning is there), or it is in no one's mind and accordingly an idle wheel in the intellectual traffic of the world' (Johnson-Laird, 1983: 195).

In brief, even if the 'true meaning' of, say, *gold*, *measles*, or *arsenic* exists in the abstract or in the minds of experts, it is clear that we non-experts bumble along quite happily with a working approximation of our own for most words, as indeed the philosophers admit. Moreover, even if we are told about an expert's viewpoint we sometimes choose to ignore it. For example, botanists tell us that an onion is simply a kind of lily (Dupré, 1981), information which seems to be unnecessary for a working knowledge of onions and lilies, and even if known is likely to be disregarded. We conclude, therefore, that even if there is somewhere a 'true' meaning for each particular word, this meaning is fairly irrelevant in relation to the mental lexicon.

In this section, then, we have found that, for some words, it seems to be impossible to identify a firm semantic core. Does this mean that the notion of fixed meanings must be abandoned? Yes it does, according to the fuzzy meaning supporters. Let us now consider their viewpoint.

Fuzzy edges and family resemblances

Fuzzy meaning supporters argue that word meanings are inevitably fluid, for two reasons: the 'fuzzy edge phenomenon' and the 'family resemblance syndrome'. Let us illustrate these. Words have fuzzy edges in the sense that there is no clear point at which one word ends and another begins. This was demonstrated by the sociolinguist William Labov when he showed students pictures of containers and asked them to label each as either a *cup*, a *vase*, or a *bowl* (Labov, 1973). The students all agreed on certain shapes. For example, they all considered tall thin containers without handles to be vases and low flat ones to be bowls. But they were quite confused when faced with something that was in between the two. Was it a vase or a cup? And suppose vase and bowl shapes were given handles (figure 4.3), what then? They had difficulty in deciding, and they came to different conclusions from one another. As Labov pointed out: 'In any kitchen, there are many containers that are obviously bowls, cups, mugs, and dishes. But there are others that might be called cups or might not; or might be a kind of cup, according to some, but a kind of dish according to others' (Labov, 1973: 340).

Figure 4.3   Vase, cup or bowl?

If it was just that they disagreed with one another, one could simply have said that people's mental lexicons differ. But it turned out that individuals were inconsistent in their own responses. For example, after confirming that a particular container was likely to be called a *bowl* when it was seen empty, Labov then asked the students what they would call it when it was filled with various things. A bowl remained a *bowl* if it was full of mashed potatoes but tended to be relabelled as a *vase* if it contained flowers, and a *cup* if there was coffee in it. Labov notes: 'A goal of some clear thinkers has been to use words in more precise ways. But though this is an excellent and necessary step for technical jargon, it is a self-defeating programme when applied to ordinary words' (1973: 341). Fuzzy edges, then, seem to be an intrinsic property of word meaning.

Let us now turn to the family resemblance syndrome. This can be illustrated by a mythical family called the Mugwumps. The Mugwumps, let us say, have certain family characteristics which tend to surface in generation after generation of Mugwumps: ears which stick out, squint-eyes, eyebrows which meet in the middle and a ferocious temper. However, it might well happen that although two or three of these features occurred in lots of Mugwumps, there was no single Mugwump who actually had all of them. The same thing happens in relation to words.

The family resemblance syndrome has been described vividly by the philosopher Wittgenstein (1958: 66): 'Consider . . . the proceedings that we call "games". I mean board-games, card-games, ball-games, Olympic games, and so on. What is common to them all? – Don't say: "There must be something common, or they would not be called 'games'" – but look and see whether there is anything common to all. – For if you look at them you will not see something that is common to all, but similarities, relationships, and a whole series of them at that. To repeat: don't think, but look! – Look for example at board games, with their multifarious relationships. Now pass to card-games; here you find many correspondences with the first group, but many features drop out, and others appear. When we pass next to ball-games, much that is common is retained, but much is lost. – Are they all "amusing"? Compare chess with noughts and crosses. Or is there always winning and losing, or competition between players? Think of patience. In ball games there is winning and losing; but when a child throws his ball at the wall and catches it again, this feature has disappeared. Look at the parts played by skill and luck; and at the difference between skill in chess and skill in tennis. Think now of games like ring-a-ring-a-roses; here is the element of amusement, but how many other characteristic features have disappeared! And we can go through the many, many other groups of games in the same way; can see how similarities crop up and disappear.'

Wittgenstein concludes that although every game has some similarity with other games, there is no one factor which links them all. We are faced with 'a complicated network of similarities overlapping and criss-crossing' (Wittgenstein, 1958: 66). He continues: 'I can think of no better expression to characterize these similarities than "family resemblances"; for the various

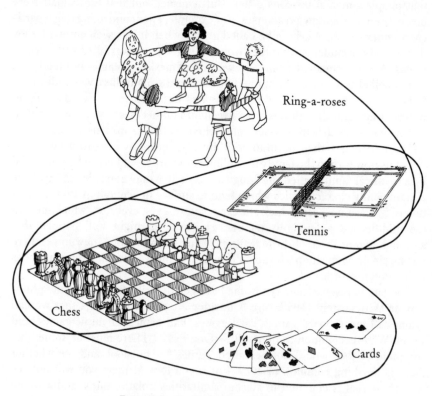

Figure 4.4 Family resemblances among games

resemblances between members of a family: build, features, colour of eyes, gait, temperament, etc. etc. overlap and criss-cross in the same way. – And I shall say: "games" form a family' (Wittgenstein, 1958: 67) (figure 4.4).

The word *game*, then, illustrates the family resemblance syndrome clearly. But this word is not an isolated, special instance and there are numerous other equally common ones which exhibit the same problem, such as *furniture*, *employment*, or *vegetable*.

The fixed–fuzziness issue

Let us now summarize the fixed–fuzziness issue. There are a small number of words such as *square* or *bachelor* which appear to have a fixed meaning, that is, they are words for which we can specify a set of necessary and sufficient conditions. The majority of words, however, do not behave in this way. They suffer from one or more of the following problems: first, it may be difficult to specify a hard core of meaning at all. Second, it may be impossible to tell where 'true meaning' ends, and encyclopaedic knowledge begins. Third, the words may have 'fuzzy boundaries' in that there might be no clear point at which the meaning of one word ends and another begins. Fourth, a single word may apply to a 'family' of items which all overlap in meaning but which do not share any one common characteristic.

These are insuperable obstacles to the fixed meaning viewpoint. We conclude that, for the majority of words, meanings in the mind are fuzzy, not fixed. Language, it seems, has an inbuilt 'property of "limited sloppiness"' and 'only some areas are marked by a degree of "terminologization"' – the setting of firm boundaries (Weinreich, 1966: 190, 186). In the next chapter we shall consider how humans cope with this hazy mush of meanings. However, before we tackle this topic we need to consider one further point. Can we assume that everyone operates with the same meanings? Or is there a huge discrepancy from person to person? Let us discuss this problem.

Plank, slab, block, brick, cube

'Plank, slab, block, brick, cube' are the first five words spoken in Tom Stoppard's play *Dogg's Our Pet*. A man called Charlie is planning to build a platform, and he shouts instructions about the pieces he wants thrown to him. A plank, a slab, a block, a brick and a cube duly arrive, in that order. But then strange things start to happen. When Charlie shouts 'Plank' again, a block arrives. When he calls for a block, he gets a brick, and when he yells 'Cube', there is no response. What has gone wrong?

It transpires that Charlie and the thrower are speaking a different language. In Charlie's language, words such as plank, block and cube have their conventional meaning. But to the thrower they mean something different, perhaps 'Here!', 'Next!' and 'Thankyou!' If Charlie had needed only the first five pieces named the discrepancy might never have been discovered, since the thrower's language fitted in sufficiently well with the context of platform-building for the work to proceed.

This is an extreme and literary situation. But the play makes a serious point. If I ask someone to fetch me a glass of water and a glass of water arrives, it is possible that the person fetching it simply thinks that the word *water* means 'colourless liquid' and so chose randomly between water, gin and vodka. Only if there is a misunderstanding, and a tumblerful of vodka arrives, would I suspect a problem. And such misunderstandings might continue for some time, only being discovered by chance, as when I overheard a schoolchild who was viewing lemurs at the London Zoo enquire of her teacher: 'Please, miss, are they extinct?', or when a horrified mother heard her teenage daughter say to an elderly lady: 'Can I relieve you of your nether garments?' as she helped the visitor out of her coat.

Furthermore, we are not in general on the look-out for problems of this kind. If someone uses a word strangely we rarely assume that their use of it is defective by our standards. If someone said, 'Look out! There's a rhinoceros sitting in the tree just above your head', we would assume that they were either joking or mad. We would be unlikely to consider the possibility that the speaker thought *rhinoceros* meant 'pigeon'. In brief, in real life we operate by assuming that, for the most part, people have beliefs similar to our own about what words mean (see Pulman, 1983, Sperber and Wilson, 1986, for further discussion on this). We as psycholinguists work in the same way. We assume that there will be sufficient overlap between the meaning of words in the minds of different speakers for us to come to some useful conclusions – though we shall be on the look-out for discrepancies which might reveal idiosyncratic ideas.

Summary

In this chapter we examined the controversy between those who claim that words have fixed meanings and those who argue that word meanings are essentially fluid.

Our conclusion was that, for many words, it is impossible to specify hardcore semantic information, and equally impossible to distinguish essential meaning from encyclopaedic knowledge. There is no firm boundary between the meaning of one word and another, and the same word often applies to a whole family of things which have no overall common characteristic. We concluded, therefore, that words are indeed slippery customers, with vague boundaries and fuzzy edges.

But if words are so fuzzy, how do speakers cope with this hazy mush of meanings? This is the topic of the next chapter.

5

Bad Birds and Better Birds
— *Prototype theories* —

The Hatter . . . had taken his watch out of his pocket, and was looking at it uneasily, shaking it every now and then, and holding it to his ear . . .

'Two days wrong!' sighed the Hatter, 'I told you butter wouldn't suit the works!'. . .

Alice had been looking over his shoulder with some curiosity. 'What a funny watch!' she remarked. 'It tells the day of the month, and doesn't tell what o'clock it is!'

Lewis Carroll, Alice's Adventures in Wonderland

If words have a hazy area of application, as we decided in the last chapter, we are faced with a serious problem in relation to the mental lexicon. How do we manage to cope with words at all? The quotation above from *Alice in Wonderland* gives us a clue. Alice appears to have some notion of what constitutes a 'proper watch'. This enables her to identify the butter-smeared object owned by the Hatter as a watch, and to comment that it is a 'funny' one.

A feeling that some examples of words may be more central than others appears to be widespread, as shown by a dialogue between two small girls in a popular cartoon strip:

Augusta   What colour did you say the Martians are?
Friend   Green.
Augusta   What sort of green? I mean are they an emerald green or a pea green or an apple green or a sage green or a sea green or what?
Friend   Well I think they're a sort of greeny green.

Humans, then, appear to find some instances of words more basic than others. Such an observation may shed light on how people understand their meaning. Take birds. Perhaps people have an amalgam of ideal bird characteristics in their minds. Then, if they saw a pterodactyl, they would decide whether it was likely to be a bird by matching it against the features of a bird-like bird, or, in fashionable terminology, a 'prototypical' bird. It need not have

Reproduced by kind permission of the *London Standard*

all the characteristics of the prototype, but if the match was reasonably good it could be labelled *bird*, though it might not necessarily be a very good example of a bird. This viewpoint is not unlike the check-list viewpoint, but it differs in that in order to be a bird, the creature in question does not have to have a fixed number of bird characteristics, it simply has to be a reasonable match.

This is an intriguing idea. But, like any intriguing idea, it needs to be tested. How could we find out if people really behave in this way? In fact, psychologists showed quite a long time ago that people treat colours like this (e.g. Lenneberg, 1967; Berlin and Kay, 1969). However, this type of study has only relatively recently been extended to other types of vocabulary items. Let us consider one of the pioneering papers on the topic.

Birdy birds and vegetabley vegetables

Just over ten years ago Eleanor Rosch, a psychologist at the University of California at Berkeley, carried out a set of experiments in order to test the idea that people regarded some types of birds as 'birdier' than other birds, or some vegetables more vegetable-like, or some tools more tooly.

She devised an experiment which she carried out with more than 200 psychology students: 'This study has to do with what we have in mind when we use words which refer to categories' ran the instructions (Rosch, 1975: 198).

Let's take the word red as an example. Close your eyes and imagine a true red. Now imagine an orangish red . . . imagine a purple red. Although you might still name the orange red or the purple red with the term red, they are not as good examples of red . . . as the clear 'true' red. In short, some reds are redder than others. The same is true for other kinds of categories. Think of dogs. You all have some notion of what a 'real dog', a 'doggy dog' is. To me a retriever or a German shepherd is a very doggy dog while a Pekinese is a less doggy dog. Notice that this kind of judgment has nothing to do with how well you like the thing; you can like a purple red better than a true red but still recognize that the color you like is not a true red. You may prefer to own a Pekinese without thinking that it is the breed that best represents what people mean by dogginess.

The questionnaire which followed was ten pages long. On each page was a category name, such as 'Furniture', 'Fruit', 'Vegetable', 'Bird', 'Carpenter's Tool', 'Clothing', and so on. Under each category was a list of 50 or so examples. *Orange, lemon, apple, peach, pear, melon* appeared on the fruit list, and so did most of the other fruits you would be likely to think up easily. The order of the list was varied for different students to ensure that the order of presentation did not bias the results. The students were asked to rate how good an example of the category each member was on a seven-point scale: rating something as '1' meant that they considered it an excellent example; '4' indicated a moderate fit; whereas '7' suggested that it was a very poor example, and probably should not be in the category at all.

The results were surprisingly consistent. Agreement was particularly high for the items rated as very good examples of the category. Almost everybody thought that a *robin* was the best example of a bird, that *pea* was the best example of a vegetable and *chair* the best example of furniture. On the bird list, *sparrow, canary, blackbird, dove* and *lark* all came out high (figure 5.1). *Parrot, pheasant, albatross, toucan* and *owl* came somewhat lower. *Flamingo, duck* and *peacock* were lower still. *Ostrich, emu* and *penguin* came more than half-way down the seven-point rating, while last of all came *bat*, which probably shouldn't be regarded as a bird at all. Similar results were found for the other categories, that is, *shirts, dresses* and *skirts* were considered better examples of clothing than *shoes* and *stockings*, which were in turn higher than *aprons* and *earmuffs*. *Guns* and *daggers* were better examples of weapons than *whips* and *axes*, which were better than *pitchforks* and *bricks*. *Saws, hammers* and *screwdrivers* were better examples of carpenters' tools than *crowbars* and *plumb-lines*.

Psychologists on the other side of America obtained very similar results when they repeated the experiment (Armstrong *et al.*, 1983), so the results are

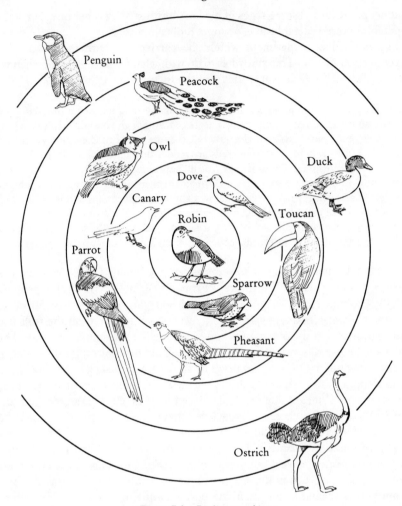

Figure 5.1   Birdiness rankings

not just a peculiar reaction of Californian psychology students. And Rosch carried out other experiments which supported her original results. For example, she checked how long it took students to verify category membership. That is, she said, 'Tell me whether the following is true', and then gave the students sentences such as 'A penguin is a bird', or 'A sparrow is a bird'. She found that good exemplars (her name for examples) of a category were verified faster than less good exemplars, so that it took longer to say 'Yes' to 'A penguin is a bird' than it did to 'A sparrow is a bird' (Rosch, 1975).

The results of these experiments are fairly impressive. But there is one obvious criticism: were the students just responding faster to more common words? After all, people come across sparrows far more frequently than penguins, and hammers more often than crowbars. Obviously, frequency of usage is likely to have some effect: in California nectarines and boysenberries are commoner than mangoes and kumquats, so it is not surprising that the former were regarded as 'better' exemplars of fruit than the latter. However, the results could not be explained away solely on the basis of word frequency. On the furniture list, rare items of furniture such as *love seat*, *davenport*, *ottoman* and *cedar chest* came out much higher than *refrigerator*, which is a standard part of every American household. On the vegetable list, *pea*, *carrot* and *cauliflower* came out higher than *onion*, *potato* and *mushroom*. And on the clothes list, *pyjamas* and *bathing suit* came out higher than *shoe*, *tie*, *hat* and *gloves*. So people genuinely feel that some things are better exemplars of a category than others, a feeling which is not simply due to how often one comes across the word or object in question.

Furthermore, these judgements were not made primarily on the basis of appearance. Peas, according to Rosch, are prototypical vegetables. If people were simply comparing other vegetables to a visual image of a pea, then we would expect carrots to come out near the bottom of the list. In fact, they come very near the top. And if visual characteristics were important, we would also expect vegetables which look similar, such as carrots, parsnips and radishes, to be clustered together. But they are not. Nor were judgements made purely in terms of use. If this was so one would expect benches and stools to come out near the top, since they are closest in function to the prototypical piece of furniture, a chair. But in fact bookcases rank higher than either benches or stools. It is not immediately obvious, therefore, how people came to their conclusions. They were making some type of analysis, though its exact basis was unclear as the criteria used seemed to be heterogeneous.

To summarize, Rosch's work suggests that when people categorize common objects, they do not expect them all to be on an equal footing. They seem to have some idea of the characteristics of an ideal exemplar, in Rosch's words, a 'prototype'. And they probably decide on the extent to which something else is a member of the same category by matching it against the features of the prototype. It does not have to match exactly, it just has to be sufficiently similar, though not necessarily visually similar.

Prototype theory is useful, then, for explaining how people deal with untypical examples of a category. This is how unbirdy birds such as pelicans and penguins can still be regarded as birds. They are sufficiently like the prototype, even though they do not share all its characteristics. But it has a further advantage: it can explain how people cope with damaged examples. Previously linguists had found it difficult to explain why anyone could still categorize a one-winged robin who couldn't fly as a bird, or a three-legged tiger as a quadruped. Now one just assumes that these get matched against the prototype in the same way as an untypical category member. A one-winged robin who can't fly can still be a bird, even though it's not such a typical one.

Furthermore, the prototype effect seems to work for actions as well as objects: people can, it appears, reliably make judgements that *murder* is a better example of killing than *execute* or *suicide*, and that *stare* is a better example of looking than *peer* or *squint* (Pulman, 1983).

However, so far we have dealt only with assigning objects and actions to larger categories. We now need to consider whether this is the way in which humans cope with individual words.

Degrees of lying

'Can you nominate in order now the degrees of the lie?' asks a character in Shakespeare's play *As You Like It* (V, iv), and the clown Touchstone responds by listing seven degrees of lying. Obviously the idea that some lies are better lies than others has been around for a long time, and still seems to be relevant today.

A 'good' lie, it transpires, has several characteristics (Coleman and Kay, 1981). First, the speaker has to assert something that is untrue. However, people often utter untruths without being regarded as liars, particularly in cases of genuine mistakes: a child who argued that six and four make eleven would not be thought of as lying. So a second characteristic of a good lie is that a speaker must believe that what he is saying is false. But even this is insufficient, because a person can knowingly tell untruths without being a liar, as in: 'You're the cream in my coffee, you're the sugar in my tea' (metaphor), 'He stood so still, you could have mistaken him for a doorpost' (exaggeration or hyperbole), 'Since you're a world expert on the topic, perhaps you could tell us how to get the cat out of the drainpipe?' (sarcasm). A third characteristic must therefore be added for a good lie, that the speaker must intend to deceive those addressed. In brief, a fully-fledged or prototypical lie occurs when a speaker:

1 asserts something false
2 which they know to be false
3 with the intention of deceiving.

A prototypical lie, therefore, might occur when a child denies having eaten a jam tart which it knows full well it has just scoffed. But consider a situation such as the following: 'Schmallowitz is invited to dinner at his boss's house. After a dismal evening enjoyed by no one, Schmallowitz says to his hostess, "Thanks, it was a terrific party." Schmallowitz doesn't believe it was a terrific party, and he isn't really trying to convince anyone he had a good time, but is just concerned to say something to his boss's wife, regardless of the fact that he doesn't expect her to believe it' (Coleman and Kay, 1981: 31).

Did Schmallowitz lie? The 71 people asked this question were quite unsure. They had been told to grade a number of situations on a seven-point scale, from 1 (very sure non-lie) to 7 (very sure lie). For many people, Schmallowitz's situation lay just in the middle between these two extremes, at point 4, where they were unable to decide whether it was a lie or not. Another situation which lay in the middle was the case of Superfan, who got tickets for a championship game, and phoned early in the day to tell his boss that he could not come to work as he was sick. Ironically Superfan doesn't get to the game, because the mild stomach-ache he had that morning turned out to be quite severe food poisoning.

Both the Schmallowitz and Superfan cases broke one of the conditions of a good lie, though each broke a different condition. Schmallowitz was not trying to deceive his hostess, he was merely trying to be polite. Superfan did not tell an untruth. Lies, then, like birds, can be graded. Lies can still be lies even when they are not prototypical lies, and they shade off into not being 'proper' lies at all.

The realization that individual words need not be used in their prototypical sense can explain a number of puzzling problems, especially cases in which people are unsure of whether they are dealing with the 'same' word or not. Consider the following sentences (Jackendoff, 1983):

I must have seen that a dozen times, but I never noticed it.
I must have looked at that a dozen times, but I never saw it.

Some people have argued that there are two different verbs *see*, one meaning 'my gaze went to an object', as in the first sentence, and the other containing in addition the meaning 'something entered my awareness', as in the second. But perhaps the first sentence contains an unprototypical usage of the verb see (Jackendoff, 1983). In prototypical instances of seeing, one's gaze goes to an object and the object enters one's awareness. But if the first characteristic is absent, one can stare at something without noticing it. If the second characteristic is absent, something can enter a person's awareness, such as a dream or hallucination, even though his gaze has not gone anywhere.

To take another example, look at the following sentences:

The staircase goes from top to bottom of the building.
The lift goes from top to bottom of the building.
The janitor goes from top to bottom of the building.

Some people might argue as to whether these are all instances of the same word *go*, since the janitor is clearly moving but the staircase is not. But a prototype approach allows one to treat this as all one word, *go* (Aitchison, 1985). In its prototypical use, *go* involves something moving from one point to another. However, the same word can be used untypically, so that something can extend from one point to another, with no movement involved. Alternatively, something can leave one point but never get to another, as in:

The train goes at ten o'clock.

Judging something against a prototype, therefore, and allowing rough matches to suffice, seems to be the way we understand a number of different words. Furthermore, a general realization that this is how humans probably operate could be of considerable use in real-life situations, as in the example below.

Mad, bad and dangerous to know

Some years ago a man who specialized in brutal murders of women was brought to trial. The Yorkshire Ripper, as he was called, divided public opinion sharply. Some people argued that he was simply bad, and therefore ought to be be punished with a long term of imprisonment. Others claimed that he must be mad, in which case he should be admitted to a hospital and treated as someone who was not responsible for his actions.

Was he mad? Or was he bad? According to newspaper reports, the judge asked the jury to consider whether the Ripper had told the truth to the psychiatrists who examined him. The discrepancies and alterations in the Ripper's story made them conclude that he had told a considerable number of lies. This led them to classify him as 'Guilty' – bad, not mad. This judgement implies, therefore, that anyone who lies cannot be mad, a somewhat strange conclusion. Perhaps the situation would have been less confusing if the terms *mad* and *bad* had been considered in terms of prototypes (Aitchison, 1981a).

'To define true madness, What is't to be nothing else but mad?' asks Polonius, on observing the deranged Hamlet (II, ii). But contrary to Polonius's opinion, madness is not an all or nothing state. A prototypical mad person has several different characteristics. A mad person is, first, someone who thinks and acts abnormally. But this is insufficient, as it would categorize as mentally deranged such people as chess champions. Someone truly mad would, in addition, be unaware that he was thinking and acting abnormally, and furthermore, be unable to prevent himself from behaving oddly. A prototypical lunatic, therefore, might be someone who covers his head with tin-foil because he fears that moon men are about to attack, or someone who walks on her hands because God has supposedly told her not to wear out her feet. On this analysis, the Ripper was partially mad, because he acted strangely and seemed unable to prevent himself from doing so. Yet he was not prototypically mad, because he was perfectly aware that his actions were abnormal.

To turn to badness, someone bad commits antisocial acts, is aware that their actions are antisocial and could control their behaviour if they wished. So a protypical villain might be the pirate Captain Hook in Peter Pan, or Shakespeare's character Iago. On this reasoning, the Ripper was partially bad in that he acted antisocially and was aware of it, but not entirely bad since he apparently could not control his actions.

To modify Caroline Lamb's statement about Lord Byron and reapply it to the Ripper, one could say that he is 'Around two-thirds mad, two-thirds bad and certainly dangerous to know'. No wonder the jury took so long to decide whether he was mad *or* bad, when he was neither prototypically mad nor prototypically bad.

The oddity of odd numbers

Prototypes seem to explain a lot. They show how people deal with the fuzziness of word meaning, and how new or damaged examples can be assigned to existing categories. Something could still be labelled a parrot if it was sufficiently like a prototypical parrot, even it if had one leg, pink and blue stripes and carried an umbrella. There remain, however, a number of unsolved questions. These will be discussed in the remainder of the chapter.

'The oddity of odd numbers' is perhaps the most puzzling problem. A group of researchers found that some odd numbers were felt to be 'better' odd numbers than others (Armstrong *et al.*, 1983). The subjects they quizzed thought that 3 was a better example of an odd number than 23, which was in turn better than 57 or 447! How could people possibly think that 3 was better than 23 when both are equally odd? Furthermore, this result had nothing to do with the ambiguity of the word *odd* which can mean either 'uneven' or 'peculiar', because the researchers found a very similar result for even numbers: 4 was considered a better example than 18, which was in turn better than 34 or 106! So what's going on? Surely when they judge whether 57 is a good example of an odd number, people are not matching it against a prototypical odd number such as 3? Can we explain all this away, or is there some fatal flaw in prototype theory?

People are still arguing about these results, but a plausible explanation is that we need to make a distinction between identification criteria and stored knowledge (Osherson and Smith, 1981). In judging whether something is a good example of an odd number, people may be using easy recognition as their yardstick rather than basic knowledge. A clash between identification and knowledge is common in some areas. Take bulls. A farmer had trouble with people breaking down fences with the result that his cattle escaped, according to a newspaper report (*The Guardian*, November 1984). He therefore put a ring through the nose of one of the cows. Since a ring usually signifies a bull, which might be dangerous, he reckoned it would successfully keep people away. Within two days he had a telephone call from the local police:

Police   You've got a bull in the park – it's illegal.
Farmer   I'm sorry but we have no bull in the park.
Police   I've seen it myself – I saw the ring in its nose.
Farmer   You'd better go and look at the other end.

The moral is obvious. People know that bulls are male but they do not normally identify them by checking their genitalia – they identify them by something which could be quite extraneous to their basic make-up. The problems such cases raise in relation to prototypes is that we do not know exactly how identification criteria are interwoven with stored knowledge in the minds of speakers.

Of course, with many words identification criteria and stored knowledge might be the same, as perhaps with *rainbow* or *lamp-post*. But in a large number of others there may be a difference, even though the two will probably overlap to a considerable extent. How we perceive and identify things cannot be entirely removed from our stored knowledge of them: 'Any sharp division between perception and conception seems questionable' (Miller and Johnson-Laird, 1976: 41). A further complication is that people sometimes have to interweave their own observations with information presented by others, since biological taxonomies and cultural beliefs may clash with instincts. For example, children often find it hard to believe that a spider is not an insect, a whale is not a fish and a bat is not a bird. And in Papua New Guinea, the Karam people of the upper Kaironk valley do not regard the cassowary as a bird, even though to us it obviously is one (Bulmer, 1967). It is unclear how such 'facts' get integrated into a person's overall view of a word's meaning. This indicates that finding out the characteristics of a prototype is enormously difficult. Let us briefly summarize these difficulties.

Further problems with prototypes

There are basically three main problems which arise in specifying a prototype: first, the diversity of the characteristics which make up the prototype; second, the difficulty of arranging them in order of priority, since some are clearly more important than others; third, the problem of knowing where to stop. Let us briefly deal with each of these.

As we have seen, the properties of a prototype are heterogeneous, involving both identification criteria and knowledge. In addition, prototypes vary quite considerably in type from one another. For example, a birdy bird seems to be treated rather differently from a reddy red (Jackendoff, 1983). A birdy bird involves a cluster of 'typicality conditions' relating to appearance and behaviour: it is likely to have feathers, wings and a beak, fly and lay eggs in a nest. But a reddy red is somewhat different in nature, unless one happens to be a physicist who can analyse the various properties of colours. For most people, a reddy red is likely to be characterized by 'centrality conditions' – it will have a central place within a range of reds. To take another example, a *table* is likely to have a set of typical table features, but the term *adult* is usually understood with reference to a central example: a man of 25 would be a more adult-like adult than a 17-year-old.

So analysing the characteristics of a prototype turns out to be enormously difficult. A further problem is deciding how to arrange these characteristics in order of importance. Take birds. It is probably fairly important for a bird to have feathers. As the humorous poet Ogden Nash once noted:

> All I know about the bird:
> It is feathered, not furred.

But what comes next? Perhaps having wings. What then? Ability to fly? Egg laying? Nest building? There are unlikely to be clear answers, as suggested by the argument between the bird and the duck in Prokofiev's *Peter and the Wolf*:

Seeing the duck, the little bird flew down upon the grass, settled next to her and shrugged his shoulders:
'What kind of a bird are you, if you can't fly?' said he.
To this, the duck replied:
'What kind of a bird are you, if you can't swim?' and dived into the pond.
They argued and argued . . .

Furthermore, in trying to sort out the features of a prototype, where does one stop? There seems to be no end to the amount of encyclopaedic knowledge which people have about things, so does someone trying to model the mental lexicon have to go on for ever? In some cases this is particularly tricky, because it seems impossible to separate out the meaning of a particular word from the whole situation in which it occurs. Consider Gus, a character in Pinter's play *The Dumb Waiter*, who seems to have a clear idea of what a prototypical bowl of salad is like:

'They've probably got a salad bowl up there. Cold meat, radishes, cucumbers. Watercress, roll mops. Hardboiled eggs.'

Gus's prototypical salad bowl seems to go way beyond the 'meaning' of the word: his mind seems to have flipped up a whole 'salad bowl situation', with particular ingredients in the bowl. Or consider the conversation between Ackroyd and Boothroyd, two characters who visit a ruined abbey in Alan Bennett's play *A Day Out*:

Ackroyd   They were Cistercian monks here . . .
Boothroyd It's an unnatural life, separating yourself off like that . . . There wouldn't
           be any kids, would there? And allus getting down on their knees. It's no
           sort of life . . .'

Here, the word *monk* has triggered not just the basic 'meaning' of the word but a whole situation, in which he imagines silent corridors and monks praying. Are all these associated scenes part of our encyclopaedic knowledge of a word? To some extent, yes. In our memory we seem to have sets of stereotypical situations, 'remembered frameworks' (Minsky, 1975), which we call up as necessary. These 'frames' or 'scenarios' provide a background into which one fits the details of the present situation. No one is quite sure how these frames might work and there have been several different proposals (for a useful summary see Brown and Yule, 1983). From the point of view of the mental lexicon, such stereotypical situations seem to be optional back-up material which is accessed if required. If a person was asked to define a *zebra*, they could do this quite efficiently without calling up a whole 'zoo' or 'safari' frame. But if they overheard someone talking about a zebra seen in London earlier in the day, then they could go deeper into their memory, and call up a zoo frame, which allowed them to fit the narrative into a predicted set-up, and be prepared for mentions of turnstiles, monkeys and elephant-rides.

This back-up information may work in two ways. Either the entries in the mental lexicon are organized so that the most important things pop up first, or, alternatively, the mind may automatically flip up considerably more information than is necessary, and humans may be very good at discarding or suppressing information that is not required. Or perhaps these two mechanisms work together. But whatever the mechanism involved, the activation of whole frames in the mind makes it even harder to specify the characteristics of individual prototypes since they interact with other elements present in the scene, and involve the optional use of a seemingly endless supply of back-up material from a person's memory.

In short, even though we suspect that humans work from prototypes when they deal with word meaning, the exact specification of the prototypes which apparently exist in a person's mind is still a long way beyond our current ability.

However, the fact that a prototype often calls up a whole scene, in which numerous other words are involved, indicates one important fact: words cannot be dealt with in isolation. We need to consider how they are stored in relation to one another. This is discussed in the next chapter.

Summary

This chapter has discussed how humans are able to cope with word meaning when it is so fuzzy and fluid. It seems likely that they analyse a prototypical exemplar of a word and then match any new example against the characteristics of the prototype. It does not have to be a perfect match, merely a reasonable fit. This explains how words can be used with slightly different meanings, and how people can recognize new or damaged examples of a category.

However, certain problems remain. It is extremely difficult to analyse the features of a prototype, since identification criteria are interwoven with stored knowledge. It is equally difficult to arrange the various features in order of importance. And it is unclear where a prototype stops, since humans have a seemingly endless amount of information about every word, and often seem to access whole situations or 'frames' in order to understand them. All these problems do not invalidate prototype theory. They simply show that there is still a lot we do not know about the human word-store. However, the fact that humans do not deal with these prototypes in isolation from one another shows that we need to find out more about how words fit together in the mental lexicon. This is the topic of the next chapter.

6

The Primordial Atomic Globule Hunt
— *The search for semantic primitives* —

> I can trace my ancestry back to a protoplasmal primordial atomic globule. Consequently, my family pride is something inconceivable.
>
> W. S. Gilbert, *The Mikado*

Words cannot be treated as if they were a swarm of bees – a bundle of separate items attached to one another in a fairly random way. They are clearly interdependent. In some cases it is difficult to understand a word without knowing the words around it: *orange* is best understood by looking at it in relation to *red* and *yellow*, or *warm* by considering it as the area between *hot* and *cold*. How, then, do humans fit words together in the mental lexicon?

As a preliminary guess, one might suggest that words are stitched together in one's mind like pieces on a patchwork quilt. The shape and size of the patches would differ from language to language, but within each language any particular patch could be defined with reference to those around it. But this simple idea will not work. Words do not cover the world smoothly, like a jigsaw with interlocking pieces. The whole situation is more like badly spread bread and butter, with the butter heaped up double in some places and leaving bare patches in others. Some words overlap almost completely, as with *chase* and *pursue*, or *plump* and *fat*, while elsewhere there are inexplicable gaps: there is no generally accepted term for 'live-in lover' or 'dead plant'.

Perhaps the biggest problem for the patchwork quilt idea is words which overlap, as with *hog*, *sow* and *piglet*, which are all pigs, or *sow*, *hen* and *princess*, which are all female, or *piglet*, *chick* and *princeling*, which are all youngsters. Every word in the language has similar links with numerous others, reminiscent of the character in Gilbert and Sullivan's opera *HMS Pinafore* who had dozens of relatives:

> His sisters and his cousins,
> Whom he reckons up by dozens,
> And his aunts!

How, then, does the mind cope with these relationships? There have been a
number of different proposals. As two psychologists warn: 'In approaching the
question, how are words related to one another, we must take care not to drown
in the diversity of answers' (Miller and Johnson-Laird, 1976: 237).

The diversity of answers is not, however, totally unmanageable, since the
theories put forward tend to fall into two broad categories, which we may call
the 'atomic globule' viewpoint on the one hand and the 'cobweb' viewpoint on
the other (figure 6.1). Atomic globule supporters argue that words are built up
from a common pool of 'meaning atoms', and that related words have atoms in
common. Cobweb supporters claim that words are recognized as related
because of the links which speakers have built between them. On the one hand,
then, words are viewed as an assemblage of bits. On the other, they are
regarded as wholes which have various characteristics and enter into relationships with other words. Both of these viewpoints are compatible with prototype
theory (Armstrong *et al.*, 1983), though the proponents of each have a different
view of the way in which people deal with a prototype. Let us therefore consider these opposing ideas. In this chapter, we will discuss atomic globules, and
in the next, cobwebs.

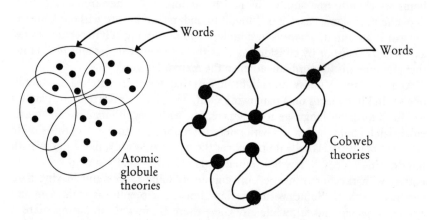

Figure 6.1   Atomic globules versus cobwebs

Primordial atoms

'But numerous primordial atoms, whirled around in numerous ways from time
immemorial, kept in motion by collisions and their own weight, have finally
come together in every possible way and tried out everything that could be
formed by their various combinations.' This sentence comes from the ancient
Roman poet Lucretius (v, 422–6), who is describing how the world may have
come into existence according to a theory current in his time. But it could

equally well describe one recurring viewpoint in linguistics, that there is some universal set of basic atoms of meaning known as 'semantic primitives' which are combined in different ways in different languages: 'Semantic features cannot be different from language to language, but are rather part of the general human capacity for language, forming a universal inventory used in particular ways in individual languages' (Bierwisch, 1970: 182).

This viewpoint was particularly dominant around 20 years ago. 'The very notion "lexical entry" presupposes some sort of fixed universal vocabulary in terms of which these objects are characterized', according to Chomsky (1965: 160). These primordial atomic globules were assumed to suffice for the description of all word meanings since they were regarded as 'presumably biologically given notions' (Fillmore, 1971: 372) built into the structure of the human mind. They represent 'certain deep seated, innate properties of the human organism and the perceptual apparatus' (Bierwisch, 1967: 3). A number of scholars still maintain this point of view (e.g. Jackendoff, 1983), so it needs to be taken seriously.

The most obvious way of promoting the atomic globule viewpoint would be to identify the semantic primitives. Unfortunately, most of those who believe in their existence have been quite vague and evasive as to what they might actually be, speaking in general terms of 'such notions as identity, time, space, body, movement, territory, life, fear, etc.' (Fillmore, 1971: 32). Only a few have settled down to producing a coherent list. Let us now consider two well-known attempts to do this. The aim of the first was to seek out the primitives underlying common verbs (Schank, 1972). The other sought to link semantic primitives to human perception (Miller and Johnson-Laird, 1976).

Approximately a dozen semantic primitives form the basis of all the verbs we ordinarily use, according to Schank (1972). Some of these primitives were physical acts, such as MOVE, INGEST, GRASP. Others were mental, such as CONC which means roughly 'to think about', or MTRANS which involved the transfer of mental information. And others were more general, such as ATRANS, which dealt with the transfer of possessions. For example, verbs such as *breathe, drink, eat, inhale* and *sniff* all had a component INGEST in common. *Buy, sell, give, take, steal* all had ATRANS in common. But a number of problems arose.

First, Schank and his colleagues found it quite difficult to specify exactly how many of these primitives there were, and what they should be. They changed their minds several times, and they never reached an entirely satisfactory conclusion. Therefore they were unable to claim that they had actually found the components out of which these verbs were made. This is perhaps a minor problem, because it often takes some time to specify things exactly. A more serious problem is that it is hard to see why several of these components are 'primitives', since each one is in fact decomposable into more basic elements: INGEST, for example, is a complex notion which could be broken down into several subcomponents. A third problem is that most verbs contain far more in their meaning than the components specified in these 'primitives', which form only the rough framework on to which more detailed specifications need to be added – yet a major claim of the atomic viewpoint approach is that the meaning atoms cover the whole meaning of the word.

In view of these problems, it seems unlikely that Schank had specified 'primitives' in any psychological sense. He had simply found a convenient way of describing 'family resemblances' between the groups of words he was dealing with. As we noted in chapter 3, it is important to distinguish between useful ways of describing things and structures which are likely to exist in speakers' minds. Judging from the work of Schank, there is no reason to believe that verbs are assembled out of pieces in the human mind – even though we might well adopt his system if we were trying to write a computer program which explained relationships between words in a helpful, though non-realistic way. And the problems found with Schank's primitives – difficulty of deciding what they are, their decomposability, and their incompleteness for specifying meaning – occur in most other attempts to identify primitives (e.g. Jackendoff, 1983).

Perhaps the most impressive exploration of the topic so far is by two psychologists who tried to link semantic primitives to perceptual primitives (Miller and Johnson-Laird, 1976). They attempted to anchor them to some kind of observable human experience, to things people can see, hear, or feel. This seems a useful enterprise, since a number of people have suggested that humans start out by dealing with the world they can perceive and then generalize from this to more abstract matters.

Their book runs to almost 800 pages and presents a thorough investigation of the subject, even though, as they admit, the whole project is based on somewhat shaky foundations, since psychologists have not yet produced an agreed, fully worked out theory of perception: 'Not having an explicit perceptual theory means that we cannot be sure what the primitives of the system are . . . The best we can do, therefore, is to limit ourselves to judgments that seem to be likely candidates as primitives. In a sense we are building on sand, but it is better to build on sand than on nothing at all' (Miller and Johnson-Laird, 1976: 38).

Miller and Johnson-Laird's proposals are quite specific. There turn out to be a lot of probable primitives. For object recognition alone they propose almost 100, such as PLACE, SIZE, STRAIGHT, HORIZONTAL, VERTICAL, BOTTOM, TOP. For example, a *table*, which can be regarded as a connected, rigid object, with a flat horizontal top, supported by vertical legs, would involve at least the primitives OBJECT, CONNECTED, RIGID, TOP, FLATFACE, HORIZONTAL, VERTICAL. However, as the researchers point out, these perceptual primitives are insufficient to deal with the meaning of table. All they do is specify the appearance of a table. Further specifications are needed in order to account for the fact that people also know what tables are used for – to eat off, work on, stand on to change a lightbulb, and so on. In brief, they came to the conclusion that the concept behind the word *table* is not simply based on the way in which tables are perceived.

And when they moved on to less tangible items, they ran into even greater difficulties. How does one tie down verbs such as *promise*, *predict*, or *disagree* to something one can perceive directly? It proved impossible. The words themselves did not contain perceivable components, and there were no obvious concrete words which could have served as a pattern. They comment: 'If a person knew only words whose meanings are given perceptually and related words interpretable by generalization from the perceptual words, his vocabulary would be severely limited' (Miller and Johnson-Laird, 1976: 688).

In brief, they concluded, first, that even words for straightforward objects such as tables had elements of meaning which were not perceptually based. Second, there were an enormous number of vocabulary items whose meaning could not be tied down to a perceptual foundation. They therefore came to the reluctant conclusion that 'much of the lexicon is based on primitive concepts that are not perceptual' (Miller and Johnson-Laird, 1976: 688). It seems, then, that even if semantic primitives exist, they cannot be based purely on perception.

Since this attempt at listing semantic primitives was the most thorough and detailed so far and has apparently failed, does it mean that we should at this stage abandon the search for them? Not necessarily, as the next section discusses.

Hunting for globule effects

Even if people have been unable to list semantic primitives, this does not prove they are not there. The presence of many things can be detected only indirectly, by the effect they produce. For example, the spread of disease indicated the existence of microbes before they were actually viewed under a microscope. Therefore, if atoms of meaning exist, they could be reflected in the way humans deal with words.

A number of people have checked to see if word comprehension could give some clues to the existence of meaning components. Their reasoning is as follows: if small components of meaning exist, then words might be stored in the human mind in a disassembled state. If so, then it would be necessary to assemble them whenever they are used in producing speech, and disassemble them into their component parts in order to comprehend them. If this scenario is a reasonable one, then words which are likely to have a large number of components would take longer for the mind to process than words which have fewer. The word *kill* might be assembled out of CAUSE DIE, and so take longer to produce or comprehend than *die* alone. *Bachelor* might be assembled out of NOT MARRIED, and so take marginally longer to process than the phrase *not married*, since additional packaging and unpackaging would be required. Such experiments would not directly test whether these components were primitives. They might, however, show whether the comprehension of words required them to be disassembled into smaller pieces: if so, the notion that words are built up out of smaller fragments would be a point of view worth taking seriously.

In one experiment, the researchers thought up a number of sentence pairs (Fodor *et al.*, 1975). For example:

1   If practically all of the men in this room are *not married*, then few of the men in the room have wives.
2   If practically all of the men in this room are *bachelors*, then few of the men in the room have wives.

The first of each pair contained an explicit negative, such as *not married*. The second contained a word such as *bachelor* where the proposed semantic representation contained a negative. The experimenters jumbled up the order of the sentences so that the paired ones did not come together, and asked subjects to evaluate the validity of the argument in each. The result was that sentences containing the explicit negative took longer to evaluate – something which should not have happened if the subjects had had to spend time disassembling a word such as *bachelor* into its component fragments.

This experiment has been criticized because it asked subjects to perform a reasoning task which might have been carried out after the original processing of the sentence. However, a similar result was found in an experiment which investigated sentences as they were processed (Cutler, 1983). The researcher used the technique of 'phoneme monitoring': 'Press a button as soon as you hear the sound [b].' As we noted in chapter 2, subjects do this slowly if there is any problem with the word preceding the one with the monitored sound. In this case, the experimenter again worked with pairs of sentences. For example:

1   The dog sniffing round the yard stuck its nose into the *yellow* bucket.
2   The dog sniffing round the yard stuck its nose into the *empty* bucket.

The words *yellow* and *empty* are both the same length when spoken, and are equally common. However, *yellow* seems to be fairly straightforward, at least when compared with *empty*, which could be glossed as 'not containing anything'. If *empty* had to be disassembled into smaller components such as NOT CONTAIN ANYTHING, one would expect the reaction time to the [b] in *bucket* to be fairly slow. In fact, there was virtually no difference between the monitoring times for the two words, so there was no reason to claim that one had a more complicated make-up than the other.

The experiments discussed so far all involve negatives, and negatives behave somewhat oddly, as psycholinguists have known for a long time (e.g. Wason, 1965). So perhaps one should pay more attention to experiments which have avoided negatives, and tested to see if a word such as *kill* involved the assemblage of CAUSE DIE, or *chase* the piecing together of TRY CATCH (Kintsch, 1974; Fodor *et al.*, 1980). But once again these experiments failed to show that the word which supposedly had more components took longer to process.

These results lead us to one of several possibilities. Either the words which have been tested have been wrongly analysed, in which case we cannot draw any conclusion. Or assemblage is so amazingly fast that it is unmeasurable by current techniques. Or people do not assemble words when they comprehend them – they are already pre-packaged.

So far, then, we have noted, first, that a number of linguists believe in the existence of a universal store of 'semantic primitives', small components of meaning out of which words are built. Second, no one agrees what these components are, and no one has been able to find them. Third, experiments have not revealed any trace of assemblage procedures when people comprehend words. All this is still not proof that semantic primitives are non-existent: 'The problem is that it is very difficult to show conclusively that something does not exist' (Pulman, 1983: 31). And some people still persist in the claim that there are meaning globules in the mind. Let us now consider why this might be so.

Atomic globule faith

Many people believe in things because they seem to provide the 'best' explanation amidst a group of not particularly satisfactory ones. And atomic globules, it is claimed, provide a possible explanation for a number of puzzling phenomena, as well as linking in with intuitions about the way the world works.

A common reason for proposing the existence of meaning atoms is, as we have noted, that they provide a convenient explanation of why certain words overlap in meaning. A group of related words such as *mother*, *aunt*, *mare*, *waitress* could all be regarded as sharing a common basic component, that of FEMALE. Or *hop*, *skip*, *run* and *jump* might all share a component MOVE. A word such as *cow* might be decomposed into BOVINE, ADULT, FEMALE, as opposed to a *bull* which could be BOVINE, ADULT, MALE, and a *calf* which might be BOVINE, CHILD. In brief, according to this view, overlapping words overlap because they share one or more components. But, as we shall see, there are other ways of explaining overlaps, so it is not conclusive.

A second reason for adopting the atomic globule viewpoint is that it fits in with the way the world appears to work. In chemistry, for example, chemicals can be decomposed into more basic elements, and some scholars have explicitly suggested that there are parallels between the breakdown of chemical structures and the decomposition of words (e.g. Katz, 1975). In the realm of linguistics, a number of linguists have drawn attention to a possible parallelism between the sound structure of words and their meaning structure (e.g. Chomsky, 1965: 160). Since the sounds of language can be broken down into more basic components such as labiality (use of lips), voice (vibration of vocal cords), and so on, which might be universal, it seems plausible that word meanings should also be broken down in this way. There is, however, no convincing evidence that mental phenomena such as word meanings behave identically to physical elements which can ultimately be identified and measured.

A third reason for proposing semantic primitives is wishful thinking. Their existence would make life easier for anybody working with problems of meaning, since they solve the problem of where definitions stop. Without semantic primitives one simply defines words in terms of each other in an endless chain. If a person asks about the meaning of *bachelor*, the reply 'unmarried man' is not particularly helpful unless the components UNMARRIED MAN are in some sense more basic than the word *bachelor*. Even if we agreed that *unmarried man* was more basic than *bachelor*, we would still need to know the meaning of *man* and *unmarried*. If the reply was that a *man* is MALE, ADULT and HUMAN, then one would want to know what was meant by *male*, *adult* and *human*, and so on. Unless we are going to come to a halt somewhere, we would go on for ever. As one group of scholars noted: 'Definitions typically apply in chains, and the further along a chain we go, the closer we get to expressions couched in the vocabulary of the primitive basis. The primitive basis is where definitions stop' (Fodor *et al.*, 1980: 266). However, wanting definitions to stop in this way does not mean that they necessarily do so.

A further reason for the appeal of 'lexical decomposition' may be that it is fairly familiar: many dictionaries work on this principle. It is in line with 'a time-honoured maxim of lexicographers "a word should be defined by using words simpler than itself" . . . In this sense, simpler should be taken to mean "of a higher order of generality"' (Ayto, 1984: 50). For example, a *mare* is defined by the *Concise Oxford Dictionary* as 'female of equine animal', and a *sow* as 'adult female pig'. *Longman Dictionary of Contemporary English* defines the meanings of 55,000 words using a total vocabulary of only 2,000. However, we are concerned not with writing dictionaries but with analysing the mental lexicon. Are all humans qualified lexicographers, at least subconsciously? It seems unlikely.

We are left, then, with the conclusion that there is no convincing evidence to support the proposal that humans split words up into 'atomic globules' in the mind. All the arguments we discussed in favour of this viewpoint have been quite inconclusive, and mostly based on descriptive convenience and wishful thinking. It is, of course, quite obvious that humans can analyse words, by noticing that different words have different characteristics. But there is no evidence that being able to identify different characteristics is in any sense similar to splitting them up into a finite number of component parts. On the whole, we conclude that these atomic globules might be a convenient artificial device for use in printed dictionaries and computer programs. But they do not exist in the mind.

Let us therefore move on to consider alternative ways in which words might be related to one another. The next chapter will discuss various versions of the cobweb viewpoint.

Summary

This chapter has dealt with the way in which words might be related to one another in the mental lexicon. It examined the atomic globule viewpoint – the suggestion that there is a universal stock of semantic components out of which all words are composed.

This theory ran into insuperable problems: no one has been able to specify what these atomic globules are, and they leave no trace in the processing of words. The arguments in favour of this viewpoint are based mainly on descriptive convenience and wishful thinking. Our overall conclusion was that they are useful descriptive devices for people such as lexicographers who need to describe things in a succinct and orderly way. But they are unlikely to exist in the mental lexicon.

Our next chapter therefore looks at 'cobweb theories' – an alternative view of how words might be related to one another.

7

Word-webs
— *Semantic networks* —

Experience is never limited, and it is never complete; it is an immense
sensibility, a kind of huge spider-web of the finest silken threads
suspended in the chamber of consciousness, and catching every air-
borne particle in its tissue.

Henry James, Partial Portraits

Words are not assembled out of a common store of semantic primitives, we
decided. So how are they are related to one another? Perhaps we should
imagine them as linked together in a gigantic multi-dimensional cobweb, in
which every item is attached to scores of others. Or, to use a more sophisticated
image: 'Suppose the mental lexicon is a sort of connected graph, with lexical
items at the nodes with paths from each item to the other' (Fodor, 1983: 80).
Theories of this type are known as network theories.

A network, according to the eighteenth-century lexicographer Samuel
Johnson, is 'anything reticulated or decussated at equal distances, with inter-
stices between the intersections'. Johnson was presumably thinking of something like a fishing net, in which the intersections must be equidistant. A
network in relation to the mental lexicon simply means 'an interconnected
system'. Researchers mostly agree that a network of some type is inevitable, but
they disagree as to how it is organized, and how to explore it.

In general, early work on the topic concentrated on finding out the strength
of a link between one particular word and another. The findings laid the
groundwork for later research, which has spent more time on trying to ascer-
tain the overall structure underlying the individual connections. In this
chapter, therefore, we will consider the outline conclusions of some early
researchers, and then try to specify the probable overall organization more
carefully.

Linguistic habits

Early work on meaning networks suggested that links between words were formed by habits: if words often cropped up together, such as *pen* and *pencil*, *envelope* and *postage stamp*, or *moon* and *stars*, then these frequently associated items were thought to develop extra-strong ties. The close links forged by these habits could be revealed quite easily, it was suggested, by means of simple word association experiments.

'Give me the first word you think of when I say "hammer"'. This, as we saw in chapter 2, is the standard procedure for word association experiments. The experimenter draws up a list of words and for each item asks a subject to name the first word which comes to mind. In such experiments, different people generally give rather similar responses. For example, out of 1,000 subjects, over half said *nail* in response to 'hammer', *low* to 'high' and *black* to 'white' (Jenkins, 1970). And for some other words the probability of a particular response was much higher: over three-quarters of the subjects responded *queen* to 'king', *girl* to 'boy' and *short* to 'long'. Moreover, in cases where there was no overwhelming single response, there were usually several very common ones: *water*, *sea*, or *blue* accounted for around two-thirds of the responses to 'ocean'. The consistency of the results suggested to psychologists that they might therefore be able to draw up a reasonably reliable 'map' of the average person's 'word-web'.

At least three important findings emerged. First, people almost always select items from the semantic 'field' of the original word. Nobody said *nail* or *poker* in response to 'needle', even though these are also thin pointed objects. The majority mentioned some aspect of sewing: *thread*, *pin(s)*, *eye* and *sew* were the words mentioned most often. Sewing items seemed to trigger one another off, suggesting that clusters of words relating to the same topic are stored together. The second finding was that people nearly always pick the partner if the item is one of a pair, as in *husband* and *wife*, or has an obvious opposite, as in *big* and *small*. The third finding (which will be discussed in a later chapter) is that adults are likely to respond with a word of the same word class: a noun tends to elicit a noun, an adjective another adjective, and so on.

Can we build up a detailed mental map from these responses? Unfortunately not, in spite of the enormous amount of information available from word association experiments (e.g. Deese, 1965; Postman and Keppel, 1970). There turn out to be a number of problems. First, thinking up an immediate response to just one word is a somewhat unnatural kind of activity, so may not reflect ordinary speech processes. Second, the standard results can be altered quite dramatically by presenting a word in a group rather than alone. People normally respond to the word 'moon' with items such as *sun*, *night* and *star*. But if 'moon' is presented alongside words such as 'elephant, hall, whale, stadium', subjects tend to reply with the word *big* (Coleman, 1964). If a word's associations can be changed so easily by the context, then it is possibly wrong to assume that we can ever lay down fixed and detailed pathways linking words in the mental lexicon.

But the most serious shortcoming of word association experiments is that they cannot tell us about the probable structure of the human word-web. This is partly because each person is asked for only one response to a particular word, and partly because the links between words are multifarious. For example, the ten most common responses to 'butter' were *bread* (the commonest), then *yellow, soft, fat, food, knife, eggs, cream, milk, cheese* (Jenkins, 1970). These responses represent several different types of link: *bread* is eaten alongside butter, *yellow* and *soft* describe 'butter', whereas *cream, eggs, milk* and *cheese* are other kinds of dairy food. One would expect the mental lexicon to treat these various connections differently from one another. Let us consider this problem more carefully.

Listing the links

The ten commonest responses in word association tests to the words *butterfly, hungry, red* and *salt* are listed in figure 7.1 (from Jenkins, 1970). As with *butter*,

	BUTTERFLY	HUNGRY	RED	SALT
1	moth	food	white	pepper
2	insect	eat	blue	sugar
3	wing(s)	thirsty	black	water
4	bird	full	green	taste
5	fly	starved	colour	sea
6	yellow	stomach	blood	bitter
7	net	tired	communist	shaker
8	pretty	dog	yellow	food
9	flower(s)	pain	flag	ocean
10	bug	man	bright	lake

Figure 7.1   Word association responses

these replies encompass a number of different types of link between the stimulus word and the response. Let us consider the four which may be the most important:

1   *Co-ordination.* The commonest response involved 'co-ordinates', words which cluster together on the same level of detail, such as *salt* and

pepper; *butterfly* and *moth*; *red, white, blue, black, green*. Opposites come into this category, as they are co-ordinates in a group consisting of only two members, as with *left* and *right*, or they are the two commonest members in a larger group, as with *hot, cold, warm, cool*.

2   *Collocation*. The next most common response involved a word which was likely to be 'collocated' (found together) with the stimulus in connected speech, as with *salt water, butterfly net, bright red*.

3   *Superordination*. Less often, a 'superordinate' occurred, the cover term which includes the stimulus word. For example, *insect* was elicited by 'butterfly', and *colour* was a response to 'red'.

4   *Synonymy*. Occasionally, a rough synonym of the original word was found, as with *starved* beside 'hungry'.

How, then, do all these connections (figure 7.2) intermesh in the mental lexicon? And are some links stronger or more permanent than others? Let us consider these questions by examining each kind of link in turn.

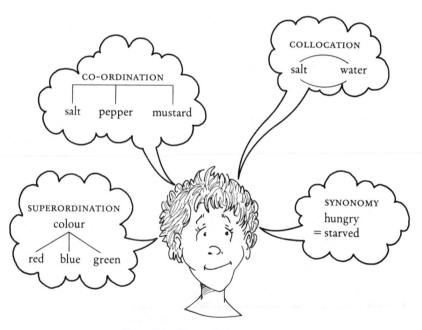

Figure 7.2   Types of link in the word-web

When left means right

The secret of good communication is to know when *left* means 'right', according to a newspaper cartoon. Muddling up *left* and *right* is possibly the

COUPLES   by Calman

Reproduced by kind permission of Mel Calman

commonest semantic tongue-slip of all, closely followed perhaps by the confusion of *yesterday*, *today* and *tomorrow*. And other similar examples can be heard daily. People say *Tuesday* when they mean 'Wednesday', *blue* instead of 'green' and *brother* in place of 'sister'.

In addition, people sometimes blend together similar words, such as:

I went to *Noshville* (Nashville + Knoxville, Tennessee towns).
I'd like some *taquua* (tequila + kahlua, Mexican drinks).
He's a born *sailure* (success + failure).

These errors confirm the results of word association experiments, that words are stored in semantic fields and that co-ordinates are closely associated. Word searches provide additional support. When looking for an elusive word, people frequently fumble around not only in the same general semantic area but often within a group of co-ordinates. Freud, when he could not remember the name 'Monaco', ran through a whole series of place-names: *Piedmont*, *Albania*, *Montevideo*, *Colico*, *Montenegro* (chapter 2; Freud, 1901/1975: 96–7). In the 'tip of the tongue' experiment (chapter 2), subjects who could not remember the word *sextant* recalled other navigational instruments, such as *compass* or *astrolabe* (Brown and McNeill, 1966).

Furthermore, aphasic patients often produce a co-ordinate or close relative of the target, as in *orange* for 'lemon', *table* for 'chair' and *diving* for 'swimming', and they may make this type of mistake in comprehension also:

Mrs P.   Do you want rice crispies?
Mr P.   Yes.

When the rice crispies arrived in front of him, Mr P., who had recently had a stroke, was surprised and angry, and Mrs P. became upset at his unreasonable behaviour (Butterworth *et al.*, 1984). It seems that poor Mr P. could no longer remember which sound sequence paired with *rice crispies*, and had perhaps thought Mrs P. meant 'cornflakes'.

Such episodes suggest that some co-ordinates are so closely linked that brain-damaged people may have difficulty in distinguishing between them. A particular sound sequence may lead into the general area of the lexicon required, at which point the matching procedure needed to pinpoint the exact word fails. This was suggested by a recent experiment in which aphasics were asked to single out one item in a picture showing several objects. If the instruction was 'Point to a lemon', patients were likely to succeed if the other objects were things quite different from it such as boot, armchair, cup, pig. But many of them found it much more difficult to pick out the lemon from among other pieces of fruit (Butterworth *et al.*, 1984).

Moreover, ties between co-ordinates tend to be retained even after serious brain damage. Aphasics were asked to squeeze a rubber ball if they recognized a relationship between pairs of words which were read aloud to them (Goodglass and Baker, 1976). They responded fastest if these words were co-ordinates, and their error rate was exactly the same as that of normal subjects. In addition, work with elderly patients indicates that these connections do not deteriorate in old age (Howard *et al.*, 1981). A number of young and old subjects were presented with two simultaneous strings of letters and asked to judge whether both were words. In general, the older group, whose average age was 70, took longer to respond than the younger group, average age 28. But if the strings were both words, and these were either co-ordinates (*rain—snow*) or contained collocational links (*rain—wet*), then the responses of both groups were speeded up equally. This result suggests that the first word was linked to the second word as strongly in the old group as in the young one.

Links between co-ordinates, then, are strong. According to one researcher (Hotopf, 1980), all the examples in his collection of semantic slips fitted into three categories: contrasting co-ordinates, as with *apple* for 'pear', *red* for 'black', *Monday* for 'Tuesday'; opposites, as with *up* for 'down', *fat* for 'thin', *man* for 'woman'; and 'semantic cousins', as with *Saturday* for 'January', which are both dates but dates of a different type. This researcher may have subconsciously concentrated on certain kinds of slip, but it is unlikely that he would have missed alternative types if there had been dozens and dozens of them.

It is difficult to be precise about the detailed organization of co-ordinates within the mental lexicon, since the structure of a group is likely to depend on the type of word involved – objects, colours and actions might be treated rather differently. It seems probable, however, that for each group there is a nucleus of closely linked words, with other words attached somewhat more loosely round the edges (figure 7.3). In some cases, as with colours, the words in the nucleus may overlap to some extent, since many words have fuzzy edges which merge into one another (chapter 5).

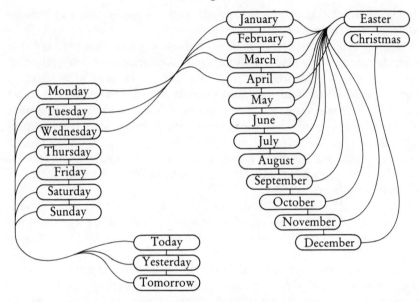

Figure 7.3   Clusters of co-ordinates

Stardust and star wars

A popular television quiz show is based on the idea that different people will come up with the same continuation for a word such as *star*: *stardust*, *starfish*, or *star wars*, perhaps. Humans seem to be fairly sensitive to collocational links of this type, as word association experiments suggested. This finding is strengthened by evidence from tongue-slips, where people sometimes start out with one phrase and then get 'derailed' on to a familiar routine, as in *Hungarian restaurant* for 'Hungarian rhapsody'. Aphasics also preserve collocational links well (Goodglass and Baker, 1976). Furthermore, the experiment involving old people mentioned earlier in this chapter showed that links such as *rain–wet* were as strong in the old subjects as the younger ones (Howard *et al.*, 1981).

These collocational links cover a wide spectrum. At one end of the range there are words which are optionally, but commonly, associated: *fresh-faced youths*, *buxom barmaids*, *rude adolescents*, *unruly hair*. These frequent associations merge into habitual connections or clichés: *agonizing decision*, *filthy lucre*, *bright and early*, *hale and hearty*. Clichés overlap with idioms, phrases whose overall meaning cannot be predicted from the sum total of the individual words: *keep tabs on*, *fall into place*, *call it a day*.

Idioms appear to be treated by humans as if they were ordinary, single lexical items (Swinney and Cutler, 1979; Cutler, 1983; Gibbs and Gonzales, 1985). They cause no special processing difficulty, even though there are thousands of them – *Longman Dictionary of English Idioms* lists over 4,500.

Collocational links, then, seem to be powerful and long-lasting. They may be as strong as connections between co-ordinates. It is not immediately clear, however, how these two different types of link intermesh, and whether one has priority over the other – though more information on this topic will crop up in the next chapter, when we consider how children acquire the meaning of words (chapter 8). Meanwhile, let us now move on to other types of links.

The old man with a beard

> There was an Old Man with a beard,
> Who said, 'It is just as I feared!
> Two Owls and a Hen,
> Four Larks and a Wren,
> Have all built their nests in my beard!'

Try reading Edward Lear's limerick about the Old Man with a beard to a friend. Then ask the friend to summarize the content of the poem. The reply is likely to be something like: 'There's this old chap with a beard, and a whole lot of birds come and build nests in it.' Almost everybody uses the word *bird* in their reply, even though it is not explicitly mentioned in the original. People, then, know that *owls*, *hens*, *larks* and *wrens* are 'hyponyms' of the cover term or 'superordinate' *bird*. Does this imply that words are always kept in bundles, labelled with the superordinate term?

There are several problems with assuming that the labelling of bundles is an inevitable procedure. First, superordinate terms do not crop up very often as errors in slips of the tongue (Hotopf, 1980), although they are commoner in aphasia. It may be that such slips are not noticed: 'That wretched *animal*'s been digging up my bulbs again' sounds quite normal and would not be categorized as an error, even though the speaker might have intended to say *cat*. But the rarity of this type of error may also be because a superordinate term is not always easily available. It is often quite difficult to think up a suitable super-ordinate, and some of the ones that exist are quite rare. Lots of people talk about *knives* and *forks*, *cups* and *saucers*, and *brothers* and *sisters*. But not all of these talk about *cutlery*, *crockery* and *siblings*. And what about *baths* and *basins*? Are these bathroom fixtures? Or sanitary fitments? Or take the tongue-slip *tin-opener* for 'nutcrackers': are these 'kitchen gadgets for opening things which are going to be consumed'? Although people appear to link groups of items together, they may not give the resulting bundle a label.

Furthermore, not all members of a category are on an equal footing (chapter 5): it turned out to be easier to categorize a prototypical bird such as a *robin* as a 'bird' than a slightly odd one such as a *pelican*. Perhaps because of this problem, almost all experiments which have tried to find out about the relationship between hyponyms and their superordinates have been somewhat unsatisfactory. Let us consider some of these.

The process of grouping and labelling can often be repeated several times, because each item in a group can usually be subdivided. *Owls* can be split into *barn owls*, *snowy owls*, *screech owls*, and so on. And a superordinate is also likely to be included in a still higher category: *birds* form a group with *fish*, *insects*, and so on, within a category of *animal*. This progressive layering can be envisaged as a type of upside-down tree (figure 7.4).

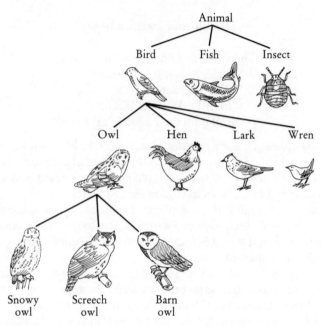

Figure 7.4   Layers of superordinates

In the late 1960s and early 1970s a number of researchers proposed that this was how the mental lexicon might be organized – in hierarchical structures of the type described above. One of the earliest papers on the topic was by Collins and Quillian (1969). They suggested that one could test this idea by asking subjects to verify sentences such as 'A canary is a canary' or 'A canary is a bird' or 'A canary is an animal', and timing how long they took to do this. They assumed that the further a person had to travel on the tree in order to verify a sentence, the longer it would take. According to this theory, 'A canary is a canary' should be verified very fast, as there is no need to travel at all. 'A canary is a bird' should take a little longer, as an adjacent node has to be reached. 'A canary is an animal' should take longest of all, since it involves travelling from *canary* to *bird*, then from *bird* to *animal* (figure 7.5).

These predictions turned out to be correct. However, their findings do not conclusively prove the existence of upside-down trees, since there are a number of other possible reasons for the result. First, *canaries* and *birds* are associated much more frequently than *canaries* and *animals*, so the effect could be caused

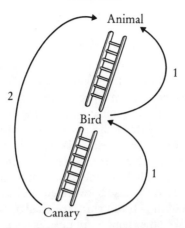

Figure 7.5   The canary—bird experiment

by a strong habitual association rather than a hierarchy. Second, there are many more possible animals than possible birds, so maybe the difficulty of assessing 'A canary is an animal' is due to the large number of items in the category *animal*. Third, the word *animal* is ambiguous: sometimes it is used in contrast to *bird*, as in 'An owl is a bird, but a dog is an animal', and at other times its includes the word *bird*, as in 'Owls and dogs are animals, but roses and oak-trees are plants'. This ambiguity might have delayed assessment time.

This last problem can be avoided by testing people on creatures which are more usually thought of as animals, such as *dogs* (Johnson-Laird, 1983: 214). The psychologists who tried this incorporated a subtle but significant difference into the task. They noted that almost all previous experimenters had contrasted the time taken to verify a link from one word to its immediate superordinate, as in 'A poodle is a dog', with the time taken to verify a link to an even higher superordinate, as in 'A poodle is an animal'. No one seemed to have checked whether 'A dog is an animal' (one step) also took less time than 'A poodle is an animal' (two steps), as the theory would predict. The researchers were unable to find any reliable difference. Subjects in general took as long to verify 'A dog is an animal' as 'A poodle is an animal'. This result suggests that even if people organize words in clumps, it is unlikely that they climb nimbly up and down lexical trees as if they were fixed scaffolding.

To summarize, superordinate labels may be easily available when the contents of a group are fairly prototypical and the label is a commonly used one. But this vertical movement, as it were, between different levels of generality seems to require somewhat more effort than horizontal movement among co-ordinates. In a number of cases, creative decision-making may have to be carried out. Faced with a question such as 'Is a tadpole an animal?', a person might well have to think this out. They might be quite sure that a *tadpole* is a small frog, and also that a *frog* is a kind of animal, but they might have to actively deduce that a tadpole is therefore an animal from these two separate pieces of knowledge.

In some cases, then, vertical links are likely to have been pre-established, and no further reasoning will be required. In other cases, humans have to make inferences on the spot. Similar active computation may also be required when one superordinate links words from different areas, such as *female*, which links *sow*, *princess*, *mare*. Humans can compare different words and decide what they have in common quite easily (to be discussed in chapter 13). However, unless the link is a commonly used one, it seems likely that humans work out the connection by performing a quick analysis rather than simply consulting a fixed chart in their mental lexicon. In brief, the treatment of superordinates suggests that firm connections, such as those between co-ordinates and those between common hyponyms and superordinates, are used in conjunction with our reasoning ability to make other temporary links as we need them.

Chasing or pursuing shadows

Humans have a pretty good idea as to which words are interchangeable. Perfect synonymy – total overlap of meaning – is somewhat rare, but many words are intermittently interchangeable. Shadows are *chased* in Matthew Arnold's poem 'The Buried Life':

> A man . . . doth forever *chase*
> That flying and elusive shadow, rest.

But they are *pursued* according to the orator Edmund Burke:

> . . . what shadows we are, what shadows we *pursue* . . .

Yet this interchangeability is not general. *Pursue* is normally preferred when the object of pursuit is desirable: we *pursue* wisdom, knowledge, 'the elusive butterfly of love', but we *chase* burglars and runaway horses. Humans control this variation in use without apparently thinking about it. How, then, does the mental lexicon cope with it?

Blends – when two words are amalgamated into one – occur most often when the words concerned mean more or less the same thing, and when either word would have been appropriate, as in:

I *climbered* (climbed + clambered) into bed.
That's *torrible* (terrible + horrible).

Words which are truly interchangeable, therefore, may well be closely connected, in the same way that co-ordinates are closely connected.

But what about words which are similar in meaning rather than interchangeable? These are sometimes found in the tongue-slips:

I don't know many *brands* (species) of tree.
These components are *extinct* (obsolete).
He has some *amending* (redeeming) features.
Facts learnt fast need to be *confirmed* (reinforced).
The *inhabitants* (occupants) of the car were unhurt.

However, this type of slip is relatively rare, according to at least one researcher (Hotopf, 1980). Why? There are two differing types of explanation. The first is that many of the near synonyms fit well into the vacant slot, so well that they are either as good as the right word or so close a fit that no one notices the error. The other is that these types of error are indeed rare, because the mental word-web deals with synonyms differently from contrasting co-ordinates, such as *black* and *white*, *robins* and *thrushes* (Hotopf, 1980). This might be because different words tend to get attached to different semantic fields: *plump* might get activated in dealing with grapes or peaches, whereas *fat*, *rotund*, or *obese* is unlikely. This point of view predicts that near synonym errors would occur mainly in word searches, as a back-up procedure when the most obvious word was temporarily unavailable.

Both points of view are possibly correct to some extent. But the lack of error involving similar meaning words in different semantic fields suggests that they are kept apart by the fact that they belong to a different semantic area. Otherwise, eggs would *curdle*, milk would *rot* and tomatoes would go *rancid* far more often than they in fact do.

Word-web conclusions

We have now considered various kinds of links found between words. Bonds between co-ordinates and collocational links were found to be particularly strong (figure 7.6), and so were links between interchangeable synonyms. Links between a word and its superordinate were firm when the superordinate was

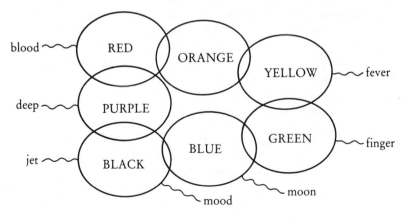

Figure 7.6   Strong links in the word-web

a frequently used term and when the words came from the same general meaning area, such as *bird* which included *robin*, *thrush*, and so on. All these findings
support the suggestion that words from the same semantic field are closely
linked.

In contrast, bonds between words from different semantic fields were somewhat weaker. Near synonyms from different semantic fields seem not to be
particularly common in slips of the tongue, and superordinate links from
different semantic fields seem to require active reasoning.

Let us now complete this chapter by considering further evidence for the
weakness of links between different semantic fields.

Saucepans yes, oranges no

'I've forgotten', said an aphasic patient, when asked to define a *needle*. Asked
about the word *carrot*, he said, 'I must once have known', to *mosquito* his reply
was 'It sounds familiar', and to *geese*, 'An animal, I've forgotten precisely'. But
the same patient defined a *pact* as 'friendly agreement', *supplication* as 'making a
serious request for help' and *knowledge* as 'making oneself mentally familiar
with a subject' (Warrington, 1981). He was able to cope with certain types of
topic but not others.

At first sight one might suggest that he simply had a neurotic block about
some kinds of word. But an ability to handle some semantic fields and not
others has now been reported in quite a few patients. One of the earliest studies
on the topic tested the vocabulary of 135 patients within a number of general
areas, such as colours, actions, numbers (Goodglass *et al.*, 1966). The researchers found that in several of these patients the performance across these
different areas was quite uneven.

One possibility is that these patients had lost the ability to deal with certain
types of lexical organization: the first patient could cope with abstract words
but not concrete objects; the other patients might have had difficulty with
colours because of their graded nature. But this explanation cannot account for
the problems of every aphasic of this type, some of whom have deficits in quite
precise areas. One man knew the names of kitchen utensils but not the names
of fruit. He could name items of clothing but not types of cloth. And he could
name tools but not kinds of metal. Another woman was significantly better on
food words than on objects (Warrington, 1981).

Fruit and vegetables were a problem for another patient (Hart *et al.*, 1985).
This 34-year-old male had a stroke in 1981 which at first left him almost totally
speechless. But he gradually recovered, and after 18 months appeared to be
better – apart from fruit and vegetables. He 'showed a striking inability to name
such common items as Peach and Orange while able to name easily less
frequent items such as Abacus and Sphinx' (Hart *et al.*, 1985: 439). He was not
entirely hopeless at dealing with these, and scored just over 60 per cent in

a naming test. But this was a strange contrast to everything else in his world, which he apparently coped with just about normally – including other food items.

These cases suggest that topic areas are stored to some extent independently, and that some semantic fields can be damaged without involving others, even though in normal speakers one would not expect this degree of isolation between areas.

Summary

In this chapter we have examined the human word-web – the way in which humans link words together in their minds. We noted that words seem to be organized in semantic fields, and that, within these fields, there are two types of link which seem to be particularly strong: connections between co-ordinates and collocational links.

Links between hyponyms and their superordinates are overall somewhat weaker. Some are more firmly established than others. Humans then use these firm connections in conjunction with their reasoning ability to make other, temporary links as they are needed. Connections between different topic areas may also be weak, and made on the spot by means of active matching and decision-making.

Let us now go on to consider how children cope with the meaning of words: finding out how the human word-web is acquired may also give us further clues as to its overall structure.

8

What is a Bongaloo, Daddy?

— *How children learn the meaning of words* —

'What is a Bongaloo, Daddy?'
'A Bongaloo, Son,' said I,
'Is a tall bag of cheese
Plus a Chinaman's knees
And the leg of a nanny goat's eye.'

Spike Milligan, 'The Bongaloo'

So far, we have discovered quite a lot about how adults cope with word meaning. But what about children? Finding out how youngsters build up a store of words may give us additional clues as to how the mental lexicon is organized. Of course, we cannot take it for granted that children store and retrieve words in the same way as adults. They may do so, or they may not.

To return to the library analogy (chapter 3), one might as a first guess suggest that children are born owning a huge room lined with empty shelves. As they acquire each new word they put it in its pre-ordained place, having been pre-programmed with the knowledge that certain words should be assigned to certain shelves, or that particular types of words should be stored together. If this scenario is a realistic one, the difference between an adult's and a child's mental lexicon is primarily one of quantity. The words would be stored and retrieved in the same way, but the child would know fewer.

Alternatively, one might assume that the child initially organized its mental lexicon along the equivalent of a tiny shelf, in a fairly haphazard order. Only when it acquired too many words for the shelf, or had problems finding a word it wanted, would it reorganize its system by setting up new shelves and arranging different types of words on different shelves. This process of enlarging the store and rearranging it might go on progressively as the child gets older. In this case, a child's mental lexicon might be somewhat different from an adult's, particularly in the early stages. We shall be considering which of these scenarios is the most likely – or whether each of them encapsulates some portion of the truth.

How, then, do children acquire word meaning? According to the nineteenth-century psychologist James Sully the task is a formidable one, so much so that the child can be likened to a 'little explorer' struggling over unknown terrain: 'Let us see what the little explorer has to do when trying to use verbal sounds with their right meanings . . . We shall find that huge difficulties beset his path, and that his arrival at the goal proves him to have been in his way as valiant and hard-working as an African explorer' (Sully, 1897, in Bar-Adon and Leopold, 1971: 31).

What are these 'huge difficulties'? Essentially, children are faced with three different but related tasks: a labelling task, a packaging task and a network-building task (figure 8.1). In the labelling task, youngsters must discover that sequences of sound can be used as names for things. In the packaging task, they must find out which things can be packaged together under one label. In the network-building task, they must work out how words relate to one another. Let us discuss these in turn.

Figure 8.1   Tasks involved in learning the meaning of words

The labelling task

Some people are surprised that one needs to ask how children learn to label things. They assume that the answer is obvious. Adults point to things, such as a toy duck or a glass of orange juice, and say, 'Duck', 'Juice'. Children in consequence learn to associate the names *duck* and *juice* with the things being pointed at.

The above viewpoint, however, is a considerable oversimplification. Symbolization – the realization that a particular combination of sounds 'means' or symbolizes a certain object – turns out to be quite a complex skill, which takes time to develop (Bates *et al.*, 1979), and possibly emerges somewhere between the ages of one and two.

Proud parents often find this comparatively late development hard to believe. Doting mothers and fathers frequently claim that babies under a year old can say *mama* and *papa*. But infants are unlikely to have attached the adult meaning to the words at this stage. In the early months of their life children experiment with making noises. Sounds formed at the front of the mouth are comparatively easy for a young child. So the sequences *mama*, *papa*, which are made with the lips, are likely to be babbled spontaneously from around six months, purely as random noises: 'Unprejudiced observers find that these babbling syllables have at first no meaning at all, are mere muscle exercises' (Leopold, 1946, in Bar-Adon and Leopold, 1971: 2).

If the child says 'Mama' as its mother approaches it, it is understandable that the average mother will misinterpret this and impose her own meaning on the child, as was recognized by some early researchers such as the nineteenth-century German physiologist William Preyer: 'For the first articulate expression of concepts, some of those easily uttered syllables are employed which have been previously uttered by the child without consciousness or aim; the meaning is introduced into them wholly by the parents or nurse. Such syllables are *pa* and *ma*, with their reduplications, *papa*, *mama*, as appellations of the parents' (Preyer, 1882, in Bar-Adon and Leopold, 1971: 31). Or, as a researcher noted some years later: 'It is natural that fond mothers, waiting for the traditional word joyfully interpret it as a reference to themselves; but dispassionate scholars should not follow them into this trap' (Leopold, 1946, in Bar-Adon and Leopold, 1971: 2).

Even if proud parents accept this explanation for the early development of *papa* and *mama*, they are likely to point out equally young children who apparently know all the names in their alphabet book. But uttering particular sounds in response to different pictures does not guarantee that the child is genuinely 'naming' anything. This whole procedure may simply be a great game for the child. At the page where a large black fuzzy blob appears, a parent might point and say 'Cat'. The child's response shriek of 'Ga' may be a ritual response to a particular page of a particular book. The discovery that 'Ga' is the name for an object, a cat, is likely to come some time later (McShane, 1979, 1980).

The notion that many early 'words' are simply ritual accompaniments to a whole situation can be illustrated by the early utterances of young Adam (Barrett, 1983). 'Dut' ('duck') shrieked this 12-month-old child excitedly each evening at bathtime as he knocked a yellow toy duck off the edge of the bathtub. Adam said 'Dut' only when Adam himself knocked the duck off. And he never said 'Dut' when the duck was swimming in the bath. So *dut* seemed to be an unanalysed cry uttered as Adam swiped at the duck. It was a ritualized accompaniment to a whole scenario, and could perhaps be best translated as 'Whoopee' or 'Here goes'. At first, then, Adam had no realization that *dut* could label a particular part of the situation. And the same was true of his other early words. He said 'Chuff-chuff' only when he, Adam, was pushing his toy train across the floor. He did not say 'Chuff-chuff' when the train was still. And he said 'Dog' only when his father, and no one else, pointed to a picture of a dog on the bib he was wearing and said, 'What's that?'

A second stage occurred when Adam started to broaden the circumstances under which he produced these ritualized utterances. For example, he began to use the word *dog* not only when his father pointed to the dog on his bib and said, 'What's that?' but also when his mother or he himself did so. A third stage occurred when Adam finally dissociated each word from a whole event and started to use it as a label for a specific object or event. *Dut* was used to refer to his yellow toy ducks in any situation, and not just when they were being knocked off the bathtub. Later the word was used for real ducks, swans and geese. Similarly, *chuff-chuff* and *dog* were eventually widened out to include proper trains and dogs.

Adam's early 'words', then, became detached from whole situations in stages. There was considerable variability, in that they went through the stages at different times and at varying speeds. In addition, some words missed out on a stage. But somewhere between the age of one and two Adam reached a 'labelling stage'. A number of researchers have remarked on a sudden increase in vocabulary size somewhere between the ages of one and two (e.g. Nelson, 1973). This may be due to the discovery that things have names, which probably leads children to try to label the objects they come across (McShane, 1979, 1980).

The ability to symbolize emerges slowly, then. It may be innate, in the sense that it may be biologically programmed to develop some time before the age of two, as long as the child is provided with a normal environment. But it is unlikely that a new-born baby or child under one year realizes that the sounds that come out of people's mouths 'stand for' things and actions. This shows that, in studying the mental lexicon, we must be quite sure that children are truly labelling things before we start to draw conclusions from their behaviour.

The packaging task

There is quite a lot of difference between applying a label such as *penguin* to one toy penguin and the ability to use that label correctly in all circumstances. How does a child come to apply the name *penguin* to a wider range of penguins?

And how does she learn to restrict it to penguins alone, and not to puffins and pandas, which are also black and white? And do children package things together in the same way as adults?

Superficially, at least, children seem to deal with words rather differently. By adult standards, both underextensions and overextensions occur: sometimes children assume that a word refers to a narrower range of things than it in fact does, whereas at other times they include far too much under a single name.

Underextensions seem quite understandable, as when 20-month-old Hildegard refused to accept that the word *white* could be used of blank pages since she herself associated it only with snow (Leopold, 1948, in Bar-Adon and Leopold, 1971: 98). She had acquired the word in a particular context, and it took time for her to realize that the word had a wider application. Similarly, a child quizzed on the words *deep* and *shallow* 'might respond correctly if he happens to be probed about ends of swimming pools . . . But if shown a picture of a deep puddle – a girl sinking into a mud puddle up to her knees – and asked "Is this a deep puddle?" the child might answer, "No, a big one" (Carey, 1978: 288). And in cases where words have abstract as well as concrete physical applications, it may be years before the child fully understands the range of meaning covered: in one experiment, three- and four-year-olds readily called milk *cold*, water *deep*, boxes *hard* and trees *crooked*, but had no idea that these words could be extended to people, and some even denied that it was possible: 'I never heard of deep people anyway!' 'No people are cold!' (Asch and Nerlove, 1960).

A period of underextension for a word, then, is quite normal, and the gradual enlarging of meaning to include an increasingly wide range does not seem particularly puzzling. Overextension, however, is more of a problem. It is probably less common than underextension but more noticeable, as the effects may be bizarre. 'One feature of the early tussle with our language is curious and often quaintly pretty', commented the psychologist James Sully. 'Having at first but a few names, the little experimenter makes the most of these by extending them in new and surprising directions . . . The name "pin" was extended to a crumb . . ., a fly and a caterpillar . . . The same child used the sound "'at" (hat) for anything put on the head, including a hairbrush' (Sully, 1897, in Bar-Adon and Leopold, 1971: 37).

Three main types of explanation have been proposed to account for this phenomenon: lack of knowledge, 'mental fog' and wrong analysis. The first of these suggests that 'the dearth of words compels the child to use words for purposes to which they are not adapted from the adult point of view' (Leopold, 1948, in Bar-Adon and Leopold, 1971: 98). He might recognize the difference between a duck and a peacock but say *duck* for both because he didn't yet know the word *peacock*. Or she might know the name *peacock* but be unable to pronounce it, since some children consciously avoid sounds they find difficult to cope with (Ferguson and Farwell, 1975). This explanation is possibly correct for some overextensions but it is unlikely to account for all of them, especially the more bizarre ones such as using the same word for a duck and a mug of milk.

'The child unquestionably perceives the world through a mental fog. But as the sun of experience rises higher and higher these boundaries are beaten back' (Chambers, 1904, quoted by Leopold, 1948 in Bar-Adon and Leopold, 1971: 99). This statement by an early twentieth-century psychologist typifies the 'mental fog' viewpoint. Its proponents argue that meanings are necessarily hazy and vague in the early stages, and that they gradually become more precise as children learn to discriminate more finely. At first, 'rough classifications suffice. With advancing maturity, finer subdivisions are needed, and new words are learned to satisfy the urge for expressing them' (Leopold, 1948, in Bar-Adon and Leopold, 1971: 101).

A more recent version of this theory suggests that 'when the child first begins to use identifiable words, he does not know their full (adult) meaning: he has only partial entries for them in the lexicon ... The acquisition of semantic knowledge, then, will consist of adding ... to the lexical entry of the word until the child's ... entry for that word corresponds to the adults' (Clark, 1973: 72). The child might have learnt the word *dog* but only noticed certain outline characteristics: 'dogginess' might have been identified with 'being four-legged'. In that case, cows, sheep, zebras and llamas would wrongly be included in the category *dog*. But each of these lexical items would gradually be narrowed down. To the lexical entry for *dog* the child might attach the additional specifications 'makes barking sounds', 'is fairly small', while to *zebra* it might add 'striped' and 'fairly large', so distinguishing one from the other. Eventually, the child's lexical entries would have all the details filled in and so be comparable to those of an adult.

This gradual narrowing down may apply to some words. But there are two facts which this type of theory does not explain. First, relatively few words are overextended – perhaps less than a third (Nelson *et al.*, 1978). If the mental fog viewpoint was correct one would expect many more words to start out by being too wide in their application. Second, many of the overextensions are bizarre and cannot easily be related to a lack of subdivisions in the adult word. This suggests that the child is not just operating in a mental fog, in which he can only see broad outlines. Instead, he has made an analysis of the items concerned, but a wrong one by adult standards.

The Russian psychologist Vygotsky (1893–1934) discusses a child who used *qua* ('quack') for a duck swimming on a pond, a cup of milk, a coin with an eagle on it and a teddy bear's eye (Vygotsky, 1934/1962: 70). In his view, children are perfectly capable of analysis but they tend to focus on only one aspect of a situation at a time and to generalize that alone. The child began with *qua* as a duck on a pond. Then the liquid element caught the youngster's attention and the word was generalized to a cup of milk. But the duck had not been forgotten, and this surfaced in *qua* used to refer to a coin with an eagle on it. But then the child appeared to ignore the bird-like portion of the meaning and focus only on the roundness of the coin, so reapplied the word *qua* to a teddy-bear's eye. Vygotsky calls this a 'chain-complex' because all the usages of *qua* are linked together in a chain. Each one is attached to the next, with no overall structure.

A more recent 'wrong analysis' theory suggests that children are working from prototypes. Like adults, they learn the meaning of words by picking on a typical example or 'prototype' which they analyse. They then match other possible examples of a category against the characteristics of the prototype, and if there is sufficient agreement they assign the new object to the same category. According to this viewpoint, discrepancies between child and adult language occur because children analyse the prototype differently from adults. For example, between the ages of 16 months and two years Eva used the word *moon* to refer not only to the moon but also to a slice of lemon, a shiny green leaf, curved cow horns, a crescent-shaped piece of paper, and pictures of yellow and green vegetables on the wall of a store (Bowerman, 1980). Most of these objects are crescent-shaped, which seemed to be an important property of moonhood for Eva. At first sight this observation supports mental fog theories: perhaps Eva simply thinks that *moon* means 'crescent'. But on examination there is more to it than this. First, Eva was able to recognize the moon in all its phases, when it was a full moon, a half moon or a quarter moon. So moons were not inevitably crescents, they were just typically crescents. Second, each of the objects labelled *moon* had something else apart from shape in common with the moon, though something different. The lemon slice shared its colour with the moon. The shiny green leaf shared the property of being shiny. The curved cow horns were seen from below. The green and yellow vegetables on the chart were seen against a broad expanse of background. So Eva had apparently identified several characteristics of the moon, the most crucial of which is its shape. Something was likely to be labelled *moon* if it shared both the shape and one other characteristic with the real moon (figure 8.2).

Similarly, at around the same age Eva took someone kicking a ball as a prototype for the word *kick* (Bowerman, 1978). She seems to have analysed this action as possessing three main characteristics: first, a waving limb; second, sudden sharp contact between part of the body and an object; third, propulsion forward of the object. This analysis could account for her labelling as *kick* a kitten with a ball of wool near its paw, dancers doing the can-can, a moth fluttering on a table, pushing a bottle with her feet and pushing a teddy bear's stomach against her sister's chest. All these things share characteristics with the prototypical *kick* but not the same ones (figure 8.2).

Prototype theory seems to account for both the broad mental fog type generalizations and the strange chain-complex ones. Furthermore, it ties in with the way adults assign words to categories. Children differ from adults in that they do not necessarily focus on the same characteristics when they analyse words, or put them in the same order of priority. They may also choose different proto-types. As they get older they gradually alter their analyses to fit in with those of the other people around them (Anglin, 1970; Keil and Batterman, 1984).

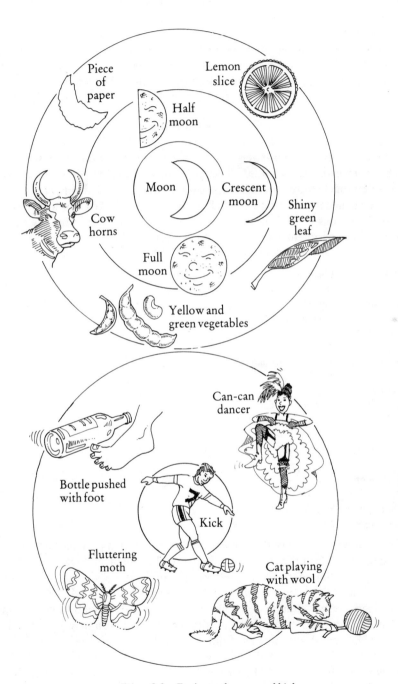

Figure 8.2   Eva's use of moon *and* kick

In terms of the library analogy mentioned at the beginning of the chapter, both the 'large empty room' and the 'rearranging shelves' viewpoints are right to some extent: the children are constantly rearranging their 'mental shelves', yet both the original classification and any rearrangement is carried out in accordance with general principles which they seem to understand instinctively, and which are broadly the same as those followed by adults.

Network building

Children pick up new words very quickly: the passive vocabulary of a six-year-old has been estimated at 14,000 (Carey, 1978). Somehow, these words have to be fitted together into a semantic network. How does this happen?

The evidence is sometimes confusing. 'What's this?' asked two-and-a-half-year-old Brian as he picked up a plastic horse. He was mimicking the behaviour of the experimenter who had just been testing him on word-names. The following conversation ensued (Macnamara, 1982):

Experimenter	It's an animal.
Brian	No.
Experimenter	Yes it is.
Brian	No (laughs).
Experimenter	Yes.
Brian	No.
Experimenter	This is an animal too.
Brian	No.
Experimenter	Yes.
Brian	Horsie.
Experimenter	It's also an animal.
Brian	No.
Experimenter	Just like you're Brian and you're a little boy.
Brian	No.
Experimenter	Yeah.
Brian	No.
Experimenter	You don't believe me.
Brian	No.

Brian would not believe that a horse was an animal. This dialogue appears at first sight to confirm the view of the Swiss psychologist Jean Piaget that Brian was too young to understand the relationship of inclusion, the fact that horses are included in the category of animal (Inhelder and Piaget, 1964). But Piaget's claim seems rather strange, since children of two can respond to commands such as 'Pick up your toys'. Perhaps, alternatively, children may just be resistant to giving an object more than one name (Macnamara, 1982). If a pig is a pig, then it can't be an animal. This seemed to be the reaction of around half of the two-year-olds tested. They reserved the word *animal* for a bunch of assorted animals.

The evidence, then, can be difficult to interpret. Apparent backward steps may be the best guide that network building is taking place (Bowerman, 1978, 1982). Two-year-old Christie used the words *put* and *give* appropriately, as in 'I *put* it somewhere', '*Gimme* more gum'. Then, when she was three, she started to use them interchangeably: 'You *put* ('give') me bread and butter', 'Whenever Eva doesn't need her towel, she *gives* ('puts') it on my table' (Bowerman, 1978). Perhaps, suggested Christie's mother, she had suddenly discovered that *put* and *give* had very similar meanings, but had not yet realized that one *puts* something on to a thing but *gives* something to a person. Two more years elapsed before Christie used *put* and *give* correctly by adult standards.

Network building takes place slowly. The 'lethargy of semantic development' (Anglin, 1970: 99) is a fairly general finding among researchers. Words which an adult would regard as related take time to get linked up in the child's mind. This fits in with the evidence from underextensions, the fact that children often learn a word in a particular context and only gradually extend it to a wider situation. Even fairly old children may find it hard to detach words from specific contexts. A group aged between eight-and-a-half and ten-and-a-half correctly guessed that the nonsense word *lidber* meant 'collect' from the sentence 'Jimmy lidbered stamps from all countries'. But when asked to interpret 'The police did not allow the people to lidber on the street', a typical response was that the police did not allow people to collect stamps on the street (Werner and Kaplan, 1950).

The tortoise-like progress of network building is confirmed by the literally dozens of studies which have explored how children cope with overlapping words, such as *tall*, *big*, *fat*, *high*, and opposites, such as *big–small*, *deep–shallow*, *tall–short*. (For a useful survey see Richards, 1979.) All the studies reported that these words acquire their adult meaning only gradually, sometimes with backward steps. One researcher found that children started out by using *big* to refer to gross overall size but then mistakenly narrowed it down to meaning 'tall' (Maratsos, 1973). Certain general trends emerge: the words *big* and *small* are used by younger children in preference to *tall–short*, *wide–narrow*, and children can cope with the larger of the two opposites better than the smaller: *fat* is learnt before *thin*, *high* before *low*, *long* before *short*. But the interpretation of these findings is disputed, since various other factors, such as children's preference for large rather than small objects, and parental usage, all complicate the situation.

Collocational links appear to have priority for children, while those between co-ordinates lag behind. This is shown by word association experiments: young children are likely to respond to 'table' with *eat*, to 'dark' with *night*, to 'send' with *letter* and to 'deep' with *hole*, whereas typical adult responses to these would be *chair*, *light*, *receive* and *shallow* (Entwisle, 1966; Brown and Berko, 1960). As children get older, the more likely they are to give an adult-like response. A suggested explanation is that 'this change in word associations is a consequence of the child's gradual organization of his vocabulary into the syntactic classes called parts-of-speech' (Brown and Berko, 1960: 14). Another explanation is that children may take time to discover the criteria by which adults classify items as co-ordinates. A study conducted with a group of three-to five-year-olds showed that they were quite happy to agree that prototypical birds, such as sparrows or robins, were birds but often argued that ducks or hens were not birds, they were ducks and hens (White, 1982). It is unclear whether the children had come to this conclusion by themselves or whether they were simply reflecting the speech of their parents, since the same experimenter noted that parents tended to refer to typical birds as *birds* more often than atypical ones: 'Oh, look there's a bird, it's a robin', 'That's a turkey, like the ones we saw at the turkey farm'.

Another explanation for the predominance of classification by co-ordinates in adult speech is that it may be more efficient for fast retrieval of a word. Fast word finding is a skill that has to be acquired, and young children can be quite slow at naming objects such as *ice-cream*, *lion* and *bed* whose names they know very well (Wiegel-Crump and Dennis, 1986). Perhaps the gradual shift-over comes in response to a need to organize and retrieve words quickly as the overall vocabulary gets larger.

This section, then, confirms our view that children are constantly reshuffling the shelves of their mental lexicon. Children are continually acquiring new words which they begin by using in restricted situations, then later fit into an overall network. Collocational links therefore have priority at first, but links between co-ordinates are gradually built up as a word is detached from the particular context in which it has been learnt. This continual integration of new words 'appears to be an extremely gradual process which may never be complete' (Anglin, 1970: 99).

Summary

In this chapter we have looked at how children acquire the meaning of words. This involved three different tasks: labelling, packaging and network building.

Labelling is not an automatic procedure. The ability to symbolize develops slowly, and probably emerges somewhere between the ages of one and two. Until this stage has been reached we cannot realistically speak of a 'mental lexicon'.

Packaging, the classification of a number of objects under a particular label, involved two common kinds of error: underextension and overextension. The gradual widening out of an over-narrow meaning was fairly straightforward. Overextension was often due to wrong analysis: children, like adults, seem to be working from prototypes, even though they tend to analyse the characteristics of the prototype somewhat differently.

Network building happens gradually, and may continue throughout a person's life. When they are first learnt, words are applied in a limited context only. So collocational links have priority in early childhood. Gradually, words are integrated into the network and links are built between co-ordinates, perhaps partly as a consequence of acquiring syntax and partly to allow for fast word finding as the overall vocabulary increases.

The last two chapters have mentioned that links between co-ordinates are closely intermeshed with a person's knowledge of their part of speech. In the next chapter, therefore, we will consider how 'parts of speech' are dealt with within the mental lexicon.

9

Lexical All-sorts
— *Parts of speech* —

Above all the noise and tumult of the crowd could be heard the merchants' voices loudly advertising their products.
'Get your fresh-picked ifs, ands and buts.'
'Hey-yaa, hey-yaa, nice ripe wheres and whens' . . .
'Step right up, step right up – fancy, best-quality words right here', announced one man in a booming voice. 'Step right up – ah, what can I do for you, little boy? How about a nice bagful of pronouns – or maybe you'd like our special assortment of names?'
Milo had never thought much about words before, but these looked so good that he longed to have some.
'Look, Tock,' he cried, 'aren't they wonderful?'

Norton Juster, The Phantom Tollbooth

In the quotation above, Milo and his dog Tock find the various types of words packaged up separately in the market-place at Dictionopolis: 'ifs, ands and buts' can be bought quite independently of 'a nice bagful of pronouns' or 'our special assortment of names'. This is not surprising. All languages divide words up into 'parts of speech' or word classes, which are conventionally given labels such as noun, adjective, verb, and so on, each of which has its own special role to play in the sentence: 'Think of the tools in a tool-box', suggested the philosopher Wittgenstein. 'There is a hammer, pliers, a saw, a screwdriver, a rule, a glue-pot, glue, nails and screws. The functions of words are as diverse as the functions of these objects' (Wittgenstein, 1958: 11).

The tool-box analogy is a useful one, in that it expresses the fact that each 'part of speech' behaves differently. However, an alternative way of viewing the situation is to regard word classes as building materials out of which a sentence is constructed. These materials are of two broad types: the bricks on the one hand and the mortar or cement on the other. The bricks can be equated with 'content' words, those which have an independent meaning, such as *rose*, *queen*, *jump*. The mortar represents the 'function' words, those whose role is primarily to relate items to one another, as in 'Queen *of* Hearts', 'work *to* rule', 'eggs *for* breakfast'.

This book is concerned mainly with content words, which are regarded by many people as constituting the 'lexicon proper'. Within content words we shall discuss primarily nouns, verbs and adjectives, which constitute the major building blocks of English. The most important task in this chapter is to find out how these are dealt with within the mental lexicon. We can then move on to other topics, in particular, problems with deciding how many word classes there are, and psycholinguistic evidence for the divide between the 'bricks' and the 'mortar'.

An eye for an eye

When people pick one word in mistake for another, the errors almost always preserve the word class of the target, whether they are based on meaning, sound, or both meaning and sound. Nouns change place with nouns, verbs with verbs and adjectives with adjectives, as in the examples below:

It's called the *Quail* (Lark) and Dove.
I looked in the *calendar* (catalogue).
It's a good way to *contemplate* (compensate).
The book I just *wrote* (read) was awful.
That model is *extinct* (obsolete).
The tumour was not *malicious* (malignant).

This characteristic of real-life errors, which has been reported by just about every researcher on the topic, is a feature which the playwright Richard Sheridan was unaware of when he created his fictional Mrs Malaprop. She sometimes gets her word classes confused, as in:

You will promise to forget this fellow – to *illiterate* (obliterate) him, I say, quite from your memory.

A confusion between *illiterate* (adjective) and *obliterate* (verb) would be unlikely in spoken speech in real life.

The finding that word selection errors preserve their part of speech suggests that it is an integral part of the word, and tightly attached to it. This cannot just be accidental, nor can it be solely due to syntactic selection procedures, as some researchers have claimed. They argue that people must, in speaking, select a syntactic 'frame' for the sentence, such as noun–verb–noun, then put appropriate words into the slots (e.g. Fromkin, 1971). They therefore suggest that the choice of a correct word class may be due to a syntactic checking device which monitors sentences as they are planned. But this cannot be entirely true, because quite often the words dictate the frame: a choice of *put* (Martha *put* the car in the garage) involves a longer frame than, say, *park*

(Martha *parked* the car). You cannot say: *Martha *put* the car (an asterisk indicates an impossible word or sentence). Furthermore, even if words are put into appropriate preplanned slots, they would still have to be 'labelled' with a word class in order to be picked for the slot. It seems likely therefore that the abstract meaning of a word is tightly attached to its word class.

A connection between the abstract meaning of a word and its part of speech is perhaps to be expected. Word class categorization is not arbitrary, and in origin arose out of semantic categories. Prototypical nouns tend to be people and things, and prototypical verbs tend to be actions. This correlation appears to be universal (Hopper and Thompson, 1984) – even though the link between a particular word and its part of speech prototype can be quite obscure: for example, verbs such as *exist, know, believe* do not involve obvious actions. Semantics and syntax therefore overlap, and linguists spend a good deal of time arguing where the boundary between them should be located. From the point of view of the mental lexicon, this suggests that we should not regard meaning and word class as separate ingredients which need to be attached, but as integrated together within the same component. In brief, we should regard words as coins, with meaning and word class together on one side and the sounds on the other. So, for example, choice of a word meaning DAISY automatically brings with it a 'label' of noun, and selection of a word meaning JUMP inevitably involves a label of verb.

Like with like

Word class 'labels', then, are attached to word meanings. This fact raises another important question. Are words from the same word class linked particularly closely together, so that a verb such as *shout* is more tightly connected to other verbs such as *yell* and *bellow* than to its own noun *shout*? Probably, yes. There are indications that on the one hand, words from the same word class are closely connected in storage, and that, on the other hand, those from different word classes are more loosely attached. Let us consider these.

First, we noted in chapter 7 that words cluster in groups of co-ordinates within semantic fields. These co-ordinates had the same word class as one another, as in *red, yellow, blue* (adjectives), *tulip, daffodil, rose* (nouns).

Second, a close connection between words from the same word class is suggested by 'tip of the tongue' guesses, in which the part of speech is mostly retained. According to one researcher, nouns and verbs retain their word class strongly (90 per cent), whereas adjectives appear to do so to a lesser extent (60 per cent), mostly eliciting nouns when the word class is disturbed (Browman, 1978). Word association experiments provide further evidence, where the commonest adult response is a word from the same class. Nouns elicit nouns around 80 per cent of the time, though verbs and adjectives do so somewhat less strongly, with a figure of just over 50 per cent (Deese, 1965).

Evidence from the bonds between co-ordinates, 'tip of the tongue' guesses and word association experiments, then, suggest that words from the same word class are closely linked, particularly nouns.

There are two types of clue that words from different word classes are relatively loosely attached. One relates to aphasics, the other to normal speakers. In certain types of aphasia, verbs seem to be the most vulnerable part of speech: 'Water . . . man, no woman . . . child . . . no, man . . . and girl . . . oh dear . . . cupboard . . . man, falling . . . jar . . . cakes . . . head . . . face . . . window . . .tap . . .' (Allport and Funnell, 1981). This is an attempt by a stroke victim to describe a busy kitchen scene, depicting a woman by an overflowing sink, a boy about to topple off a stool as he reaches for a jar of cookies, and a girl looking on. Yet to deal with this action-packed picture, it is mainly nouns which spring to the patient's mind.

In another study, a normal person and an aphasic were given the same set of questions. In her reply, the normal speaker used 67 different nouns and 56 different verbs. The aphasic, on the other hand, used 80 different nouns but only 28 different verbs (Hand *et al.*, 1979). The aphasic had developed a number of strategies in order to cope with the unavailability of verbs. She tended to reuse the same verb repeatedly: 'I love the sailboat', 'I love the music', 'And I love hiking', 'I love mother', 'I love outside'. She also used a general all-purpose verb *did* several times: 'I did the sailboat', 'I did the line', 'I did the kitchen and kitchen and kitchen'. But mostly, she used the phrase *this is*, or *it was*, in place of the appropriate verb: 'It was Charlton Avenue' (= I lived on Charlton Avenue), 'And then it was the stroke' (= And then I had a stroke), 'And right here this is Eddie the telephone' (= Eddie worked for the telephone company). At other times she omitted the verb entirely, which made her speech difficult to interpret: 'And the cookies jam cookie jam', 'And the arts Susie', 'Right here and me boom boom boom boom'.

Why should verbs present extra difficulty? A possible explanation is that, in the mental lexicon, verbs are perhaps attached to information about the constructions normally associated with them. English nouns require relatively little syntactic information attached to them – mainly whether or not they can be preceded by *the* (*the cat*, but not **the happiness*) and whether they can be counted (*six cats*, but not **six happinesses*) – even though aphasics can sometimes get this wrong, as suggested by the patient discussed above who said, 'I love *the music*', meaning apparently 'I love music'. Verbs, on the other hand, need at the very least to specify the constructions which must, or must not, follow them in a sentence, which often involves reference to other parts of speech: we cannot say **Stella put*, **Stella put the cat*, or **Stella put outside*: it has to be *Stella put the cat outside*.

A further, more controversial piece of evidence for the relative separation of verbs and nouns is their apparent rarity in semantic selection slips, even though there are plenty of verbs in all other types of tongue-slip (Hotopf, 1980). Out of 101 semantic errors in English there were only 3 verbs (compared with 81 nouns and 17 adjectives and adverbs). Yet judging by the proportion of verbs in English as a whole, one would have expected about 30 errors involving verbs. And in a collection of German errors, nouns, adjective and adverbs accounted for over 90 per cent of the semantic errors, and verbs less than 10 per cent. The explanation for this may be that when speakers produce a sentence they pick the verb very early from a special verb store which gives the syntactic framework for the rest of the sentence, and then the other words are slotted in around.

Overall, then, nouns seem to be the most robust and independent word class, in that people can remember some nouns when all else fails. This is not just because there are many more nouns than verbs. It is probably because they are relatively free of syntactic restrictions. Verbs, on the other hand, are some-what more vulnerable, perhaps because they are inextricably entangled with the syntax of the sentence. At all events, their differential treatment suggests that words from the same class are bonded together in the mental lexicon, whereas links between word classes are in general relatively weak – even though the collocational links between particular words may be powerful (chapter 7).

However, so far we have discussed only nouns, verbs and adjectives, yet most grammar books list many more parts of speech than this. Let us therefore briefly mention some of the problems raised by these other classes, and explain why it is impossible to give a definitive list of the word classes in the mental lexicon.

The adverbial rag-bag

There is a deeply ingrained belief among many well-educated English speakers that there are eight parts of speech in English, a belief usually derived from schooldays. School textbooks usually pick on this figure because eight was the number decided on by Greek grammarians for ancient Greek – and up until relatively recently descriptions of English were based on Latin grammars, which were themselves based on Greek ones. Greek is not entirely useless as a model, since Greek and English are ultimately descended from the same language, so some of the categories – noun, verb, adjective, preposition – work quite well. But the fit is bad in some other respects: for example, there is no obvious category for 'determiners', words such as *a*, *the*, *this*, *that*.

Furthermore, according to some linguists eight word classes may be too few, reflecting a 'common prejudice that the number of "parts of speech" should be small . . . That prejudice, of course, is as baseless as the once equally common prejudice that the number of chemical elements should be small' (McCawley, 1983: 263). The number eight is largely preserved by treating the category adverb as a rag-bag which contains a heterogeneous collection of words, many of which are there principally because they do not fit into any other category (McCawley, 1983). For example:

The parrot has *presumably* been taught *not* to swear.
The bird *nevertheless* swore *fluently* at Aunt Jemima.
Aunt Jemima was *really quite* upset.
Astonishingly, she was *almost completely* speechless.

The words underlined are all traditionally classified as adverbs. Yet they behave quite differently from one another. Words from the same word class can often be interchanged without altering the basic structure. But hardly any of the adverbs can change places with one another. If we try this kind of switching around, we get a quite unacceptable result:

*The parrot has *really* been taught *quite* to swear.
*The bird *presumably* swore *not* at Aunt Jemima.
*Aunt Jemima was *completely astonishingly* upset.
**Almost*, she was *fluently nevertheless* speechless.

In the case of adverbs, then, words which behave somewhat differently are lumped together under the same label. An even more confusing example of this occurs with prepositions (*to, for*, etc.). In this case, the same preposition can have two radically different uses. The situation fits an analogy suggested by Wittgenstein: 'It is like looking into the cabin of a locomotive ... We see handles all looking more or less alike ... But one is the handle of the crank ... another is the handle of a switch ... a third is the handle of the brake lever' (Wittgenstein, 1958: 12). Take the sequence *to*. Sometimes, it seems to have an independent meaning, as in:

The wart-hog trotted off *to* the forest.

Here *to* can be glossed as 'towards', 'in the direction of'. But at other times, *to* appears to be quite empty of meaning, serving only to show the relationship between the words on either side of it, as in:

The wart-hog wanted *to* eat.

One would expect the mental lexicon to make some distinction between these radically different uses, as indeed seems to be the case: aphasic patients find it easier to produce prepositions in their speech if they have intrinsic meaning (Friederici, 1982).

Examples such as these show, first, that care should be taken in assigning words to word classes; second, we are unlikely to be able to work out with any accuracy exactly how many different word classes are distinguished by the mental lexicon. In particular, it is not clear whether one should regard a clump of words which behaves partially like another clump as a subcategory within an overall category or as a category in its own right.

In spite of these cautions, however, a large number of English words can be readily identified as nouns, verbs, or adjectives, on the basis both of their position in the sentence and their general make-up. This is why we have kept mainly to these categories, dealing with clear-cut cases as far as possible. Let us now go on to consider possible psycholinguistic evidence for the broad-based distinction made earlier in this chapter, that between content words (the bricks) and function words (the mortar).

Bricks versus mortar

Word classes involving content words are mostly 'open' in the sense that they readily allow in newcomers: one can make up any number of new nouns, verbs and adjectives without any problem, as shown by some lines from Anthony Burgess's novel *A Clockwork Orange*:

Dim was a lot more *starry* and grey and had a few *zoobies* missing as you could see when he let out a *smeck*, *viddying* me, and then my *droog* Georgie said, pointing like at me: 'That man has filth and *cal* all over his *platties*', and it was true.

In contrast, word classes containing function words seem mostly to be 'closed', in the sense that they keep out newcomers.

The divide between open and closed class words is not absolute. Prepositions span both. They are usually regarded as a closed class, but they are marginally more welcoming to new members than the other closed classes. For example, in horse-racing, *upsides* meaning 'up alongside, up beside' is heard increasingly: 'Phantom Kipper has come *upsides* Happy Cheese'; and in sailing, people can fall *overside* the boat. But for the most part each of the closed classes has a fixed number of words, and any alteration in number is likely to be a slow change, occurring over centuries. One would suspect, therefore, that there might be an identifiable difference between open and closed word classes in the mental lexicon, which correlates roughly with the content–function distinction. However, the evidence for differential treatment is controversial – even though, as mentioned earlier, aphasics seem able to cope with prepositions with 'content' better than those without (Friederici, 1985).

The disputed evidence involves both aphasics and normals. Consider the following conversation:

Interviewer   What happened to make you lose your speech?
Patient   Head, fall, Jesus Christ, me no good, str, str ... oh Jesus ... stroke.
Interviewer   I see. Could you tell me, Mr. Ford, what you've been doing in the hospital?
Patient   Yes, sure. Me go, er, uh, P.T. nine o'cot, speech ... two times ... read ...
              wr ... ripe, er, rike, er, write ... practice ... get-ting better.
Interviewer   And have you been going home on weekends?
Patient   Why, yes ... Thursday, er, er, er, no, er, Friday ... Bar-ba-ra ... wife ...
              and, oh, car ... drive ... purnpike ... you know ... rest and ... tee-vee.

The patient in this dialogue (Gardner, 1974: 61) is suffering from a disorder usually labelled 'Broca's aphasia', after the nineteenth-century neurologist

Broca, who tried to pinpoint the area in the brain affected in patients who showed symptoms such as those of Mr Ford. Their speech is slow and effortful, they have difficulty thinking up the words they want and problems in pronouncing those they do find. But their most noticeable symptom is a lack of word endings, and a dearth of the 'little' words which normally hold the content words together: there appears to be no mortar between the bricks, as it were.

Such patients have been at the centre of a controversy in recent years. Some researchers have regarded them as evidence that the content versus function word distinction is valid: the patients still have access to the main portions of the mental lexicon but they are mostly unable to cope with the syntax of sentences, the processes which tie words together. This viewpoint has been around for quite a long time (Jakobson, 1956). If this interpretation is correct, then it is reasonable to assume that the 'lexicon proper' is stored separately from function words.

However, this is not the only possible explanation. A second possibility is that the missing words are just too small and insignificant to be retrieved easily. Maybe the aphasic described above is perfectly aware of what the sentence should be like but something has gone wrong with retrieving the sounds, so that short unstressed items are just too small to get hold of. Metaphorically, such a patient might be like a short-sighted person who knows quite well that a shirt needs buttons sewn on to the front and cuffs but is entirely unable to locate and select such tiny items as buttons. In linguistic terminology, this theory suggests that 'the manifested linguistic deficits of Broca's aphasics can only be accounted for in terms of the interaction between an impaired phonological capacity and otherwise intact linguistic capacities' (Kean, 1977: 10). Supporters of this hypothesis point out that the items affected are linguistically quite varied in character. The main thing they have in common is their insignificance, from a phonological point of view. If this viewpoint is correct, then there is no reason to believe that the function words are separated off from the content words – they are just written in more faintly, as it were, because of their lack of stress.

Can we decide between these viewpoints? The question is still under discussion, and both may be right to some extent, in that patients with these symptoms could be suffering from a mixture of disorders (Goodglass and Menn, 1985). However, some researchers have been trying to probe the problem further by the use of lexical decision tasks (Bradley, 1983; Bradley *et al.*, 1980). They argue that normal speakers treat open and closed class words differently in lexical decision tasks, whereas aphasics apparently do not. When normal speakers are asked to judge whether a string of letters such as CAT or PUDDLE or CUG or PLIGN is a word or not, they say 'Yes' faster to a real word if it is a common one. This is a well-known effect for open class words. Closed class words differ in frequency, just as open class ones do, so one might expect the same frequency effect to be found. But this seems not to be the case.

All closed class items are reportedly responded to in approximately the same time as each other. This suggests that they are perhaps treated differently from the open class items, and stored separately. Broca's aphasics, however, did not show this difference. They seemed to treat closed class items on a frequency basis, as they did the open class words, suggesting that a whole area of their brain, that dealing with syntax, had been disconnected.

These findings have been disputed by researchers who were unable to replicate this result (Gordon and Caramazza, 1982). However, some work done on German partially supports the original claim (Friederici, 1985) – though it is not definitive, since care must be taken in generalizing from one language to another. Subjects were asked to press a button as soon as they heard a target word, such as *Geld* 'money', as they listened to a couple of sentences. The speed with which open class items were responded to depended on whether or not the previous sentence had involved the general area of the target word. For example, when a casino was mentioned in the sentence preceding *Geld* 'money', the listeners spotted the word for 'money' more quickly. But the speed with which closed class items were accessed remained the same, whatever the previous context. This supports the claim that these two types of word are normally coped with in different ways by normal speakers. The aphasics tested showed a rather similar pattern to the normals, even though their responses were much slower, especially for closed class words.

These experiments suggest, then, that in normal speakers it is possibly justifiable to regard the words people know as divisible into two major categories: content words, which constitute the 'lexicon proper', and function words, the latter being linked to the syntax – though further work is still needed in relation to the aphasics.

Summary

This chapter has examined how the human mind copes with the different 'parts of speech'. Word class 'labels' seem to be tightly bonded on to the abstract meaning of a word, so much so that these two ingredients can be regarded as overlapping, and integrated within the same overall component of the lexicon.

Words within each of the three major word classes of English – nouns, verbs and adjectives – are closely bonded together. Furthermore, there is evidence that nouns and verbs are kept distinct in the minds of speakers, and that links between them are relatively weak.

We decided that it was impossible to say exactly how many word classes exist in the mental lexicon, though we found some evidence for a broad distinction between content words and function words, with the former constituting the 'lexicon proper'.

Let us now go on to discuss the other side of the word-coin, beginning with the internal architecture of words.

10
Bits of Words
— *The internal architecture of words* —

Are your pillows a pain in the neck?
Are they lumpy, hard, or torn?
Are they full of old influenza germs?
Are the feathers thin and forlorn?
Bring 'em to us,
We do the trick;
Re-puff,
Replenish,
Re-curl,
Re-tick,
We return your pillows, spanned-and-spicked,
Re-puffed, replenished, re-curled, re-ticked.

Ogden Nash, 'Any Millenniums Today, Lady?'

From the point of view of internal architecture, there are two kinds of English words. On the one hand, there are words such as *owl*, *wallaby* or *giraffe*, which seem to exist as wholes. On the other hand, there are items such as *replenished*, *uncaring* and *disagreement*, which are internally complex, in that they can be divided into chunks which they share with other words. *Disagreement*, for example, can be split into three sections: a base *agree*, with a prefix *dis-* tacked on to the front and a suffix *-ment* attached to the end (figure 10.1). Each of these components figures in other words also, such as *disintegrate*, *agreeing*, *merriment*, and so can be categorized as a morpheme, which is sometimes defined as 'the smallest grammatical unit' (see Brown, 1984, for a useful outline discussion).

Are these bits of words relevant to the mental lexicon? This is a matter which has been much discussed: 'A central question in the psychology of language is whether the mental lexicon – the dictionary in our heads – is a lexicon of words' (Jarvella and Meijers, 1983). Are words stored as single items ready for use? Or are they stored disassembled into morphemes and then put together

PREFIX	STEM	SUFFIX
dis-	*agree*	*-ment*

Figure 10.1　Bits of a word

when needed, as some people have suggested (e.g. Mackay, 1979)? And if they are disassembled, how does one find the word one wants? Would *disagreement* be listed under *dis-*? Or under *agreement*? Or under *agree*? Or under all three? These are fundamental questions which need to be answered in order to understand how humans cope with words.

'Common sense' can provide the answer, according to some people. The common-sense viewpoint claims that if a prefix or suffix can be added on to a stem by a regular rule, then it is unlikely to be already attached in the lexicon: 'Regular variations are not matters for the lexicon, which should contain only idiosyncratic items' (Chomsky and Halle, 1968: 12). This may be a useful guideline for a written grammar but it is not inevitably true of the mental lexicon, where a common sense view of speech processing would allow us to argue either way (Butterworth, 1983a). On the one hand, listing each word separately puts a heavy load on human memory, especially when the forms are predictable by a regular rule. On the other hand, attaching suffixes each time they are needed adds considerably to the burden of 'on-line processing'. Since humans have so much to cope with when they speak, perhaps they minimize the amount of on-the-spot assemblage.

Of course, even if words are stored as wholes, humans are still likely, on consideration, to be able to analyse them into sections, just as a car-owner can recognize that her car engine has a number of different components when she peers under the bonnet (hood). The point at issue, then, is not whether humans *can* analyse words but whether these words are normally stored in a disassembled state. This is the topic of this chapter.

Various attachments

There may not be a blanket answer to the assemblage question: some morphemes may already be attached to stems, others not, depending on their type. Lines from Ogden Nash's poem 'The Joyous Malingerer' illustrate a fundamental distinction, that between *inflection* and *derivation*:

> If faced with washing up he never *gripes*,
> But simply drops more dishes than he *wipes* . . .
> Stove-wise he's the perpetual backward *learner*
> Who can't turn on or off the proper *burner* . . .

> He can, attempting to *replace* a fuse,
> Black out the coast from Boston to Newport News.

The words *gripes* and *wipes* at the end of the first two lines illustrate the process of inflection: an ending (in this case *-s*) adds extra information to an existing word (*gripe*, *wipe*) without fundamentally altering it. *Dishes* in the second line is another example, consisting of *dish* + plural ending.

Learner and *burner* at the end of the middle two lines exemplify derivation: a morpheme (in this case *-er*) is attached to an existing word (*learn*, *burn*), and the result is a new word. *Replace* in the next to last line is another example of derivation, though in this case via a prefix: *re-* is added to *place* to form a new word, *replace*.

For the most part it's fairly easy to distinguish inflection from derivation. A rough rule of thumb for telling them apart is that you can add inflectional endings after derivational ones but not vice versa. You can say *comput-er-s* (derivational *-er* then inflectional *-s*), but not **compute-s-er*. You can say *comput-er-ize-ed* (derivational *-er* and *-ize*, then inflectional *-ed*), but not **comput-er-ed-ize*. This suggests that derivational endings may be more firmly attached than inflectional ones – as turns out to be the case. We will deal with the matter in the order indicated in figure 10.2: inflectional suffixes, then derivational prefixes, then derivational suffixes.

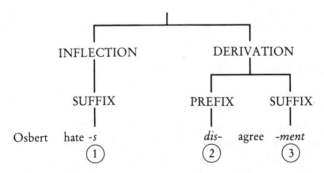

Figure 10.2   Inflection and derivation

Wash upping the dishes

An amalgam of smallish clues suggests that inflectional suffixes are quite often added on in the course of speech. First, consider slips of the tongue, as in the following:

> He *go backs* (he goes back).
> They *point outed* (pointed out).
> She *wash upped* the dishes (washed up).

She *come backs* tomorrow (comes back).
Stop him *go offing* (going off) and doing that.
I'd *forgot abouten* (forgotten about) doing that.

These tongue-slips provide strong evidence that at least some inflectional endings are added on as needed. The examples listed involve phrasal verbs – verbs which consist of more than one word such as *pick up*, *go back*, *point out*. If endings were already attached, one should always get *picks up*, *goes back*, *points out*. But if the ending needs to be attached in the course of speech, then it is quite probable that someone in a hurry might accidentally attach it at the end of the whole sequence, and say things such as *pick ups*, *go backs*. Furthermore, since these slips sometimes produce non-existent words, such as *abouten*, *outed*, these cannot be examples of wrong lexical selection – they must be examples of an ending added in the wrong place.

Care must be taken, incidentally, as to which kind of errors we use as evidence. Sometimes stems change places, resulting in wrongly attached suffixes, as in *It waits to pay* (It pays to wait), *I want to get a cash checked* (I want to get a check cashed) (Garrett, 1976, 1980). But since this type of switch-over also occurs with unsuffixed words as in *Fran Sanisco* (San Fransciso), *The scan is a Sundal sheet* (The Sun is a scandal sheet), the detachment of suffixes is in this case probably a late error which occurred as the phrases were about to be uttered, rather than a misplacement of suffixes during the planning process (Butterworth, 1983a).

On-the-spot attachment of suffixes is also suggested by the occasional accidental regularization of irregular forms:

All the men who *fighted* in it (fought).

Further examples occur in the plurals of complex lexical items such as *mother-in-law*. Is the plural *mothers-in-law*? Or *mother-in-laws*? Some people are uncertain, and fluctuate between the two. All these examples suggest that, at least in some cases, inflectional suffixes are added on when needed, rather than being already glued to words in the mental lexicon.

Some people with speech disorders provide additional support for the attachment of suffixes as speech proceeds, especially those aphasics who produce strings of words with very little syntax: 'Jar . . . cakes . . . head . . . face . . . water . . . tap' (chapter 9). In severe cases, the only inflectional endings found are in rote phrases, such as *I don't know what happened*, or forms which are more usually plural, as in *arts*, *crafts*, *cookies*. Such patients indicate that inflectional endings are usually added on in the process of speech production, apart from some common phrases, or words which are habitually inflected.

In another kind of aphasia, patients produce fluent speech but have difficulties both with comprehension and word finding. In their struggle to remember words, such patients sometimes utter non-existent ones. In chapter 1 we gave an example of a brain-damaged man who was unable to remember the name for a box of matches: 'Waitresses. Waitrixies. A backland and another bank. For bandicks er bandiks I think they are, I believe they're zandicks, I'm sorry, but they're called flitters landocks.' He also talks about a *pidland* – possibly a telephone dial, and then comments, 'each of the pidlands has an eye in, one two three and so on'. In these examples he appears to be putting plural -*s* on to nonsense words. Elsewhere, he adds on verb endings: 'She wikses a zen from me', 'He mivs in a love-beautiful home'. The fluency with which he does this suggests that the addition of inflectional suffixes is something which he is used to coping with routinely (Butterworth, 1983a).

The inconsistent behaviour of some normal speakers points to a similar conclusion. For example, teenagers in Reading frequently attach a non-standard -*s* to verbs which are typical of their subculture, as in the sentences below (Cheshire, 1982):

We fucking *chins* (hit on the chin) them with bottles.
I *legs* it (run away) up Blagdon Hill.
We *kills* (beat in a fight) them.

They also attach this -*s* to other verbs, but not so often, and they do this more often in casual than in formal speech. This suggests that -*s* is variably added most of the time, but there may be a few verbs to which it is already firmly attached in the mental lexicon.

A number of experimental psychologists have come to the conclusion that regular inflections are added on in the course of speech (e.g. Cutler, 1983). Several experiments have found that prior exposure to a regularly inflected form of a word such as *jumps* appeared to speed up recognition time of the base *jump* as much as prior presentation of the word itself (Murrell and Morton, 1974; Stanners *et al.*, 1979). Irregular forms of the same verb, as with *hung* and *hang*, did not produce the same effect. The experimenters interpreted the result as indicating that *jumps* and *jump* led subjects to the same lexical entry *jump*. Although this particular type of experiment is not always reliable (Fowler *et al.*, 1985), it supports the other pieces of evidence which suggest that inflectional suffixes are commonly attached as speech proceeds.

Our general conclusion, then, is that inflections are added to words as we speak, for the most part. However, they may already be attached to a few words used commonly in their inflected form such as *peas*, *lips*, having become welded on over the years. Humans develop routines for common procedures which gradually become automatic, and the adding on of frequently used inflectional suffixes probably comes into this category of behaviour (Stemberger, 1985). Let us now move on to prefixes.

The *pertoire question

Suppose, in a lexical decision task, you found that the non-word *pertoire* was rejected faster than the non-word *juvenate*, what would you conclude? *pertoire* was dismissed fast because there was no sign of it in the mental lexicon, according to the researchers who reported the finding (Taft and Forster, 1975). People did not link it up with *repertoire*, since the *re*-in this word is not a proper prefix. But *juvenate* was rejected slowly because it actually existed as an entry, though with a small *re*- attached under it, showing that it could not be used without a prefix. The time taken to read through the entry slowed down reaction time. According to this view, words are entered in the mental lexicon in their stem form, with the prefixes stripped off, and listed underneath the relevant stems:

JUVENATE	PLENISH
RE-	RE-

And this conclusion seemed to be supported by another experiment (Taft, 1981), in which it took subjects longer to recognize 'pseudo-prefixed' words – words such as *precipice* which look as if they have a prefix but do not in fact do so – than either prefixed words or unprefixed words. Perhaps hearers mistakenly think such words are prefixed, and so strip away the pseudo-prefix and look for a non-existent lexical entry under its presumed stem. So *precipice* would take a long time to find because the subjects mistakenly spent time searching under *cipice*. The experimenter concludes: 'In summary, then, from the finding that pseudo-prefixed words are indiscriminately treated as prefixed words, it can be concluded that prefix stripping occurs in word recognition, and this, in turn, implies that prefixed words are accessed through a representation of their stem' (1981: 296).

There are a number of criticisms which can be levelled at these findings. In the first experiment, *juvenate* is very like *juvenile*, so the presence of the entry for *juvenile* might have slowed down reaction time. The main stress has been stripped off in *(re)pertoire*, but not in *re(juvenate)*. Subjects may have adopted artificial strategies to deal with this rather strange task (Rubin *et al.*, 1979). Above all, the experiment used written words, so perhaps did not reveal anything about the way spoken words are stored.

Defenders of 'prefix stripping', however, argue that it is supported by slips of the tongue which involve apparent prefix switching, as in *constraint* for 'restraint', *advice* for 'device'. These superficially support the claim that words are listed in the mental lexicon primarily by their stems, with the various prefixes listed underneath, perhaps in order of frequency of usage, so words from the same stem would be likely to get confused if they begin with equally common prefixes (Fay, 1977).

In answer to the 'prefix strippers', proponents of 'ready-made' words have put forward a number of counter-claims. First, in many cases there is no consistency in the meanings of either prefixes or stems (Aronoff, 1976). There is no discernible semantic link between *con*-in *consume*, *confer*, *conceive*, *condemn*, and there is no obvious connection between the various occurrences of *-fer* in *confer*, *defer*, *infer*, *prefer*, *refer* unless you happen to know Latin. Humans would have enormous difficulty in dealing with all these arbitrary pieces separately. If words were really stored in fragments, one would expect there to be far more confusion than in fact exists, or alternatively, one would predict a move to restore some kind of consistent meaning to each stem and prefix. And even apparently meaningful prefixes sometimes resist detachment from their base: *uncanny* and *uncouth* do not mean *non-canny* and *non-couth*.

There are several other reasons for thinking that prefixes are glued to their stems (Aitchison, 1983–4). In slips of the tongue, prefixed words preserve their beginnings as often as unprefixed words, something which one would not expect if prefixes were easily removable. Also, prefixed words often interchange with non-prefixed words, suggesting that they are not regarded as a different special category:

> The emperor had many *porcupines* (concubines).
> Those lovely blue flowers – *concubines* (columbines).

Concubines has the prefix *con*-, whereas *porcupines* and *columbines* are unprefixed. One could, of course, argue that only people who know Latin would recognize *concubines* as prefixed: but 'He's a very *combative*, I mean, *competitive* man' shows a word *combative*, whose make-up is similar to *concubine* – Latin prefix followed by a stem which does not occur elsewhere – changing place with a word which should probably be regarded as prefixed because the stem occurs elsewhere, in *repetitive*. Furthermore, in word searches people seem to be fairly sure about the way in which words start, and often use the prefix as a fixed point around which their search revolves, as shown in the following rooting-around by someone who was mildly drunk: 'I met a man at the party who said he'd written an article on the IRA, on its *contemplation*, no *combination*, I think I mean its *construction*, not quite, it's something like *consistency* or *constitution*, it's make-up, ah, *composition*!' These findings suggest that the prefix is an aid in remembering the word, not an appendage to be added later.

How, then, are we to account for the examples of 'pure prefix change', such as *advice* for 'device'? If the context in which these occurred is examined, it turns out that many of them – possibly the majority – are blends (Aitchison, 1983–4):

> I don't *expose* (expect + suppose) anyone will eat that.
> At the moment of *compact* (impact + collision).
> Plastic bags are *dispendable* (disposable + expendable).
> The numbers aren't *consequential* (consecutive + sequential).

Most of those that are not obviously blends have unstressed prefixes, as in a most *extinguished* (distinguished) professor, suggesting that unstressed syllables are less prominent in storage, and perhaps cannot be retrieved as fast as stressed ones (to be discussed in chapter 11).

All this suggests that prefixes and stems are epoxied together in the mental lexicon, at least when stems obligatorily occur with a prefix, as in *rejuvenate*. With words such as *happy* and *unhappy* it is difficult to be quite so definite, though one suspects that the prefix is already added on, at least with all common words – otherwise one would get far more cases of wrong prefix attachment, such as *dishappy*, *non-happy*.

Prefixes, then, are normally attached to stems. But what about suffixes? There are many more of these in English, which is a language which prefers suffixes to prefixes. There is therefore no reason to expect them to behave identically in the minds of speakers.

Reproductive furniture

It is possible that most individual and international social and
economic *collisions*,
Result from humanity's being divided into two main *divisions*.
Their lives are spent in mutual *interference*,
And yet you cannot tell them apart by their outward *appearance*.

These four lines from Ogden Nash's poem 'Are You a Snodgrass?' encapsulate the problem of derivational suffixes. In a large number of cases a derived form can be related to a more basic one from which it was originally formed, as in the words at the end of each line: so *collision* was formed from *collide*, *division* from *divide*, *interference* from *interfere*, and *appearance* from *appear*. Some people regard this as a purely historical fact, of no relevance to the production of speech (e.g. Aronoff, 1976). Others assume that these words are reassembled each time we use them: they claim that we store a base form of a word (e.g. *appear*) with an extra note about the possible suffixes (e.g. *-ance*) and how to attach them (e.g. Mackay, 1979). Let us consider these points of view.

The main argument in favour of words being stored as wholes is the unpredictability of the link between a base and its derivative (Chomsky, 1970; Aronoff, 1976). Above all, there are a number of 'baseless derivatives' in English, words such as *perdition*, *conflagration*, *probity* which have no base from which they could have been formed (Aronoff, 1976). Furthermore, the meaning link between a base and its derived form is often unpredictable, as in *comprehend / comprehensive*, *revolve / revolution*, *succeed / succession* (Aronoff, 1976). In addition, words with similar stems are fairly idiosyncratic as to which suffixes they allow: we find *induce*, *inducement* and *induction*, but *produce*, *production* only, with a gap where *producement* might have existed (Butterworth, 1983a). The examples above, then, all indicate the chaotic nature of the relationship between stem and suffix. This would make dismembered words extraordinarily difficult to remember.

Slips of the tongue also suggest that words are stored as wholes, with their suffixes tightly attached. In malapropisms, suffixes are usually maintained, as in *provisional* for 'provincial', *detergent* for 'deterrent', especially in long words (Aitchison and Straf, 1982). Preservation of the end of the word occurs more often in suffixed words than in those without a suffix (Aitchison, in press). Indeed, sometimes the suffix alone survives intact:

He has a terrible speech *predicament* (impediment).
She goes in for *pornographic* (hydroponic) gardening.

And when the suffix is changed, other portions of the word are usually changed as well, as in *malicious* for 'malignant', *prostitute* for 'protestant'. In a study of the six commonest suffixes in a collection of malapropisms, the suffix was maintained in over 150 cases, and changed in 29. Twenty-one of these 29 involved changing other parts of the word as well as the suffix. There were only eight examples of 'pure' suffix change – cases when only the suffix was altered, and the rest of the word maintained, as in *reproductive furniture* for 'reproduction furniture', *indulgement* for 'indulgence', *industrial* for 'industrious' (Aitchison, in press).

The sporadic cases of pure suffix error seemed to have three main causes. The first, as with prefix errors, is blending:

It might be fun to *speculise* (speculate + surmise).
It's a *contential* (contentious + controversial) matter.

The second reason is 'derailment' – cases in which a speaker starts on a word but, by not paying attention, gets 'derailed' on to another, more common word, just as someone who walks into the kitchen might without thinking put a kettle on to boil, even though she actually went into the kitchen for some quite different reason, perhaps as in:

Bees are very *industrial* (industrious).

A final reason for wrong suffixes is the use of a fall-back procedure. If people cannot think of the word they want, they know methods of producing new ones, which might in any case produce the word they cannot think of, though it sometimes results in an error:

Children use *deduceful* (deductive) rules.

Here, the speaker has temporarily forgotten the relevant word and has attempted to recreate it afresh from its verb, possibly after analysing a similar example, such as *resent/resentful*. (This process will be discussed more fully in chapter 13.) These findings suggest that suffixes are normally glued to their stems, and that they often aid retrieval (Brown and McNeill, 1966).

The arbitrary links between bases and suffixes, and the preservation of suffixes in malapropisms, then, suggest that words are entered into the mental lexicon as wholes, not as bits. So far we have not yet mentioned experimental evidence on this point. Unfortunately experiments which have tried to examine this question are somewhat inconclusive (Cutler, 1983). On the whole they have shown two facts: first, it does not take any longer to recognize a word with a derivational suffix such as *dust-y* than a word without, such as *fancy* (Manelis and Tharp, 1977), which supports the 'whole words' view. Second, people can split words up if they need to – something which may happen in the course of comprehension but is not inevitable. For example, when people were asked to judge whether two sequences were both words, the process took longer if one was suffixed and the other not, as with *printer* and *slander* (Manelis and Tharp, 1977). This slightly complicated task probably led subjects to attempt to disassemble them. It seems clear, then, that people can, on reflection, decompose words into morphemes. They use this ability as a back-up procedure in order to construct a complex word if their normal memory for the word fails them, or if they are asked to perform a complex task. It's also probable that they disassemble a word if they are faced with a long, complicated one whose meaning they are not quite sure about. Let us now consider how this back-up information might be stored.

Back-up information

So far, we have concluded that words are stored primarily as wholes but that speakers are optionally able to split words up if necessary. We therefore need to ask where this back-up information is stored. One possibility is that this extra information is in a secondary store, attached to the lexicon proper. A human may be like a shopkeeper who keeps extra information about his goods in a back room. Words which can be split up are linked to others with similar make-up, and this may involve a subsidiary network attached perhaps between the 'lexicon proper' and the 'lexical tool-kit' – the procedures for making new words (to be discussed in chapter 14). Some of the links in this subsidiary network are strong ones, others weak. Some are perhaps non-existent until the need to split up a particular word arises. The human mind is able to analyse and match elements continuously, as speech is processed. So it will automatically be reaffirming old links and creating new ones in the course of speech, and using the back-up information to do this. Words previously unanalysed will be moved into the back-up store as links with existing words are recognized. For example, it is quite possible to find adults who are unaware that the word *Plymouth* means 'at the mouth of the river Plym', even though they may have correctly analysed *Dartmouth* and *Exmouth* as towns at the mouth of the Dart and the Exe. When they come across the river Plym, perhaps on a map, *Plymouth* is moved to the back-up store (figure 10.3). These back-up links are therefore revised continuously.

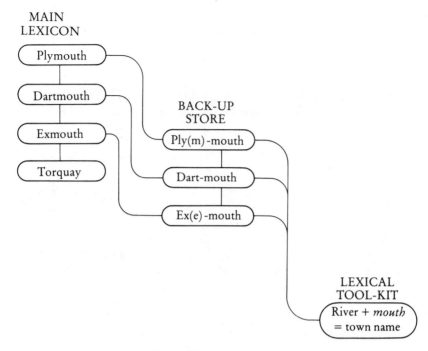

Figure 10.3   The back-up store

But if words are stored as words, then people sometimes have to deal with quite long sequences. How therefore is their sound structure represented in the mental lexicon? This is the topic of the next chapter.

Summary

In this chapter we discussed whether the mental lexicon contained words, or bits of words, which had to be assembled when required. We concluded that inflectional suffixes are commonly added on as needed in the course of speech, but that derivational prefixes and suffixes are already attached to their stems. However, even though words are already assembled in the main section of the mental lexicon, speakers can, if necessary, disassemble them, by using a back-up store attached to the 'lexical tool-kit', the procedures for making new words.

Meanwhile, we need to discuss how the sound structure of words is stored in the mental lexicon. This is the topic of the next chapter.

11

Taking Care of the Sounds
— *Dealing with the sound patterns* —

'Ah, well! . . .' said the Duchess, digging her sharp little chin into
Alice's shoulder . . . 'the moral of that is – "Take care of the sense and the
sounds will take care of themselves".'
'How fond she is of finding morals in things!' Alice thought to herself.

Lewis Carroll, *Alice in Wonderland*

Most of us hope that if we think of the meaning of the word we want, then the
sounds will take care of themselves by following immediately, like a train
attached to an engine. This happens most of the time, but not always. This
chapter considers how humans cope with the sound structure of words. In
particular, what is an entry like in the mental lexicon from the point of view of
sounds? And how are the various items organized in relation to one another?

For a printed dictionary, these questions could be answered quite straightforwardly by saying that each word consists of a sequence of units known as
letters, and that all words are listed in alphabetical order, a conventional but
arbitrary arrangement. As far as the mental lexicon is concerned the answer is
unlikely to be so simple, even though, at a superficial level, it is possible to
characterize each word as a row of sound segments or phonemes, of which
English has around 40. Speakers must subconsciously be aware of these: they
know, for example, that [r] and [l] are different English sounds, because they
distinguish words which are otherwise the same, as in *rid* and *lid*, or *rook* and
look – though this is a distinction not made by some other languages, such as
Japanese.

Furthermore, each language has its own rules for permitted phoneme
sequences: English does not allow the combination [pt] at the beginning of
words, though this is common in ancient Greek, as shown by the spelling of
borrowed words such as *pterodactyl*. Speakers subconsciously know these
sequencing rules, since they can for the most part reliably judge if a nonsense
word is a possible word, such as *scrad*, or an impossible one, such as **ptad*
(Greenberg and Jenkins, 1964).

However, the observation that humans 'know' the phonemes and phoneme sequences of their language does not necessarily imply that lexical entries are just a string of phonemes, all given equal value, like coaches on a train, especially as each English word has its own stress pattern which intermeshes with the sounds. And compared with the entries in a written dictionary, words turn out to be stored somewhat unevenly, with some parts more prominent than others.

The bathtub effect

The 'bathtub effect' is perhaps the most commonly reported finding in the literature on memory for words. People remember the beginnings and ends of words better than the middles, as if the word were a person lying in a bathtub, with their head out of the water one end and their feet out the other. And, just as in a bathtub the head is further out of the water and more prominent than the feet, so the beginnings of words are on average better remembered than the ends (figure 11.1).

an _ _ _ _ _ _dote

Figure 11.1   The bathtub effect

The 'bathtub effect' was first pointed out by Brown and McNeill (1966). As we noted in chapter 2, these two Harvard psychologists tried to induce a 'tip of the tongue' (TOT) state by reading out definitions of relatively uncommon words to around 50 students. This procedure resulted in over 200 'positive TOTs', situations in which the subjects, on later being told the target, claimed that it was the one they had in mind. The psychologists quizzed those in a TOT state about other items which came to mind in their search, and found a clear bathtub effect when the words judged to be similar sounding – such as *sarong*,

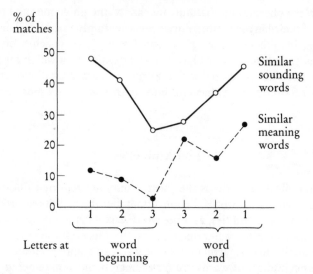

Figure 11.2   Similar sounding versus similar meaning words (from Brown and McNeill, 1966)

Siam, sympoon for 'sampan' – were matched against the target. This was not due to chance, since the effect was not repeated for similar meaning words – such as *houseboat, junk* for 'sampan' (figure 11.2). And the observation that people tend to recall the beginnings and ends of words they cannnot otherwise remember has been confirmed by other researchers (e.g. Koriat and Lieblich, 1974; Rubin, 1975; Browman, 1978).

In malapropisms – cases in which a similar sounding word has been wrongly selected, as in *cylinders* for 'syllables', *anecdote* for 'antidote', *facilities* for 'faculties' – the effect is even stronger. The same bathtub-shaped curve was found in a study of around 200 errors involving numerous common words, such as *goof* for 'golf', *my* for 'me', *psychotic* for 'psychological' (Tweney *et al.*, 1975), which showed that the phenomenon did not relate only to low frequency words. The data in subsequent studies show over 80 per cent of word initial sounds as either identical or very similar to the target, and over 70 per cent of word endings. The middles, however, do not show such a high level of agreement (Fay and Cutler, 1977; Hurford, 1981; Aitchison and Straf, 1982).

Length of words has some influence in the bathtub. In a collection of almost 500 malapropisms, the initials of short words were marginally better remembered than those of long words, and memory for the end of long words was considerably better than for the end of short words (Aitchison and Straf, 1981):

	INITIAL CONSONANTS	FINAL CONSONANTS
SHORT (1–2 syllables)	86%	70%
LONG (3 or more syllables)	82%	82%

The bathtub effect, then, suggests that particularly the beginnings, and to a lesser extent the ends of words are prominent in storage. The effect is not just due to 'selective attention', paying attention to particular parts of the word when all sections are stored equal, because words that get confused in memory show similar characteristics. When people forget the difference between two words and merge them in their mind, these items usually have similar beginnings and endings. A large proportion of the entries in a well-known book of 'confusibles' (Room, 1979) begin and end with the same sound, as in *flaunt/ flout*, *fluorescent/phosphorescent*, *hydrometer/hygrometer*, *prodigy/progeny*, *hysterics/histrionics*.

How far along the word does the bathtub effect extend at each end? The bathtub starts sloping down almost immediately, it seems. In a study of around 500 TOT guesses (Browman, 1978) the beginning phoneme was recalled in 51 per cent of cases, and the final in 35 per cent. Taking pairs of phonemes, the first two and the last two were each recalled 19 per cent of the time. Beyond this, the near misses had more segments in common with their targets than could be expected by chance, though these were not necessarily in the same order. The chunks remembered at the beginning and end did not correspond with either morphemes or syllables: CV (consonant + vowel) sequences tended to be remembered at the beginning of a word, and VC sequences at the end, as in *binomial* for 'bimodal', *rebuttal* for 'retrieval'. Vowels, it seemed, were prepared to attach themselves either to consonants in front of them or to ones after them: 'Vowels are the swingers of the phonetic world' (Browman, 1978: 48).

Beginnings and ends of words, then, seem more prominent in storage, and are more likely to be remembered than other sections of the word which one might expect to be prominent, such as stressed vowels. Stressed vowels are moderately well recalled in short words but match their target in fewer than 60 per cent of long words, according to one study of malapropisms (Aitchison and Straf, 1982). In another, stressed vowels matched their target in 65 per cent of words, a retention rate that was less good than the first vowel in the word, which matched in 83 per cent, after the elimination of cases in which the stressed vowel and the first vowel coincided (Fay and Cutler, 1977: 514 n.).

The bathtub effect relates to sequences of sounds. But words are a complicated amalgam of sounds and rhythm. Let us now consider how these two facets of a word are integrated.

The skeleton underneath

A word can be likened to a body: flesh (the sounds) covers an underlying skeleton (the rhythmic pattern) which gives it its shape. One way of representing this internal structure is by means of a 'tree diagram' (Liberman and Prince, 1977; Selkirk, 1980). This rhythmic or 'metrical' tree shows how syllables combine to form larger units, sometimes called 'feet', which in turn build up

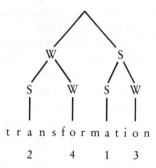

Figure 11.3   A metrical tree

into words. The stronger branches on the trees are labelled S (strong) and the weaker ones W (weak). By following a syllable up through the various nodes – points at which branches join – it is possible to see the relative strengths of the different syllables (figure 11.3): (1) is the strongest (an S under another S), (2) is the next strongest (an S under a W), (3) comes next (W under S) and (4) is the weakest (W under W). The number underneath any particular syllable shows how strong or weak it is in relation to the others.

The exact way in which trees should be drawn is still under discussion (Liberman and Prince, 1977; Halle and Vergnaud, 1980; Selkirk, 1980, 1984). Also under discussion are the 'rules' which specify how the rhythm alters when words come into contact: *hot, water* and *cylinder* will be rather different when they come together in *hot water cylinder* from when they are pronounced separately. However, in spite of minor differences, all researchers agree on one thing: words have a rhythm which is likely to be specified in the mental lexicon. The important point about this rhythm is that it is relative. The exact amount of stress given to each syllable may vary. But it is essential to get the relationship of strong to weak right along the whole length of the word.

An alternative way of showing the basic rhythmic pattern of strong and weak is by means of a 'metrical grid', in which asterisks replace numbers (Hayes, 1983, 1984). On a grid, the strongest syllable has the greatest number of asterisks and the weakest has the least (and sometimes people leave the weakest syllable unmarked, which reduces the number by one all along) (figure 11.4).

From the point of view of the mental lexicon, it may be more revealing to imagine the grid the other way up, as a series of peaks and troughs, like a complex wave formation, with the strongest syllable having the highest peak.

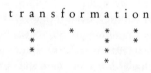

Figure 11.4   A metrical grid

t r a n s f o r m a t i o n

Figure 11.5   A rhythmic wave pattern

On this diagram, as on the tree, the relationship between the various syllables is more important than the exact amount of stress on each one (figure 11.5).

How, then, is this rhythmic contour stored in the mind? In particular, is it stored separately from the segments, so that rhythm and stress have to be assembled at some point? Or are the two inextricably intertwined?

Recall for number of syllables

A basic feature of the rhythmic wave is the number of syllables. 'Tip of the tongue' experiments and tongue-slips show that people have a reasonable knowledge of this when they try to recall words. When subjects were asked to make explicit guesses about the number of syllables in their TOT words, 57 per cent of these were correct (Brown and McNeill, 1966). This is exactly the same percentage as were correct for guesses about initial consonants, though the result is somewhat less remarkable for syllables, since there are fewer possibilities to choose from. However, this figure of 57 per cent is still considerably above the chance level, which is around 25 per cent (Goodglass *et al.*, 1976). And a similar figure was found by Browman (1978), in her study of TOT approximations, who found that the number of syllables was recalled 56 per cent of the time.

As with recall for segments, slips of the tongue show a higher rate of syllable preservation than TOT phenomena, though there is some disagreement between researchers as to the percentage retained. One study of malapropisms found that 87 per cent agreed with the target in number of syllables (Fay and Cutler, 1977), and another came out at 67 per cent (Aitchison and Straf, 1982). One possible reason for the discrepancy is that shorter words maintain the number of syllables better than longer ones, and the two studies may have included different length words. If one averages the figures, we may conclude that, as with the TOT data, the number of syllables is remembered about as well as the beginnings and endings, even though this is less remarkable, since there are almost four times as many possible phonemes as likely word lengths.

In spite of minor disagreements over the recall of the number of syllables, all studies agree in finding that if someone gets the syllables right they almost always get the stress pattern right. So, if we find out what went wrong when the syllables failed to match, we can also see what went wrong in the case of the stress pattern.

When syllable length was misremembered, shorter words tended to get lengthened and longer ones to get shortened, in both TOTs and mala-propisms. People were likely to remember both two-syllable and four-syllable words as having three syllables, whereas three-syllable words moved in either direction (Brown and McNeill, 1966; Aitchison and Straf, 1982). These omissions and additions almost always involve weak syllables, as in *translation* for 'transformation', *comment* for 'compliment', *tactical* for 'tactful', *castigated* for 'castrated'. Unstressed syllables, therefore, fade away easily, and get inserted easily.

People therefore tend to have a general rhythmic pattern in their heads, with the weakest syllables being the least well recalled. This pattern seems to be interwoven with the sound sequence. Weakly stressed syllables cause problems at the beginning of words – even though, as we noted earlier, sounds in this position are normally recalled best of all: the biggest single category of word initial errors comprises those with unstressed first syllables, as in *fire dis-tinguisher* (extinguisher), *a touch of vagina* (angina) (Aitchison and Straf, 1982, Browman, 1978). Furthermore, middle sequences, which are normally not as well recalled as the beginning and ends, are better remembered if they involve the stressed syllable (Browman, 1978). If rhythm and segments were independent, one would not expect them to intermesh in this way.

Our general conclusion, then, is that certain features of a word are more prominent in storage than others, and people home in on these when they are selecting a word. Above all, people seem to know about the beginning, to a lesser extent the end, and the general rhythmic pattern. This finding relates not only to normal speakers but also to aphasics, who are able to make better than chance guesses about word beginnings and number of syllables (Barton, 1971), though some types of aphasics are better than others (Goodglass *et al.*, 1976). The rhythmic pattern and the segments are intertwined, much in the way that flesh and bones are inextricably intermeshed on a body.

The conclusions reached above suggest that words with the same or similar beginnings and endings are closely linked. However, we now need to discuss what we mean by 'similar' in relation to the mental lexicon. Just as A and B are near together in a book dictionary, so certain sounds seem to be treated as close in people's minds – even though they need not be spatially close, just hooked up with strong connections. Let us consider the evidence for this.

Natural clusters

In the previous section we likened sounds to the flesh covering the rhythmic skeleton. But in another respect they are more like clothes than flesh, in that like garments they fall into certain categories. Just as shirts and blouses fall together as opposed to pants, jeans and shorts, so particular sounds can be grouped into 'natural classes' (for a useful summary see Halle and Clements, 1983). For example, [p], [t] and [k] share a number of phonetic similarities – the vibration of the vocal cords starts relatively late and there is a complete stoppage of breath – and so do [m] and [n] – the vocal cords vibrate throughout, and air is expelled through the nose.

Speakers of a language seem to group sounds into their natural classes in the mental lexicon. When malapropisms differ by only one segment from the target, these segments often come from the same natural class:

My *brain* (drain) is clogged.
A religious *profession* (procession).
The clutch *petal* (pedal).
Transcendental *medication* (meditation).

One study (Fay and Cutler, 1977) analysed the point at which malapropisms diverged from their targets, starting from the beginning of the word. Almost half the malapropisms studied turned out to veer off on to a sound from the same natural class. For example, *convention* for 'confession' veered from [v] to [f], *windows* departed from 'winters' with [d] instead of [t]. But this happened with less than a quarter of the similar meaning errors. In other words, when people are searching around their mental lexicon among the word beginnings, *conf-* and *conv-* are closely linked, and so are *wind-* and *wint-*.

Overall, then, segments which belong to the same natural class seem to be arranged near one another in the mental lexicon. A natural clumping principle in the mental lexicon therefore replaces the arbitrary alphabetical system of a printed lexicon. The exact workings of this are unclear, because there is no overall agreement as to the categorization of sounds into natural classes (for overlapping but divergent views see Jakobson *et al.*, 1952; Chomsky and Halle, 1968; Ladefoged, 1982; Van den Broecke and Goldstein, 1980). In addition, the natural classes themselves overlap, and the sounds may therefore fall into more than one category. So [p] has some similarities with [b], [t] and [f], but a different type of similarity with each one.

Since each sound can be regarded as having a composite structure, a few people have suggested that the mental lexicon might split phonemes up into their various components (Fay and Cutler, 1977), which would then have to be assembled. This is somewhat unlikely. If segments had to be fitted together from a heap of components or 'features', one would expect numerous examples of incompetent bundling together within words, with the wrong atoms attached to the wrong phonemes, as in *tebestrian* for 'pedestrian', where a component of [p] has changed place with one belonging to [d]. In fact such errors are extremely rare, and after extensive searching, two researchers who examined this question concluded that 'features are not independent movable entities' (Shattuck-Hufnagel and Klatt, 1979). Splitting sounds up into components is undoubtedly a useful descriptive device, a convenient way of characterizing similarities and differences between segments. But it is not the way in which sounds are dealt with in the mental lexicon where whole segments only seem to be the rule.

Overall structure

In general, then, words which have similar beginnings, similar endings and similar rhythm are likely to be tightly bonded. 'Similar' in this context means either identical or coming from the same natural class. Words seem to be grouped in clumps rather than in a list, suggesting that once again, we are dealing with a network (figure 11.6). Those that are most alike will be closely

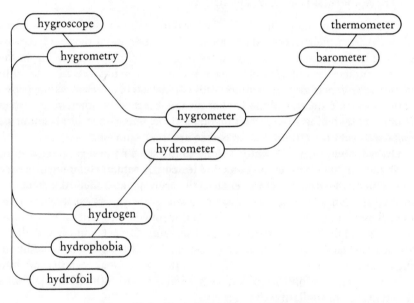

Figure 11.6   Network of similar sounding words

linked, such as *antidote* and *anecdote*, *hydrometer* and *hygrometer*, *musician* and *magician*. These are particularly likely to get confused. Those that are slightly less similar will be somewhat more loosely linked, such as perhaps *specialization* and *specification*, *tambourines* and *trampolines*, *funicular* and *vernacular*, but still sufficiently near to get muddled up occasionally. As with other aspects of the lexicon, these links are not fixed and immutable. New ones are being created all the time, as existing words get shuffled into their place in the network, or as people get exposed to a new joke or rhyme in which they suddenly see a link between the sound of words which they had not noticed before: '*Cleopatra*, Egypt's answer to *Montmartre*'.

A final point: what about the 'rules' which deal with the permissible sequences of sounds? Where do they fit in? These rules for permitted sound sequences do not appear to be particularly relevant for the storage of existing words. They may not be in the 'lexicon proper' but part of the back-up information attached to the 'lexical tool-kit' which speakers use for coping with new words (chapter 14). The overall reason for limiting the number of patterns may be as an aid to memory, to prevent the mind from being overloaded with thousands of unpatterned sound sequences. However, there is one important topic which we have not yet covered: how do children cope with this sound structure? Do the entries in their mental lexicons resemble those of adults, and are words clumped together in the same way? The answer to these questions might tell us whether humans automatically store words in the way outlined in this chapter, or whether the effects we have discussed are found only among adult speakers of English. This is the topic of the next chapter.

Summary

In this chapter we have considered the sound structure of words in the mental lexicon. It seems that some parts of the words are more prominent in storage than others. They are, as it were, more deeply engraved in the mind. These are the sounds at the beginning and the end (the 'bathtub effect') and the general rhythmic pattern, which is inextricably linked with the sounds.

Words are possibly clumped together in groups, with those having a similar beginning, similar ending and similar rhythmic pattern clustered together.

We next need to consider whether these findings are also relevant for children. This will be discussed in the next chapter.

12

Aggergog Miggers, Wips and Gucks
— How children cope with the sound structure of words —

Listen to me, angel tot,
Whom I love an awful lot . . .
When I praise your speech with glee
And claim you talk as well as me,
That's the spirit, not the letter.
I know more words, and say them better.

Ogden Nash, 'Thunder over the Nursery'

Children mutilate words, by adult standards. Anyone who listens for only a few minutes to a young child is likely to hear forms such as *guck* for 'duck', *wip* for 'ship', *tat* for 'cat', or even *aggergog migger*, which appeared to mean 'helicopter' and 'cement mixer' interchangeably for one child (Smith, 1973). In order to understand how children cope with the sound structure of words we need to probe into these 'deformations'. Do they accurately represent the contents of the mental lexicon? Alternatively, perhaps the child's stored forms are more advanced but unpronounceable, so only a mangled approximation remains: 'His articulatory organs cannot master the terrible words we put in his way, and he is driven to these short cuts and other makeshifts' (Sully, 1897, quoted in Bar-Adon and Leopold, 1971: 36). These and other possible explanations need to be considered.

To an outsider, it may seem like a waste of time to try and unravel this gobbledegook. But the alterations are by no means haphazard, and in normal children there are consistent links between the child and adult forms. If a child says *dee* instead of 'tree', substituting [d] for [tr], then she is likely to say *dain* for 'train' and *duck* for 'truck' as well. Similarly, if she says *wip* for 'ship', then she will probably say *woo* for 'shoe' and *weep* for 'sheep'. Furthermore, the same types of alterations occur in languages all over the world. Certain substitutions seem to be typical of early child utterances. For example, sounds made near the back of the mouth are often replaced with sounds made near the front, as in *doose* for 'goose' or *tat* for 'cat'. Two consonants separated by a single vowel tend to 'harmonize', in the sense that they are likely to become similar, so 'cream' might become *meem* and 'lorry' might become *lolly*. Sounds at the ends of words tend to be devoiced – produced without vibration of the vocal cords – as in *bet* for 'bed' and *ek* for 'egg'. And there are numerous others (for fuller lists see Ingram, 1986; Chiat, 1979). What, then, causes them?

There are three main types of explanation put forward: physical incompetence, pre-ordained paths and unsolved puzzles (figure 12.1). Incompetence explanations emphasize that children are just physically incapable, when compared with adults. The poor little darlings can't hear properly, or they can't get their tongue round the required sounds. Pre-ordained path theories suggest that children are pre-programmed to cope with sounds in a certain way, or certain order, and the deformations are therefore predestined steps which the child must pass through before acquiring the adult form. Puzzle-solving theories argue that the sound structure of a language is a puzzle which each child has to slowly solve, and until it has done so, deformations will remain. Let us consider each of these in turn.

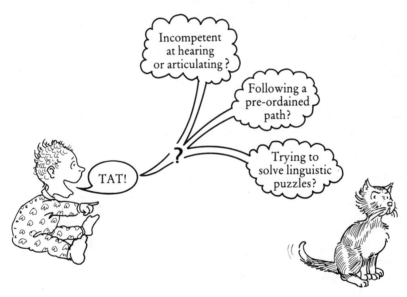

Figure 12.1   Theories about children's word 'deformations'

The cloth ears theory

'The child acquires the adult phonological system by way of his perception of certain limited features of the adult form. These he reproduces ... As his perception improves, the responses change. He discriminates more and attempts to reproduce more' (Waterson, 1970: 23). This represents the simplest hypothesis in relation to children's 'deformations', since it suggests that they are, to a large extent, reproducing what they hear. At first children hear, or pay attention to, only certain gross features in the sound waves. Only later does their discrimination become 'fine-tuned'.

To some extent this seems to be true. Children do not perceive sounds in exactly the same way as adults (Fourcin, 1978), and they frequently mis-perceive words (Vihmann, 1981). Misperceptions can be identified primarily when a child gives an irrelevant response. For example, one French child, on hearing the word *Angleterre* 'England', responded with his word for *pomme de terre* 'potato' (Bloch, 1921, quoted in Vihmann, 1981).

But misperception cannot be the sole or even the main cause of children's 'deformations', because there is plenty of evidence that youngsters perceive considerably more than they produce. For example, two-year-old Amahl had the same forms for *bus* and *brush*, *jug* and *duck*, *cart* and *card*, *mouse* and *mouth*. His father drew pictures of these objects and placed them in the next room. When asked 'Bring me the picture of the mouse' or 'Bring me the picture of the mouth', Amahl always responded correctly (Smith, 1973). Furthermore, he was quite aware of some of the deficiencies in his pronunciation, as when his father tried to persuade him to say 'Jump':

Father   Say 'jump'.
Amahl   Dup.
Father   No, 'jump'.
Amahl   Dup.
Father   No, 'jummmp'.
Amahl   Oli daddy gan day dup (= Only Daddy can say 'jump').

Further evidence of the discrepancy between what a child hears and what she says are provided by dialogues such as the following between an uncle and his niece Nicola, who called herself *Dicola*:

Uncle   What's your name?
Nicola   You know.
Uncle   Is it Dicola?
Nicola   No, Dicola.
Uncle   Oh, Nicola.
Nicola   Yes.

This is sometimes called the 'fis phenomenon' because of a child who called a plastic fish a *fis*. 'Is this your *fis*?' the researchers asked. 'No', replied the child, 'My *fis*' (Berko and Brown, 1960). As in this case, children are quite often puzzled if they are addressed in speech which resembles their own output. When a French mother addressed her child using his own deformations, the indignant youngster replied, 'Talk French to me, mummy' (Jakobson, 1941/1968). This would be unlikely to happen if they were reproducing what they hear.

'Backward steps' in pronunciation provide even stronger evidence of the gap between perception and production. At one point, two-year-old Amahl said *dut* for both 'lunch' and 'shut'. Later he distinguished them in pronunciation, saying *lut* for 'lunch' and *dut* for 'shut' (Smith, 1973). But later still, he suddenly started pronouncing both of them as *lut*! Anyone maintaining that children say what they perceive would have to assume that this child at one time perceived the distinction between *lunch* and *shut* but then suddenly failed to hear the difference any more. Furthermore, this is not an exceptional case. Forms which were once separate but later merge in the child's output are found quite often (Vihmann, 1981). This phenomenon suggests that more is going on than simple misperception.

There is plenty of evidence, then, to suggest that children do not have 'cloth ears', perhaps not surprisingly, considering the acuteness of the mammalian ear. Babies only a few weeks old can hear the difference between [b] and [p] (Eimas *et al.*, 1971; Eimas, 1985), and so can rhesus and chinchilla monkeys (Morse, 1976; Kuhl and Miller, 1974, 1975). The babies in the experiment were given dummies to suck, and were played a sequence of [p] sounds: *pah-pah-pah-pah* ... Then this [p] was changed to [b]. A sudden change in the rate at which they sucked showed they had detected the alteration.

The difference between what children perceive and what they say, therefore, suggests that the words which they utter might be somewhat different from those stored in their mental lexicons. So let us now go on to consider the theory that the problem is purely a mechanical one. According to this view, children have the words in their minds – they just can't get their tongue round certain sounds.

The tongue-twister theory

'I believe I can, on the foundation of my observations, state the following basic law: that the speech sounds are produced by children in an order which begins with the sounds articulated with the least physiological effort, gradually proceeds to the speech sounds produced with greater effort, and ends with the sounds that require the greatest effort for their production' (Schultze, 1880, in Bar-Adon and Leopold, 1971: 28). This pronouncement in 1880 by Fritz Schultze, Professor of Philosophy and Pedagogy at Dresden, became known as 'Schultze's Law' and was widely accepted at that time.

This 'tongue-twister' theory, like the 'cloth ears' theory, encapsulates a certain amount of truth. Particular sounds, such as English *th* [θ], as in *think*, are more difficult to cope with than others: they require extra precision and muscular tension. And some sound sequences, such as the cluster of consonants in *explain* [eksplein], may require more neuromuscular co-ordination than the child can manage. Nevertheless, children are physically capable of producing more sounds than they in fact do. Sounds which are not found in

actual words may be present in babbling: a child may replace every [k] with
[t] when it attempts to pronounce words, but may still babble long *kakaka-
kaka* sequences (Jakobson, 1941/1968). Furthermore, a sound apparently
unavailable in one word may be used in another word. Young Hildegarde
used the sequence *moush* [mauʃ] for *mouth*, with a clear *sh* [ʃ] at the end, but
she did not use *sh* in a word such as *shoe* (Leopold, 1947). In addition, she
repeated the word *pretty* correctly when she first heard it, but later reverted to
saying *pity*. This less accurate pronunciation fitted in with the way she dealt
with other occurrences of [pr] which she pronounced as [p].

It is over-simple, therefore, to argue that children just can't pronounce
things properly. Their muscles are not too floppy, nor their tongue too
clumsy, as is sometimes supposed. The realization that children can both
hear and pronounce more than they actually do has suggested to some
researchers that there is some universal pre-ordained path which they are
obliged to follow: some inbuilt constraint prevents them from articulating
sounds they are physically capable of producing, because they are genetically
programmed to follow a particular route as they acquire sound patterns. Let
us consider this viewpoint.

Pre-ordained path theories

The best-known pre-ordained path theory is that of Roman Jakobson, one of
the pioneers in child language phonology, who claimed that speech contrasts
are pre-programmed to emerge in a set order (Jakobson, 1941/1968). He
proposed a set of 'implicational laws', according to which certain contrasts
are unable to emerge until certain others have been acquired. For example,
he stated that the first consonantal contrast a child makes will be between a
nasal consonant (in which air is expelled through the nose) such as [m] and a
non-nasal stop (sound produced with a complete stoppage of breath) made
near the front of the mouth such as [p], as in *mama*, *papa*. After this, he
suggested, the stop will be subdivided into labial – made with the lips such as
[p] – and dental – made with the tongue against the teeth as in [t]. A contrast
between these front stops must be acquired before one between a front stop
and a back stop, such as [k], can be brought into the child's sound system.
And so on (figure 12.2).

A number of researchers have examined these claims. There seems to be
general agreement that Jakobson's 'laws' are statistical tendencies rather than
obligatory universals (e.g. Macken, 1980). Many children fit Jakobson's
pattern to a reasonable extent, and some fit it perfectly (e.g. Leopold, 1947).
But a number of others break it (e.g. Velten, 1943). A statement of general
tendencies can provide a useful guideline for charting normal development
but it does not explain why children 'deform' words.

A somewhat different pre-ordained path theory suggests that the human

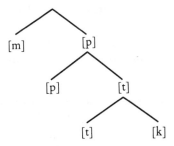

Figure 12.2   Jakobson's pre-ordained path theory

vocal organs are organized in such a way that certain sounds, or sound sequences, are more 'natural' than others (Stampe, 1969, 1979). For example, it is natural to have alternating consonants and vowels, so *abu* may be more 'natural' than 'apple'. Similarly, it is natural to devoice sounds (produce them without vibrating the vocal cords) at the end of words, so *pik* may be more 'natural' than 'pig'. According to this theory, words in which the natural tendencies are followed will be easier to learn, and those which do not – perhaps the majority – will be harder. In producing words, then, children must gradually suppress the universal tendencies they are born with, and learn the idiosyncratic rules of the particular language they are acquiring.

This theory, unlike Jakobson's, does not require all children to develop phonological structure in exactly the same order. Variation occurs partly because different processes may clash and children may choose to resolve the clashes in different ways, and partly because they may suppress different processes at different ages. For example, a word such as *duck* might be pronounced by one child as *dut* with the second consonant harmonizing with the first (both articulated at the front of the mouth) and by another as *guck* with the first consonant harmonizing with the second (both articulated at the back of the mouth) (figure 12.3). A mild tendency for the first consonant to harmonize with the second clashes with a tendency for sounds to be produced at the front of the mouth.

However, the fact that the theory allows so much variation is also its greatest weakness: whatever the child says can be attributed to a different natural process, or a different order of suppression, with no overall guiding principle. One concludes that certain 'natural processes' – the ones which occur very widely, such as a tendency to devoice consonants at the end of words – are indeed built in to the way the articulatory organs work, but that the others – the weaker ones – do not 'explain' the deformations since they need not happen.

But the main problem with the natural processes viewpoint is that it treats the child as a fairly passive individual, flattened by these universal tendencies and attempting to struggle out from under them. This does not tie in with the general impression that people have of children in the early stages of language development. They are mostly energetic little people who treat the world as a kind of puzzle which they are actively trying to solve. The third type of theory concerning children's deformations, then, regards the child as an active puzzle-solver, though one who often takes the 'easy way out' by using natural tendencies as intermediate solutions to the problems provided by the sound structure.

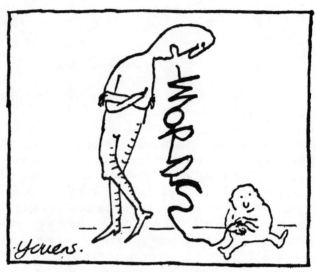

Reproduced by kind permission of the *Observer*

Puzzle-solving theories

Puzzle-solving theories argue that the sound structure of language presents children with a series of different but interlinked problems which have to be solved before they can have an adult-type grasp of the system. They have to identify words, work out which articulatory movements are paired with which sounds, discover which sound sequences are permissible and become skilled at producing them fast and in the right order. The way children cope with these tasks is likely to affect both the way they store words, and the way they pronounce them (figure 12.3). Let us therefore consider some of these problems in more detail.

A child must first identify lexical items by dividing up the stream of sounds into word-size chunks. Words are not spoken one by one but in a continual flow in which the end of one word often sounds as if it begins the next, a fact exploited sometimes by humorous writers, as in the following extract from Eugene Field's poem 'A Play on Words':

> Assert ten barren love day made
> Dan wood her hart buy nigh tan day;

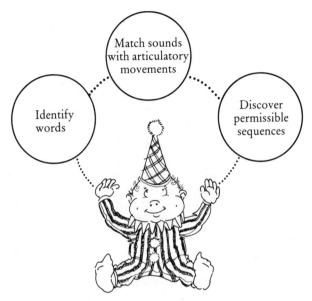

Figure 12.3   The sound puzzles facing children

> Butt wen knee begged she'd marry hymn,
> The crewel bell may dancer neigh.

(A certain baron loved a maid / And wooed her heart by night and day; / But when he begged she'd marry him, / The cruel belle made answer 'Nay'.)

At first, children may learn off whole chunks of sound, which are simply ritual accompaniments to particular actions (chapter 8). Fourteen-month-old Minh said 'Obedide' apparently in imitation of adult 'Open the door', since he was pounding on a closed door and shouting to his older brother on the other side (Peters, 1983). Another child used the phrase 'I carry you' as a request to be picked up, presumably imitating adult 'I'll carry you' (Clark, 1974). Both these utterances seem to be unanalysed wholes, not yet divided into words. One can regard the mental lexicon 'proper' as being under way as soon as consistent sequences get used as symbols for particular items (chapter 8).

Youngsters may be able to build up a small repertoire of words they have heard alone, which they then might recognize in the stream of speech. But if they waited to hear every word in isolation it would probably take years to learn to talk. They therefore have to analyse those which they do know and draw conclusions from these as to how to identify other words. For example, almost all English words have a strongly stressed syllable, and in the words which a child hears early and in isolation, this will often be the first: *daddy*, *mummy*, *kitty*, *dinner*, *broken*. So he might make a preliminary guess that words start with stressed syllables. It would then be fairly easy to identify words at the end of sentences, a hypothesis supported by the observation that children often make attempts to pronounce final words in an utterance, saying 'Teddy' in response to 'Let's look for teddy', or 'Garden' when mother says, 'We're going into the garden' (Dupreez, 1974; Blasdell and Jensen, 1970).

As the child gets better acquainted with English she can utilize certain additional clues. For example, [h] can never occur at the end of a word, and [ŋ] as in *sing* can never occur at the beginning. Overall, though, the most important factor in splitting words up is probably the rhythm, and this is likely to affect word storage in the mental lexicon. (For a fuller account of how children identify words see Chiat, 1979, 1983.)

Once the child has isolated a number of sequences as 'words' in the adult output, his next major task is to find out which sounds are paired with which movements of the articulatory organs. For example, one day Amahl rushed to his father and said, 'Daddy, I can say *quick*' (Smith, 1973). He may well have had a good auditory image of the sound sequence *qu* [kw], but he had to discover the complicated set of articulatory movements needed to pronounce it by trial and error. As one writer notes: 'The situation is analogous to the problem which the older child faces in learning to draw geometric figures. It is well-known that pre-schoolers can visually discriminate square, cross, triangle, etc., long before they can draw them. Learning to copy such figures involves progressive analysis of the forms in terms of the nature and position of the lines needed to make them' (Braine, 1974: 283).

Matching the auditory image of a word to its actual pronunciation seems to be a fairly conscious process. Children sometimes intentionally exploit their existing abilities and avoid things which cause them trouble (Ferguson and Farwell, 1975; Menyuk and Menn, 1979). For example, one child when asked 'Show me your thumb' could happily wiggle his thumb. Yet he himself referred to his thumb as *winger* (finger). He appeared to be purposely avoiding the sound *th* [θ] which he found hard to say (Drachman, 1973). Another child, Philip, substituted nasals as often as he could, often using consonant harmony, so he said *mim* for 'cream', *nanu* for 'sandwich', *nangu* for 'candle' and *mannow* for 'hammer' (Ingram, 1986). A further, somewhat strange strategy, by adult standards, is for children to seek out words they can say, and then to use the same output for words which they know are different but have certain similarities (Vihmann, 1981). *Aggergog migger*, mentioned at the beginning of this chapter, for both 'cement mixer' and 'helicopter' seems to be one of these, and another is *ebenin* used both for 'elephant' and 'ambulance' (Smith, 1973).

The problem, especially with longish words such as *elephant* and *helicopter*, is not just one of matching individual segments but also of stringing the sounds together fast, and in the right order. If a child hits on a whole sequence it can reproduce quite easily, then it tends to overuse this. Learning to speak is partly learning to build up a library of these 'articulatory sub-routines' (Menn, 1978). The sub-routines which the youngster learns to cope with early are likely to be those which fit in with the natural tendencies inherent in the human vocal apparatus – though some might be quite idiosyncratic. One boy, Christopher, had a strong preference for producing words ending in *-yat* or *-yan*. So he said *bayan* for 'banana', *payan* for 'panda', *kajat* for 'carrot', *pijat* for 'peanut' and *miyat* for 'steamer' (Priestley, 1977).

It seems, then, that we have come to a reasonable understanding of why children deform words. Alongside a certain number of perceptual and pronunciation problems they are actively trying to solve sound structure puzzles, and they follow certain natural tendencies as they do this. The puzzle solving involves segmenting speech into words, matching articulatory sequences with auditory images and learning to produce these smoothly and fast.

So far, we have discovered that there is a considerable mismatch between the words in children's minds and what they say. Children's pronunciation can give us only very rough clues as to the form of words in their mental lexicons. Let us now go on to consider how words might be organized in their minds.

Mini-malapropisms

Please daddy, can I have an ice-cream *toilet* (cornet = cone).
At school we have a *concussion* (percussion) band'.
We parked our car in a *naughty story* (multi-storey) car park.
Mummy, why have you got so many *burrows* (furrows) on your forehead?
Our new car's a *mistake* (estate) car.

The above are all cases in which children have, by adult standards, used the wrong word. The words which a child chooses to clump together with the same output, either intentionally or accidentally, can provide useful clues as to how they are stored, since presumably these words have been identified as 'similar' in some way.

An analysis of 170 'mini-malapropisms' (Aitchison, 1972) revealed that the rhythmic pattern was the feature most often retained, followed by the stressed vowel. The consonants, both those either side of the stressed vowel and those at the beginning and end, seemed to have lower priority, even after possible pronunciation problems had been taken into account. And this agrees with the findings of another researcher, who analysed a further 150 from several different languages (Vihmann, 1981). This suggests that children, like adults, have some characteristics of the word stored more prominently than others, though these conspicuous characteristics do not seem to be the same as those in adult words, since children appear to give higher priority to the rhythm and a lower priority to the consonants.

One study looked specifically at adult–child differences in malapropisms (Aitchison and Straf, 1982). It found that in the majority of cases both adults and children preserved the same set of phonetic characteristics: number of syllables, rhythmic pattern, stressed vowel, consonants at the beginning and end of the word. However, when something went wrong, children preserved the number of syllables and rhythmic pattern and tended to change the initial consonant. Adults, on the other hand, almost always preserved the initial consonant, preferring to change the number of syllables or the stressed vowel. Children gave the initial consonant the lowest priority of all, and preserved it less well than the consonant at the end of the word – a finding reported elsewhere (e.g. Slobin, 1973; Vihmann, 1981). The situation can be illustrated by a word which occurred as a target among both the child and adult malapropisms:

Small girl   Pass the *monuments*, please.
Her brother   Don't be silly, you mean the *ornaments*.

In the adult example, a woman was boasting of old treasures she possessed: 'We have a lovely Victorian *condom* set in the attic.' The children could presumably have picked on a word beginning with *c* [k], and the adult could have chosen a three-syllable word. But they were naturally predisposed to make certain kinds of mistakes.

Children, then, seem to have mental representations of words which are in a number of ways similar to those of adults but which have different sections prominent: the 'bathtub effect' (chapter 11) is important for adults, but for children the rhythmic pattern and the stressed vowel are more important – and the younger the child, the more likely she is to preserve the rhythmic pattern (Vihmann, 1981).

In addition to certain sections of the word being more prominent for the child, certain types of words seem to be easier to remember than others. In one experiment, children between the ages of four and nine were shown picture-books containing animals which they could mostly recognize easily, such as cows, dogs, elephants and rabbits (Aitchison and Chiat, 1981). But among these common creatures there were a few strange ones: a bandicoot, a racoon (strange to British children), a lemming, a yak, and so on. Whenever a strange one occurred the child was taught its name, then was asked to continue naming the well-known animals. After a few minutes the strange animal would reappear and the child would try recall its name, usually having partially forgotten it: 'Was it a *gandigoose* (bandicoot)?' 'It might have been *rack* (yak).' 'Something like *lemon* (lemming).' Certain words, or sections of words, turned out to be more memorable than others. It was easier for children to cope with words which began with the stressed syllable and in which nearby consonants agreed in voicing with one another. The beginnings of *lemming* and *bandicoot* were well remembered, but the first syllable of *racoon* and *kudu* turned out to be quite difficult.

When a word was difficult to recall, the children tended to implement 'natural' processes such as consonant harmony: 'racoon' was sometimes recalled as *cocoon*, and 'kudu' as *kuku* or *kutu* (a finding also found by Vihmann,

1978). And they tended to reproduce syllables composed of consonant + vowel, so 'armadillo' was remembered as *marmadillo*, and 'bandicoot' as *bandicoo*. These findings suggest that perhaps a few of the strange forms produced by children may be due to 'gap-filling' procedures when they cannot remember the exact sounds, as in *riductor*, *ritack* and *rilastic* for 'conductor', 'attack' and 'elastic' (Smith, 1973), where the initial unstressed syllable might have proved difficult to recall. Possibly words which are relatively easy for the child to remember are in their mental lexicon in a fairly complete form, though with different sections prominent compared to an adult's lexical entry. But difficult words may be somewhat different from the 'correct' form since the details are liable to be forgotten.

The re-organization process

If children have different sections of a word prominent in storage compared with adults, then this suggests that the overall organization of words by sounds is partially different, in that they are likely to clump together different words in storage. Those with a similar rhythm will possibly be closely linked, whereas the beginnings of words will not be as important. They therefore gradually reorganize their lexicons as the years go by. In the animal learning experiment, four-year-olds had more examples of consonant harmony than older children, but nine-year-olds still had some (Aitchison and Chiat, 1981). This suggests that the rearrangement might go on at least into adolescence, with minor re-orderings perhaps continuing throughout a person's life as more words are built in to the lexicon.

However, perhaps we should ask why this reorganization is necessary. The portions of the word which children concentrate on seem to be the most naturally noticeable. So why do adults switch over to the 'bathtub' system (chapter 11)?

Learning to read is an obvious factor. This focuses attention on the beginning of a word, especially when a person becomes familiar with dictionaries. But a more important reason may be the need for fast retrieval. An adult is likely to have a lexicon of around 50,000 actively used items (chapter 1), whereas up to the age of five a child's is probably less than a tenth of that number (if one averages the figures quoted by various writers). As a person's vocabulary gets larger, fast retrieval may require an altered storage system, one which allows the speaker to home in on the required word fast. A beginnings and endings strategy for clumping words together is fairly efficient, since it can narrow down the choice to a relatively small number of words. A rhythmic pattern and stressed vowel strategy, on the other hand, would produce much larger clusters, once the lexicon gets large: *ability*, *debility*, *facility*, *hostility*, *mobility*, *sterility*, *virility* and numerous others would all be together. So attention to the consonants is likely to be more useful for pinpointing a word.

Our general conclusion over how children store words from the point of view of the sound pattern, then, is as follows. To a large extent children recall the same features as adults do. But their priorities are different. They pay attention above all to the rhythmic pattern and the stressed vowel, and they possibly organize their lexicon into clumps based on these features. The consonants, particularly those at the beginning of words, are ranked less highly. Then as children get older, learn to read and acquire a much larger vocabulary they gradually switch to an adult-type system which is more efficient for finding words fast.

Summary

This chapter has looked at how children cope with the sound structure of words. We started by considering why children apparently 'deform' words, since we needed to know whether these deformations represent the contents of the mental lexicon.

We noted that children can perceive more than they produce, and the deformations are not simply due to articulatory problems either. Overall, children seem to be actively trying to solve the puzzles involved in acquiring sound structure – identifying words, linking up auditory images with articulatory routines and learning to cope with them fast. Word identification led them to concentrate on the rhythmic structure, and many of the deformations are intermediate attempts to match up words and sounds, in which children use 'natural processes' as fall-back procedures.

Children and adults possibly have somewhat similar lexical entries overall, though children appear to have different characteristics prominent in storage, in particular the rhythmic pattern and the stressed vowel. They turn to an adult-like system gradually, as they learn to read and as their vocabulary increases.

We have now dealt with the core components of the mental lexicon. In the next two chapters we will consider important back-up abilities which supplement this core: how people extend old words and create new ones.

Part 3

Novelties

13

Interpreting Ice-cream Cones
— *Extending old words* —

> Your body is a mountain-chain, your bones
> Ridges of rock, your nipples ice-cream cones.
> Others have said the same, and others will,
> In rearranged comparisons, until
> The mountains have subsided to the plain,
> And the world's meanings have to start again.
>
> Laurence Lerner, 'Meanings'

Nipples are not ice-cream cones, nor are ice-cream cones nipples. Yet no one would be likely to suggest that the author of this poem was mentally deranged. Humans are amazingly good at extending the application of words: 'The lexical mosaic is constantly being stretched to cover more than it should' (Miller and Johnson-Laird, 1976: 292). This stretching is not restricted to poetry: 'Cougars drown Beavers', 'Cowboys corral Buffaloes', 'Air Force torpedoes the Navy', 'Clemson cooks Rice' are all perfectly comprehensible headlines describing football games in American newspapers (Smith and Montgomery, 1982). And in everyday conversation one is likely to hear numerous examples of super-ficially bizarre expressions: 'His new boss is a dinosaur!', 'A donkey is the car of the islanders', 'The chimney provided a back-door to the cave', 'The ham skated across the kitchen floor', 'The brandy tobogganed down his throat'.

As these examples suggest, humans use words in creative and innovative ways, and this is an intrinsic part of a human's lexical ability (chapter 1). The mental lexicon contains equipment which enables a person to continually expand old words and coin new ones. In this chapter therefore we shall con-sider the extension of existing words, and in the next, the creation of new ones – even though the distinction between these two processes is not always clear-cut. We shall be discussing what guidelines humans follow when they produce these novelties and how others manage to comprehend them. Our overall aim is to understand how this creative ability is integrated into the mental lexicon.

Metaphor will be our main concern in this chapter, a term which encompasses all the examples mentioned in the first paragraph. We shall then move on to the type of creative extension involved in the instruction 'Please do a Napoleon for the camera' (Clark and Gerrig, 1983), which listeners apparently interpret quite readily. Such usages provide a bridge between the word extension of this chapter and the new formations to be discussed in the next.

Ice-cream cones and cabbages

Metaphor, according to the ancient Greek philosopher Aristotle, involves 'the application to one thing of a name belonging to another'(*De Arte Poetica* 1457b). One might expect humans to be puzzled by this apparent use of wrong labels, such as calling nipples 'ice-cream cones'. But instead they are amazingly good at thinking up plausible explanations when they encounter a metaphor: perhaps ice-cream cones and nipples have a similar shape, or they can both be licked or sucked. In fact, it is quite difficult to think up an inapplicable metaphor because people are so good at finding potential explanations. Try out 'Her breasts were . . .', and then make a list of random objects. They almost all work. 'Her breasts were cabbages' (shape). 'Her breasts were rabbits' (perhaps soft feel). 'Her breasts were bricks' (feel again – perhaps she'd had a breast-enlargement operation). 'Her breasts were snow-drifts' (pale colour). 'Her breasts were doors' (perhaps the way in to deeper love-making). 'Her breasts were peas' (size). 'Her breasts were question-marks' (perhaps symbols of tentative sexual exploration). These metaphors all work, to some extent, even though breasts are not cabbages, rabbits, bricks, snow-drifts, doors, peas, or question-marks, nor even particularly like them.

Interpreting a sentence such as 'Breasts are cabbages' might seem a complex task. Yet the basic mechanism behind metaphor is straightforward. It is simply the use of a word with one or more of the 'typicality conditions' attached to it broken. As we noted in chapter 5, words have fuzzy edges, in that for the majority of words it is impossible to specify a hard-core meaning at all. Humans understand words by referring to a prototypical usage, and they match a new example against the characteristics of the prototype. A tiger can still be a tiger even though it might have three legs and no stripes: it just wouldn't be a prototypical tiger. Seeing can still be seeing, even if your mind doesn't register what your eye fell on: it just wouldn't be a prototypical instance of seeing.

Use of words with broken typicality conditions happens all the time, in fact so often that one ceases to notice it. If anyone does, there is sometimes an argument as to whether a word is being used 'metaphorically' or not, as in:

The price of mangos *went up*.

Is *went up* a metaphor, since the price did not literally travel up a hill? Or is this simply the use of *go up* with a typicality condition broken, since *going* typically involves travelling between two physical points, and covering the distance in between? Similarly, what about:

Marigold is *coming out* of a coma.
Felix is *under* age.

Coming out typically involves physical movement, and *under* typically involves a physical position underneath. So are these metaphors? Or ordinary uses with a typicality condition broken? As these examples show, the two are indistinguishable. One can therefore say either 'Our ordinary conceptual system . . . is fundamentally metaphorical in nature' (Lakoff and Johnson, 1980: 3), or 'Metaphors . . . are in no sense departures from a norm' (Sperber and Wilson, 1985/6). The two comments are equivalent and interchangeable.

The necessity of breaking typicality conditions – or in other words, the inevitability of metaphor – is so high in some semantic fields that one cannot communicate without it. Music and art cannot be discussed intelligently without words such as *austere, balanced, charming, complex, empty, flamboyant, forceful, graceful, insipid, majestic, rough, soft, sweet, warm* – words which are also used for the description of wine (Lehrer, 1983). Indeed, if one were restricted only to a prototypical use of words, wine would be undiscussable: 'You can talk about wine as if it were a bunch of flowers (fragrant, heavily perfumed); a packet of razor blades (steely); a navy (robust, powerful); a troupe of acrobats (elegant and well-balanced); a sucessful industrialist (distinguished and rich); a virgin in a bordello (immature and giving promise of pleasure to come); Brighton Beach (clean and pebbly); even a potato (earthy) or a Christmas pudding (plump, sweet and round)' (Derek Cooper, quoted in Lehrer, 1983: 1). Quite often, if particular extended usages have become conventional, as in the wine examples, they are classified as 'dead' metaphors, on the assumption that they must once have been new and vivid but are now old clichés: 'The music flowed over her', 'The evening staggered on', 'Her heart drummed against her rib-cage', and so on.

Prototypical metaphors

If every broken typicality condition is, in some sense, an example of metaphor, why do people make value judgements and say 'It's not a proper metaphor' for some extended usages, but 'That's a nice metaphor' for others? Some 'metaphorical' usages are less satisfactory because not all broken typicality conditions result in 'prototypical' metaphors. People seem to have some notion of what is a 'proper' metaphor, which is perhaps partly instilled by poetry lessons at school and partly by the ease with which they have recognized the speaker's intention. What, then, constitutes a prototypical metaphor?

At first sight, such an analysis might seem impossible. If breasts can be cabbages, bricks, peas, rabbits, or question-marks, it might seem a hopeless task to find any guidelines underlying the choice. Furthermore, the literature is confused, since some writers stress the similarity of the items that are compared and others stress the dissimilarity (for a summary of the main views see Tourangeau and Sternberg, 1982). In fact, both similarities and dissimilarities must exist, but of different types.

First, the items must not be too similar, because the metaphor will either be incomprehensible or it will not be a metaphor. One would not normally say 'Wine is whisky', or 'Cars are lorries', or 'Jam is honey', or 'Marmalade is jam'. In the first three of these examples the hearer is likely to be simply baffled, and in the last would probably regard 'marmalade' and 'jam' as being rough synonyms. In a good metaphor, therefore, the items compared should not share major characteristics. So 'Breasts are cabbages', 'Nipples are ice-cream cones', 'Life is a subway train', 'Women are thistles', 'He posted the toast down to his stomach', 'The brandy tobogganed down his gullet' would be far 'better' metaphors, where the subject of the metaphor is compared to something which is quite different from itself, in the sense of coming from a different semantic field.

Second, although the items involved must not share major characteristics, they must share some. Statements such as 'His feet were stars', 'Her cheeks were typewriters', 'Her knees were penguins' are fairly unlikely and difficult to interpret, even though humans can usually think up some kind of joint characteristic, given enough time to ponder. In a prototypical metaphor, the words involved share some fairly obvious characteristic, usually a minor one. In 'Her breasts were cabbages', the hearer would probably interpret the metaphor as one of size or shape, even though when thinking of a breast or cabbage separately the shape and size of each might not be the first thing which springs to mind. Similarly, 'His boss is a dinosaur' cannot refer to the most important characteristics of dinosaurs, that they are extinct and often enormous. It presumably relates to some additional piece of knowledge which people have about these animals, the fact that the species probably died out because it was slow-moving and failed to adapt to new conditions. In 'The brandy tobogganed down his gullet', the drinker's throat cannot be lined with snow, a major typicality condition of tobogganing. It must instead refer to the speed and downhill movement involved.

In a prototypical metaphor, then, the items compared are likely to be dissimilar, in that they come from different semantic fields, and similar in that they share obvious, minor characteristics. The dissimilarity of the semantic fields signals to the hearer that active matching has to be carried out in order to interpret the sentence. The listener sets about doing this because she routinely assumes that the speaker is trying to communicate intelligently (Grice, 1975), unless there are clear indications that he is a lunatic. The computations required are no different in kind from those in 'ordinary' word interpretation (chapter 5), though some may require extra mental agility since certain types of brain damage apparently limit a person's ability to deal with extended usages (Brownell *et al.*, 1984).

Narrowing down the range

Unfortunately, matters are not always as simple as in the prototypical meta-phor outlined above. Sometimes items may share more than one minor charac-teristic. The ice-cream cones and nipples metaphor could refer either to shape or lickability, 'Her eyes were coins' could refer to their roundness or their shininess, 'Mavis was a panda' could refer to her cuddliness, her large size, or a preference for black and white clothes, or even all three. How is the choice narrowed down? Sometimes speakers explicitly explain their metaphors: 'Life is a foreign language: all men mispronounce it' (Christopher Morley, in Cohen and Cohen, 1980: 240); 'Hollywood money isn't money. It's congealed snow, melts in your hand' (Dorothy Parker, in Cohen and Cohen, 1980: 260). 'Many people find it helpful to think of wines as having a shape . . . A round wine has its skeleton (the alcohol) adequately and pleasantly covered with flesh (the fruit) and is enhanced by a good skin (the fragrance)' (Pamela Vandyke Price, quoted in Lehrer, 1983: 14). But mostly the context will limit the possibilities, and allow the hearer to come to a plausible solution.

In some cases, however, it may not be possible to narrow down the metaphor to one exact comparison. This is particularly true of poetry, where the poet may intentionally have included several layers of interpretation. When Chaucer in the *Canterbury Tales* said that the prioress's eyes were 'greye as glas' (*Prologue* 152), he overtly chose colour as the basis of the comparison. But he presumably intended other qualities of glass, such as translucence and brilliance, to be considered. 'Grey as rabbits' would hardly be as effective. Similarly, in the ice-cream cone example the reference to a mountain-chain and ridges of rock sug-gest very strongly that shape, rather than lickability, is the major comparison, though something deliciously edible in a peak-like shape is still more appro-priate for a lover's body than, say, a pine-cone or a sun-hat.

Occasionally, there may be no obvious interpretation at all for a metaphor. The creator may intentionally have made understanding difficult, perhaps in order to force the hearer to think about the subject. For example, 'There is pleasure in exploring the metaphor of the Church as a hippopotamus even if we do not believe anything about the Church at the end that we did not believe at the beginning' (Blackburn, 1984: 175). Or take the following lines by Emily Dickinson:

> We barred the windows and the doors
> As from an emerald ghost;
> The doom's electric moccasin
> That very instant passed.

What on earth is an 'emerald ghost' or 'doom's electric moccasin'? Each time one thinks about these metaphors some new idea about the links comes to mind: people wearing moccasins creep up stealthily, electric shocks make one tingle, and so on. But it would be hard to claim that one had finally interpreted it: the possible layers go on and on, as the poet perhaps intended.

The arousing of multiple associations raises another characteristic of some metaphors. Many of them go much further than a comparison of just two words. They require the activation of whole situations or 'frames' (chapter 5): Shakespeare's 'Sleep that knits up the ravell'd sleave of care' (*Macbeth* II, ii) requires the activation of a whole knitting scenario, and we imagine drunken dollars staggering about in Maynard Keynes's comment (in Cohen and Cohen, 1980: 183): 'The recent gyrations of the dollar have looked to me more like a gold standard on the booze than the ideal managed currency which I hope for.' Here, hearers have to pick out the relevant similarities in the whole situation, they cannot just compare two words. As we noted in chapter 5, humans continue to delve within their mental lexicons, activating more and more material, until they have acquired as much as they need for interpreting an utterance.

Ideas for metaphors

Producing and understanding metaphor, then, requires complex matching skills, even though the mechanisms involved are fundamentally the same as those used in ordinary speech comprehension. Yet this ability is present in young children. They sometimes use figurative language quite intentionally, and not simply because they do not know the word involved. For example, a young child asked to describe an Afro hairstyle said: 'Lots of snakes are coming out of his head.' When asked if this was truly so, the child said, 'Of course not, but his hair's all wiggly like snakes are'. This spontaneous use of metaphor decreases with age, according to one study (Pollio *et al.*, 1977). It fades fastest among children who attend reputedly good schools, and more slowly among those who go to supposedly bad ones. This suggests that education channels children towards conventional usages and less colourful speech.

Of course, adults still initiate metaphor quite often, as we have seen. However, metaphors coined by adults are not quite as unpredictable as they seem at first sight. A goodish number are based on conventional topics. In every decade certain metaphors tend to be prominent (Sperber, 1930). The most pervasive current metaphor may be the computer: it is standard to talk about topics in terms of software, hardware, input, output, and so on. American politics in the 1960s was particularly characterized by repeated imagery of athletic competition: it was important to win, not lose, to be ahead, to defeat one's opponents. As Richard Nixon commented: 'This nation cannot stand still because we are in a deadly competition . . . We're ahead in this competition . . ., but when you're in a race the only way to stay ahead is to move ahead' (quoted in Pollio *et al.*, 1977: 4). And sport continues to inspire political metaphor today. The 'arms race' in particular is still with us.

Certain areas permanently attract a large number of metaphors. An analysis of figurative language between 1675 and 1975 showed that the human body had consistently been the highest source of metaphor for these 300 years, and that the subject of the metaphor was most often a human's psychological processes, as when W. Irving, in *Legend of Sleepy Hollow*, spoke of 'In his devouring mind's eye' (Smith *et al.*, 1981). The partial predictability of topics, then, helps to narrow down the range of metaphor, so making it easier for human beings to understand one another without effort.

To summarize the characteristics of metaphor, it utilizes normal processes of word interpretation, in that a metaphor is primarily the use of a word with a broken typicality condition, something which happens all the time (chapter 5). There is therefore no difference between a word used in a non-prototypical way and a metaphor. However, when humans consciously use metaphor they subconsciously follow certain guidelines. They tend to compare items which come from different semantic fields, which share minor but obvious character-istics. This enables hearers to realize that an unusual comparison is being made, and helps them to pinpoint the relevant similarities. Comprehension is also aided by the fact that, in any era, certain topics tend to become the focus of metaphors.

However, although metaphor is perhaps the most noticeable form of extended word usage, it is by no means the only one. Let us now go on to con-sider another, which bridges the gap between the extension of old words and the creation of new words.

Doing a Napoleon

'Suppose a friend, taking your photograph, asks you with a glint in her eye, "Please do a Napoleon for the camera". Most people to whom we have offered this scenario report imagining, quickly and without reflection, posing with one hand tucked inside their jacket à la Napoleon. Arriving at this sense is a remarkable feat' (Clark and Gerrig, 1983).

The feat is remarkable because Napoleon never had his photo taken, and he did a considerable number of things in his life, including dying from arsenic poisoning. Moreover, people do not habitually tuck their hands in their jacket for photos. This sucessful assessment of a new situation occurred not only with well-known figures such as 'doing a Napoleon', 'doing a Richard Nixon', but also, as we saw in chapter 1, when people were presented with entirely new characters about whom they had been given a few sentences of description. How do hearers arrive at the right conclusions? Can speakers just say anything and be understood, or are there pointers, as with metaphor, which lead listeners in the right direction?

A couple of experiments were devised to test this point (Clark and Gerrig, 1983). In the first, students were read out sentences which included the name of a famous person, such as 'I met a girl at the Coffee House who did an

Elizabeth Taylor while I was talking to her', 'After Joe listened to the tape of the interview, he did a Nixon to a portion of it'. They were asked to interpret the sentence, and say how sure they were of their interpretation.

Hearers were fairly good at this. They seemed to utilize both knowledge of the character concerned and an assessment of the context. They were able to match a known and fairly obvious characteristic, possibly only a minor one, against the needs of the situation, much as people had when they interpreted metaphor. But they were much surer of their interpretations when they were pointed in the right direction by the speakers. If the context was vague, and failed to help, people were puzzled.

In the second experiment, subjects were read out short descriptions of invented characters (as described in chapter 1): 'Imagine your friend told you about his neighbor, Harry Wilson. Harry Wilson decided that it was time to rejuvenate his house and property. He started by using his electric shears to carve his hedges into animal shapes – an elephant, a camel with two humps, and a fat seal balancing a ball on its nose. Then he decided to paint the exterior of his house. He painted the clapboard walls with bright white and the trim with royal blue. For the final touch, Harry moved his furniture out to the porch, so that he could enjoy the evening breezes. Later your friend told you, "This summer I plan to do a Harry Wilson "'. Once again, the students had to interpret these vignettes and say how confident they were in their interpretation, though not all students were given the same ending. Others were presented with alternatives such as 'This summer I plan to do a Harry Wilson to the hedges' or 'do a Harry Wilson to a bar of soap'. And some stories were more complex than others.

People had no difficulty in picking out the unusual actions which typified the character in question, though they coped better if the context was narrowed down for them. So, in the example above, 'doing a Harry Wilson to the hedges' was the easiest to interpret, and the subjects felt fairly confident that their interpretation was correct.

These experiments show that humans are prepared to make a guess at anything, but mostly their options are narrowed down by speakers, so that hearers are able to successfully select the relevant interpretation. A remarkable amount of active matching is involved, since existing knowledge has to be judged alongside the current situation, but it is matching in which the possibilities are not totally wide open. Humans are able to exploit the clues given by the speakers, and so limit the number of solutions they consider. Overall, then, this type of extension, like metaphor, shows that the human mind cannot be regarded as a machine which gives a fixed set of responses. Active computation is required, in which the various factors involved have to be assessed and a decision reached. And this seems to be true of the creation of new words also, as we shall see in the next chapter.

Summary

This chapter has considered how people extend the usage of existing words. We examined primarily metaphor, then went on to a second type of extension which overlapped with the creation of new words.

Metaphor involves broken typicality conditions, something which is very common in word meaning. So the basic mechanism is fairly straightforward, and is routinely found in 'ordinary' word interpretation. A prototypical metaphor involves comparison of items from different semantic fields, which share some obvious minor characteristic. These two characteristics enable the hearer to compute the probable meaning by narrowing down the range of probabilities – even though some poetic metaphors purposely lead hearers into multiple interpretations.

The second, 'Napoleonic' type of extension showed that there were no fixed constraints on its working, but narrowing down the context enabled the hearer to be guided towards the intended interpretation. As with metaphor, hearers have to actively match their existing knowledge against the requirements of the situation in order to interpret the sentence. This type of extension bridges the gap between the extension of old words, and the creation of new ones, which will be discussed in the next chapter.

14

Globbering Mattresses
— *Creating new words* —

The mattress globbered. This is the noise made by a live, swamp-dwelling mattress that is deeply moved . . .
'I sense a deep dejectedness . . .' it vollued . . . 'and it saddens me. You should be more mattresslike. We live quiet retired lives in the swamp, where we are content to flollop and vollue and regard the wetness in a fairly floopy manner.'

Douglas Adams, Life, the Universe and Everything

Humans are enormously clever at making up new words, as the passage above shows. This is a literary example, so the novelties are perhaps more carefully thought out than those produced in everyday speech. But they exemplify a skill permanently available to humans, the ability to coin new words at any time, even in the course of a conversation.

These new usages occur continually, though most are quite temporary visitors to the language. They may be used only once, or by one person. 'Come and see my fishling', said a friend who had just acquired a tiny fish. A travel journalist noted that a small airline had gone in for *jumbification* – the use of jumbo jets (Alex Hamilton in *The Guardian*, November 1984). And in an advertisement, *Autoguzzlosaurus Rex* is a large car-like animal with an excessive thirst for petrol (gas) and in danger of extinction. It's possible that these novelties will come into general use, though not particularly likely. Many, many more new words are invented than come into firm existence, in the sense of eventually being listed in a printed dictionary. Only if a new coinage is sufficiently useful, and used by someone influential, is it likely to catch on. The few which spread to a wider audience and get accepted into the language are like the raindrops which get caught in a bucket. They are only a minute proportion of those which fall from the sky. The majority soak away into the ground without trace. How then do humans perform this creative task?

The rarity of googols

Word formation is the 'deepest, most secret part of language', according to the nineteenth-century philosopher-linguist Wilhelm von Humboldt (quoted in Bauer, 1983: 292). This viewpoint is probably wrong, in that the mechanisms behind word formation are fairly easy to identify. Most new words are not new at all, they are simply additions to existing words or recombinations of their components. Words which are invented out of nothing are extremely rare: the writer of a book on word formation was able to find only six words in this category (Bauer, 1983) – though a seventh is *googol*, meaning 'the figure 1 followed by 100 zeroes' (*Webster's New Collegiate Dictionary*), supposedly coined by a mathematician after he had heard the gurgles of his baby grandson. There are, however, a few more if one includes trade or product names, such as *Kodak*, *Teflon*, which are sometimes computer-generated. But even these are only partially new, since they always follow the existing sound patterns of the language which, as we noted in chapter 11, form a limited number of combinations: one might invent a new bath-cleaner called *Woft*, or *Drillo*, or *Frud* – but certainly not one called **Sfog*, or **Bdift*, or **Wozrfeh*.

At any one time in a language there are numerous possible word formation devices, though only a few of these are likely to be in common use. These 'productive' processes – those in active use for the production of new words – are attached to the mental lexicon, perhaps as an auxiliary component. The use of this 'lexical tool-kit' is always available, and always optional (Aronoff, 1976). The situation may be somewhat like name-labelling at conferences. The organizers usually have name-labels ready for delegates, but there are some-times unexpected arrivals, for whom the organizers simply write out extra labels as required. The lexical tool-kit, then, contains back-up mechanisms which supplement the existing lexicon with instructions as to how to make up new words if they are needed.

No two researchers agree exactly on the nature of these instructions (for differing but overlapping views see Aronoff, 1976; Selkirk, 1982; Dressler, 1985), but certain outline facts are fairly clear. The devices used differ from language to language, though some recur widely (Cutler *et al.*, 1985). In this chapter we shall consider some that are common in English (figure 14.1). First, we shall look at compounding – the juxtaposition of existing words, as in *cow-tree*, perhaps 'tree where cows shelter'. Second, we shall discuss conversion – the changing of one part of speech into another, as in 'He jam-jarred the wasp'. Third, we shall consider affixation – the addition of a morpheme to the end, beginning, or middle of an existing word, as in *Donald Duck-ish*. Finally, we shall discuss the human ability to split up existing words in order to create new ones, as in *flopnik* from 'sputnik'. The aim of this investigation is to see how humans do this, and how others manage to comprehend them. In this way we

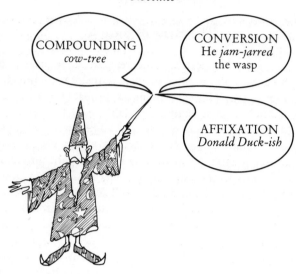

Figure 14.1   *Common ways of creating new words*

shall find out more about the working of the 'lexical tool-kit', and how it is attached to the 'lexicon proper'.

Owl bowls and pumpkin buses

Headache pills demolish headaches, *fertility pills* produce fertility and *heart pills* aid the heart. Moreover, *slug powder* kills slugs, *talcum powder* is made of purified talc and *face powder* goes on faces. As these examples show, words can be put together in so many superficially illogical ways that one wonders how on earth people manage to understand one another when this is done afresh, as in 'You can have the owl bowl', meaning 'You can have the bowl with the picture of the owl on it'.

There are quite a lot of different ways in which words can be combined together (Adams, 1973; Bauer, 1983). The largest group of existing compounds involves nouns alongside other nouns, and this is possibly the commonest category for novel ones. Children can produce compounds of this type from around the age of two, as in *sky-car* 'aeroplane' (age 18 months), *car-smoke* 'car exhaust' (age two years four months) (Clark, 1981).

There are no absolute constraints on the way in which nouns can be combined, though speakers show certain preferences, in that a smallish number of relationships are favoured (Downing, 1977). Objects tend to be involved in compounds which specify their use, as in *banana fork* 'fork used for bananas', *spaghetti saucepan* 'saucepan for cooking spaghetti'. Animals and plants are likely to occur in compounds which describe their appearance or habitat, as in the *Widmoor fox*, *marsh tulip*, and humans are likely to have their occupation or sexual or ethnic identity specified, as in *police demonstrators*, *women sailors*.

The new compound must, it seems, convey further information: the sequence *egg bird* was judged unacceptable as a compound on the grounds that all birds come from eggs, and *head hat* was rejected because 'All hats are worn on the head – so all hats are head hats' (Downing, 1977: 832). Furthermore, the relationship between the two parts of the compound was normally expected to be a permanent or habitual one: 'The person who says *owl-house* does not expect his hearer to interpret this as "a house that owls fall on" or "the house my owl flew by". Houses are not characterized by a general tendency to be fallen upon by owls' (Gleitman and Gleitman, 1970: 92). Similarly, the interpretation of 'a bus that ran over a pumpkin' was considered unlikely for the compound *pumpkin-bus* (Downing, 1977). People were happier to consider it a bus that habitually carried pumpkins, or that looked like a pumpkin.

These preferences, therefore, help to narrow down the likely possibilities. They subconsciously guide speakers, and also aid hearers in their interpretation, and so must be regarded as part of the lexical tool-kit. However, exact interpretation depends above all on the context, and the intelligence and co-operation of hearers: *plate-length hair* is hair which drags in the food, and *the apple-juice seat* was the chair in front of which the apple-juice was placed (Downing, 1977). Once again, human word comprehension requires active matching skills, in which pre-existing information has to be combined with information extracted from the context.

There is, incidentally, some intriguing evidence that highly educated people find it easier to cope with compounds, at least in the absence of strong contextual clues. Seven Ph.D. candidates, and seven clerical workers were each asked what they thought *house-bird glass* was. Six of the Ph.D. candidates thought that it was some kind of glass relating to house-birds, but only one of the clerical workers made this suggestion. The six others made fairly bizarre proposals, such as 'a glass bird-house', 'a house-bird made from glass', 'house-bird that's in a glass' (Gleitman and Gleitman, 1979). This finding suggests that familiarity with the particular compounding processes used by one's own language is important for understanding less obvious combinations of words – and is a question which requires further research. Let us now turn to conversions.

Lightning conversions

'Marigold chocolated the cake', 'Peregrine abouted the car', 'Let's do a wash-up'. The process of converting one part of speech into another is particularly common in English (Adams, 1973; Bauer, 1983), possibly because the basic form of verbs and nouns is often identical, as with *play* (noun or verb). This process is easily extended, not only by adults but also by children: 'He's keying the door', commented a three-year-old, watching someone unlock a door. 'Is it all needled?' queried another three-year-old as a pair of pants were mended. 'I'm shirting my man', said a five-year-old dressing a doll. 'Will you nut these?' requested a six-year-old, when she wanted some walnuts cracked (Clark, 1982).

There are many more nouns than verbs in a language, so the conversion of a noun to a verb is considerably more common than the other way about. One simply has to add a verbal ending. The point of doing this, for an adult, seems to be to use fewer words: 'Marigold chocolated the cake' is shorter than 'Marigold covered the cake with chocolate'. As with compounding, there are relatively few constraints on this process but a number of preferences can be detected (Clark and Clark, 1979). It is particularly common when the noun involves some type of implement, and so the corresponding verb means to use the implement in a characteristic way: 'Henry Moulinexed the vegetables' (referring to a brand of food processor), 'John squeegeed the floor' (a type of floor-mop known as a squeegee). It also occurs in order to describe where something has been put: 'Henry kenneled the dog', 'The dog treed a raccoon', 'Mavis jam-jarred the wasp'.

Other relationships are possible but are not so common in adult language. Adults do not normally say 'I'm caking' for 'I'm eating a cake' – though children sometimes use this activity construction: 'I'm souping', said a two-year-old as he ate soup. 'I'm lawning', said another, playing with a toy lawnmower (Clark, 1982).

In general, then, adults will use these conversions in certain conventional ways, which will simplify the problem of interpretation for the hearer. The hearer, however, as in the previous examples of extended and novel formations, has to take the current context into consideration since the same word might mean something different on different days: *Sammy pizza-ed the floor* might mean 'Sammy dropped pizza all over the floor' on one day, but *Felicity pizza-ed the dough* could signify 'Felicity made the dough into pizzas' on the next. As elsewhere, active computation is essential, integrating existing knowledge with the current situation. Let us now move on to affixation.

The undebeakability of Donald Duck

'Undebeakability is the test of true Donald Duckishness.' This sentence, though containing 'words' which have probably never been uttered before, would be quite comprehensible to a speaker of English, especially if it occurred in an article explaining that Donald Duck could be easily distinguished from fakes by the fact that his beak could not be twisted off. The new words make use of highly productive word formation processes – prefixation and suffixation – which allow them to be easily produced and readily understood.

Suffixation is the commonest method of forming new words in English, with certain suffixes being particularly favoured. The suffix -*ness*, for example, is enormously productive, so much so that an article in *Time* magazine entitled 'The Nesselrode to ruin' suggested that it may be a 'formidable enemy' of good English when it is extended indiscriminately to all kinds of words (*Time*, May 1962). It is primarily added on to adjectives in order to create a new noun as in *goodness*, *happiness*, *reasonableness*, but can also be attached to phrases as in *broken-heartedness*, *matter-of-factness*, *up-to-dateness*, *hump-backed whaleishness*, *Donald Duckishness*, and occasionally other types of word as well, as in *whyness*, *thusness*, *whereness*, *oughtness*.

The suffix -*ness* illustrates several important characteristics of the suffixes found in the lexical tool-kit (Aronoff, 1976). First, they are normally attached to whole words or phrases, not bits of words: we find *politeness*, not **poliness*, *prettiness*, not **prettness*. Second, they are mostly added on to the major word classes – nouns, adjectives, or verbs – in order to create another noun, adjective, or verb: it is somewhat rare to find an ending added to a minor part of speech, as in *this-ness*, *about-ness*. Third, each word class has its own characteristic suffixes: nouns can be turned into adjectives by adding a suffix such as -*al* or -*ish*, as in *jumbificational*, *duckish*, but turning a verb into an adjective requires a different suffix, one such as -*able*, as in *debeakable*.

These three major characteristics are perhaps not surprising, in view of what we already know about the mental lexicon. We have noted that words are listed as wholes, so it seems reasonable that the most productive process is one which simply adds a piece on to a complete word. We know that 'full' words are treated separately from function words, which are closely related to the syntax, so it is not strange that only the former can normally employ the lexical tool-kit. Finally, we have seen that words are stored in word classes, so it makes sense that each class should have its own attachments.

Over time, words can accumulate several suffixes, as in *reason-able-ness*, or *department-al-iz-ation*. Like an onion, these words seem to have gathered increasing layers of outer skin. In general, this heaping-up of suffixes happened gradually. Each word became accepted as a lexical item before the next suffix was added, though it is not impossible to find two suffixes which appear to get added on at the same time, as in *Donald Duckishness*.

Prefixes, on the other hand, are not often combined, though this is not impossible, as shown by *undebeakability*. They are less numerous than suffixes, and only one or two of these change the word class, such as *de-* which can make nouns into verbs, as in *de-frost*, *de-bug*, *de-beak*. Infixes are even rarer. 'Ain't that fantastic! Oh, Jeez, isn't that fangoddamtastic! ... Ain't that fanfuckingtastic?' This overexcited comment by a character in John Gordon Davis's novel *Leviathan* illustrates the use of infixes – a minor, occasional process in English, which never changes the word class. A long word might change its word class several times in the course of being built, as with *Donald Duckishness*, which changes from a noun, to an adjective, and then back to a noun:

Donald Duck (NOUN) + ish
Donald Duckish (ADJ) + ness
Donald Duckishness (NOUN).

A useful way of showing this layering is on a tree diagram, where the topmost join or 'node' shows the overall result of adding various suffixes, which can be peeled off one by one (figure 14.2).

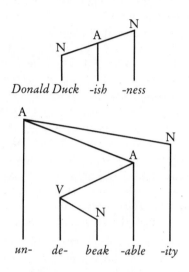

Figure 14.2   Layering of affixes

Speakers, then, obviously have tools in their tool-kit which allow them to do this. Moreover, the tool-kit deals not only with sound segments but also with adjustments to the rhythm of the original word, which may alter when a suffix is added (Selkirk, 1982). However, there is a further question which we need to discuss. Quite often there is more than one possible suffix in the tool-kit. How do speakers decide between them?

Scronkiness or scronkity?

Suppose one came across a new word, *skronky*, meaning, perhaps, *scruffy* and *wonky*, and were asked to guess the noun which went with it, what would you say? *Scronkiness? Scronkity?* Most people judge that either is possible, but generally prefer *skronkiness*. Let us consider the guidelines which may have led to this decision.

There appear to be several 'rules of thumb' which speakers follow (Aronoff, 1976; Romaine, 1983). Frequent usage is the most obvious. There are more existing words ending in -*ness* than words in -*ity* (Lehnert, 1971). So -*ness* might just 'sound right' because it is so common. However, frequency of usage is not the only guideline.

The sound structure of the word is another factor taken into account. When people are asked to form a noun from a nonsense word such as *runcile*, the preference is for *runcility*: *runcileness* is judged possible but not very likely. And this turns out to be the most usual suffix in the dictionary for adjectives ending in -*al*, -*ible*, or -*ile*, as in *nationality*, *possibility*, *fragility* (Lehnert, 1971). So small portions of the lexicon have their own most probable ending (Romaine, 1983).

A third consideration is the extent to which the existing word needs to be altered in order to produce the new one. In general, people try to retain the stress pattern of the base (Cutler, 1980, 1981). If you ask people to choose between *tulsivity* and *tulsiveness* as the noun for a nonsense adjective *tulsive*, they tend to choose *tulsiveness* not only because -*ness* is common but also perhaps because it keeps the rhythm of the base word unchanged. This finding is supported by a moderately rare type of tongue-slip, in which new words are formed in the course of speech, probably because the existing one can't be accessed immediately, such as *deduce-ful* for 'deductive', *professor-al* for 'professorial' (chapter 10). The speaker tends to coin a word in which the base word is wholly reproduced. And in an experiment where people were asked to think of related words, the subjects sometimes replaced the base word even when it had been altered historically, initially saying *pompous-ity* instead of 'pomposity' (Romaine, 1983). Furthermore, if there is no way of keeping the original word whole, speakers prefer to keep the early part of the word intact and alter the sounds at the end, according to one researcher (Cutler, 1980): subjects who were asked if they preferred a verb *languidify* or *languify* as a derivative of the adjective *languid* came out in favour of *languify*. The experimenter attributed this to the fact that *languidify* would have altered the stress of the beginning of the word and so made it hard to recognize – though another reason may be that the stress pattern of *languify* sounds more usual.

A further guideline which speakers use is the meaning. They are likely to prefer a suffix if it has a consistent meaning, so that there is a straightforward relationship between the old and the new word (Aronoff, 1976; Romaine, 1983). This is another reason for the general favouring of -*ness* over -*ity*. Words formed with -*ness* almost all denote abstract qualities, such as *kindness*, *cautiousness*, *mulishness*. Those in -*ity*, however, are less consistent. Some are abstract, as with *stability*, *equality*, but many of them also denote concrete people or institutions, as in *celebrity*, *university*. Furthermore, -*ty* endings can sometimes occur on adjectives, as in *crotchety*, *pernickety*.

The last two guidelines mentioned – a preference for keeping the base word intact and a preference for consistency in meaning – are both examples of a more general tendency found in language, a predilection for choosing formations which are 'transparent' or easily analysable and an avoidance of ones which are 'opaque' or hard to analyse (Aitchison, 1981).

These guidelines – frequency of use, the sound structure of the base and a desire to avoid altering it, consistency of meaning in the suffix – are the main 'rules-of-thumb'. And there may be others which work intermittently. For example, there seems to be a resistance to having a suffix which repeats the previous sound: no one would be likely to agree to a formation *crotchety-ity* – *crotchetiness* would gain unanimous support (Menn and MacWhinney, 1984). Other sporadic preferences are less predictable: for example, a group of students thought -*ity* sounded better on nonsense words with a Latin flavour, such as *orbitality*, than on non-classical ones such as *plentifulity* (Randall, 1980). In infixes, rhythm has to be taken into account: *licketyfuckingsplit* is possible, but ** lickfuckingetysplit* is not (Bauer, 1983: 90). Speakers have to weigh up the guidelines. If they all reinforce one another, as sometimes happens, then the choice will be obvious. But where they clash, different speakers might assess the situation in different ways. In brief, the lexical tool-kit does not work automatically – it quite often requires active decision making, above all from the creator of the word, but also from the hearer.

A tronastery for trunks

> I wish I were a Tibetan monk
> Living in a monastery.
> I would unpack my trunk
> And store it in a tronastery;
> I would collect all my junk
> And send it to a jonastery . . .

Ogden Nash, in his poem 'Away From It All', uses the fact that monks live in monasteries to reason that perhaps things that rhyme with *monk*, such as *trunk* and *junk*, are stored in places which rhyme with *monasteries* – *tronasteries* or *jonasteries*.

This is clearly a carefully thought-out play on words, but it parallels the type of analysis that goes on in everyday life:

Steven   This TV sure doesn't recept very well.
Mother   What do you mean, 'recept'?
Steven   You know, the reception's bad.

This conversation occurred between a woman and her 11-year-old son (Taylor, 1978: 352). It shows that speakers can sometimes form new words by analysing existing ones into segments – in this case the speaker had probably noted existing pairs of words in the lexicon, such as *select*, *selection*, *adopt*, *adoption*, and figured that *recept*, *reception* was another pair in this category.

Analyses of this type form the basis of numerous new words. After the word *sputnik* was borrowed from Russian, following the launching of a Soviet satellite called a *sputnik*, -*nik* was detached and -*nik* words were coined in profusion: a satellite launched with a dog inside it was referred to as a *dognik*, and a failed American satellite was referred to as a *flopnik*, a *goofnik*, an *oopsnik*, a *pfftnik*, a *sputternik* and a *stayputnik* (Bauer, 1983: 255).

This particular type of construction – splitting words and forming new ones – relies above all on the assumption that the hearer can refer back to the original word which formed the pattern and analyse its make-up. In brief, 'words are formed from words' (Aronoff, 1976: 46).

From the point of view of the mental lexicon, the important point is that humans are able to split up words in this way, even though (as we saw in chapter 10) this ability is not strictly necessary for existing words since they are stored as wholes. The primary purpose of this ability, therefore, seems to be to enable speakers to make up new words of their own, and to comprehend the novelties coined by others. Its secondary purpose may be as a memory aid to enable people to link up words containing similar morphemes. We noted in chapter 10 that many words had a set of back-up information attached to them, which showed how they are split up, and specified links with other words containing the same morphemes. This back-up store also contains pointers to the lexical tool-kit, and may be intermediate between it and the main lexicon. For example, *kindness* will be listed as *kindness* in the central lexicon, but in the back-up store it will be divided into *kind-ness*. There will be a link both to other words in -*ness*, as *goodness*, *happiness*, and also to the tool-kit, to the rule which says a new noun can be formed by adding -*ness* on to an adjective (figure 14.3).

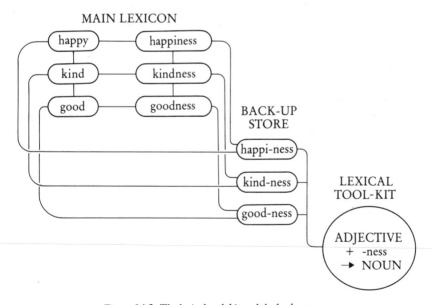

Figure 14.3 The lexical tool-kit and the back-up store

In this chapter, then, we have considered four types of word formation process which are common in English: compounding, conversion, affixation and reanalysis. Although we have dealt with them separately, they can be combined. A possible word *spaghetti-sniffer*, presumably 'someone who sniffs spaghetti' involves putting a suffix on a verb, then attaching it to a noun, probably after analysing a word such as *glue-sniffer*. These mixed types behave in certain moderately predictable ways (Marchand, 1969), though they appear to be more complex, in that they take longer for children to learn (Clark *et al.*, 1986).

Above all, then, the process of creating new words shows how enormously flexible the human mind is in coping with vocabulary. The lexical tool-kit contains instructions and guidelines as to how to make up new words, and in order to do this it makes use of the back-up information attached to each word, showing how it can be split up, and other words to which it is related. The creation of new words reinforces a viewpoint which we have already reached: that the mental lexicon is not a fixed dictionary with a set amount of information about each word, but an active system in which new links are perpetually being formed.

Summary

In this chapter we examined the lexical tool-kit, the human facility for creating new words, an optional and always available ability. We examined a number of common word formation processes in English – compounding, conversion, affixation, reanalysis – and noted that these rules were flexible, in that there were very few overall constraints. However, there were a number of guidelines which narrowed down the range of new formations, and made interpretation easier for the hearers. Furthermore, the lexical tool-kit does not work in isolation. It has access to back-up information about each word, which helps it to deal with cases in which new words are formed by reanalysis.

We have now dealt with a number of facets of the mental lexicon. But we have not yet explored how all these intermesh with one another. This is our next topic.

Part 4

The Overall Picture

15

Seeking and Finding
— *Selecting words* —

Mrs Rooney	I remember once attending a lecture by one of these new mind doctors. I forget what you call them. He spoke . . .
Mr Rooney	A lunatic specialist?
Mrs Rooney	No, no, just the troubled mind. I was hoping he might shed a little light on my lifelong preoccupation with horses' buttocks.
Mr Rooney	A neurologist?
Mrs Rooney	No, no, just mental distress. The name will come back to me in the night.

Samuel Beckett, All That Fall

Humans behave like jugglers when they use the mental lexicon, in that they have to deal with semantic, syntactic and phonological information at the same time. We have not yet considered how all these ingredients are combined. Tracing through the processes involved in putting them together, therefore, is likely to shed light on the organization of the various components in the human word-store.

In outline, production and recognition seem to be mirror images of one another. When producing a word, humans must pick the meaning before the sound. When recognizing a word, they must start with the sounds, then move on to the meaning. However, we cannot take it for granted that they utilize the same processes in a different order, just as we cannot automatically assume that going upstairs uses identical muscles to going down but in the reverse sequence. In this chapter, therefore, we shall consider word production, and in the next, word recognition.

However, before we look at the intersecting processes involved in producing a word, the question of choice needs to be considered. Do people normally weigh up alternatives when they select words? Everyone knows that poets, in particular, are always seeking for the apt word among the various possibilities in their mental lexicons. T. S. Eliot in 'Little Gidding' vividly expresses the search for

The word neither diffident nor ostentatious,
An easy commerce of the old and the new,
The common word exact without vulgarity,
The formal word precise but not pedantic . . .

And Emily Dickinson describes a similar word selection process:

Shall I take thee, the Poet said
To the propounded word?
Be stationed with the Candidates
Till I have finer tried –
The Poet searched Philology. . . .

There are also special occasions, such as wedding speeches, when words must be selected carefully, so much so that the phrase 'a few well-chosen words' has become a cliché. But in everyday conversation, when one is chatting to friends in a relaxed way, there is a general impression that decision making is unnecessary: one just utters the first words that come to mind, as the poet Samuel Coleridge implied when he claimed that prose consisted of 'words in their best order', but poetry of 'the best words in the best order'. Is this assumption correct?

An embarrassment of riches

The notion that decision making might be involved even in ordinary speech, though perhaps at a subconscious level, was suggested by the nineteenth-century psychologist William James: 'And has the reader never asked himself what kind of a mental fact is his intention of saying a thing before he has said it? It is an entirely definite intention . . . But as the words that replace it arrive, it welcomes them successively and calls them right if they agree with it, it rejects them and calls them wrong if they do not' (James, 1890/1981: 245). There are several indications that James was quite right.

'Blends', when two words are melded into one, provide the clearest evidence that alternative words are often considered in the course of speech. 'Shun the frumious Bandersnatch', said Lewis Carroll in the nonsense poem 'The Jabberwocky'. For those in doubt, he explains the word *frumious*: 'Take the two words "fuming" and "furious". Make up your mind that you will say both words, but leave it unsettled which you will say first. Now open your mouth and speak. If your thoughts incline ever so little towards "fuming", you will say "fuming-furious"; if they turn, by even a hair's breadth, towards "furious", you will say "furious-fuming"; but if you have that rarest of gifts, a perfectly balanced mind, you will say "frumious"' (Carroll, 1876/1967: 42).

This example is a contrived, literary one, but it exemplifies a phenomenon which occurs quite unintentionally in real life, as in:

It's quite *ebvious* (evident + obvious) that you disagree.
Don't *frowl* (frown + scowl) like that!
Not in the *sleast* (slightest + least).
She *chuttled* (chuckle + chortle) at the news.
My *buggage* (baggage + luggage) is too heavy.
My *tummach* (tummy + stomach) hurts.

The large number of such examples suggests that we consider both options when there are two equally useful words to fill a slot, especially when these words have sounds in common. These are clear examples of cases in which speakers have failed to make up their mind between 'competing plans' (Baars, 1980).

Blends can also be found in the speech of some aphasics. 'I forget seeing you before, sir. I remember the other documen and was plazed to see the other documen. My brother was with me. And he was queen that I was hoddle with our own little mm . . . bog, my thing of mogry, you know' (Butterworth, 1979). This aphasic patient, a 72-year-old solicitor who has had a stroke, does a great many things wrong. But amidst this jumble, blends appear to predominate among the different types of errors (Bickerton, 1981). *Documen* may be a blend of 'doctor' and 'gentleman', perhaps reinforced by 'document', a word which would have been very common in the patient's profession. *Plazed* might be a combination of 'pleased' and 'glad'. *I forget seeing you* may be a replacement of 'don't remember' with 'forget'. By themselves, these examples are not definitive evidence of blending, since it is easy to be fanciful in interpreting garbled utterances. But they are reinforced by other examples in this patient's speech (Bickerton, 1981). At least part of his problem, therefore, is that he is unable to choose the words he wants from the various alternatives which flash up, as it were, on his mental screen.

Both ordinary people and some aphasics, then, suggest that it is normal to consider more than one possibility, if there are several plausible candidates. There are, however, a number of indications that the selection process goes beyond this, and that humans automatically consider words that are inappropriate, provided they are in some way connected with the topic concerned.

Noshville, Greeceland and Freudian slips

Blends are typically composed of two equally suitable words. But this is not inevitable. In some examples one word fits the sentence better than the other, as in *Noshville* (Nashville and Knoxville) where the speaker meant to name only one of these Tennessee towns, or in *taquua* (tequila + kahlua) when only the first of these Mexican drinks was being ordered, or in *Greeceland* (Greenland + Iceland) where Iceland alone was intended. Such errors suggest that it may be normal to activate a number of words in the area of the required word and then suppress those which are not wanted. Furthermore, overactivation might also be the explanation for errors such as *left* for 'right', *myrtle* for 'mimosa'. So far, we have assumed that the speaker accidentally picked up a neighbour and passed over the one which was required. But this is not the only possible explanation. Alternatively, the speaker may have activated both of them, and then erroneously suppressed the wrong one. Let us consider further evidence for this point of view.

The mind appears to inadvertently over-prepare itself quite often, as suggested by errors such as:

> The beach was flowing with *pebbles* (water).
> I bought eels and *snake* (skate).

In the first sentence, the speaker was describing a pebbly beach after a rainstorm, and there was no need for the word *pebbles* to have been uttered, but it had been subconsciously activated. In the second, the thought of eels triggered *snake* as well, which sounded sufficiently like *skate* to take its place. Sometimes, also, surrounding objects arouse words, even when they are not part of the topic of conversation:

> I'm waiting for the *snow* (butter) to melt.

Here, a woman was planning to make sandwiches, while watching the snow falling outside.

Such examples are akin to genuine 'Freudian slips' – cases in which a person's secret thoughts and anxieties slip into the conversation. Although there are not as many of these as Freud assumed (as noted in chapter 2), they do sometimes occur. For example, Freud describes how, at a stormy meeting, the chairman announced: 'We shall now *quarrel* (streiten) to point four of the agenda', instead of 'proceed' (schreiten) (Freud, 1901 /975: 112). Recently, after a fruitless discussion, a meeting was abandoned with the words: 'And now, in *confusion* (conclusion) . . .' Such examples indicate that more words are prepared than normally surface. Usually the unwanted ones are suppressed, but occasionally they pop up inconveniently.

This state of affairs has been reproduced experimentally. When a provocatively dressed female asked male subjects to read out pairs of words, many more subjects said *fast passion* for 'past fashion', *happy sex* for 'sappy hex' and *bare shoulders* for 'share boulders' than in a comparable control group (Motley, 1985). In another experiment, bogus electrodes were wired on to subjects and they were told that at some random moment they would be given a painful electric shock. Of course, as the 'electrodes' were not real ones no shock was given. But the anxiety produced by this procedure was sufficient to make many more subjects say *damn shock* when they should have said 'sham dock', *carried volts* instead of 'varied colts' and *cursed wattage* instead of 'worst cottage' than in a comparable control group who had no anxiety about electricity. These experiments, therefore, give support to the notion that words get easily aroused in relation to topics one is thinking about, and so strengthen the idea that it is normal to activate many more words than one could ever use in a conversation.

The word salads – jumbles of apparently disconnected words and thoughts – of some schizophrenics may represent a similar phenomenon: 'I have distemper just like cats do, 'cause that's what we all are, felines. Siamese cat balls. They stand out. I had a cat, a manx, still around somewhere. You'll know him when you see him. His name is GI Joe: he's black and white. I had a little goldfish too, like a clown. Happy Hallowe'en down' (Chaika, 1974: 261). Here the notion of cats leads on to different types of cat – Siamese, Manx – then cats lead on to goldfish. The goldfish presumably had big lips, like a clown, which triggers the idea of Hallowe'en, perhaps because in America this is a night when people sometimes dress up as clowns. And *clown* rhymes with *down*. When the same patient had a cigarette in her hand, she commented: 'This is holy smoke. It's a holy one. It goes in one hole and out the other and that makes it holy' (Chaika, 1974: 260).

Part of this patient's problem is that her mind is overexcited. It is flashing up too many associations, and she cannot seem to distinguish between associations which should be secondary, and in the background, and those which are of vital importance to the topic under discussion. In this situation she jumps about among all of them, producing a seemingly incoherent jumble of images and ideas. Cases such as this indicate that when things go wrong, an inability to control and manipulate normal mechanisms may be the primary difficulty (Green, 1986). There is no need to assume that bizarre symptoms involve abnormal mechanisms. The opposite situation occurs with some aphasics, whose brain does not arouse sufficient information: only the occasional not particularly appropriate word is thrown up into their mental screen.

There seems to be a good deal of evidence, then, that in speech production it is normal for the mind to activate many more words than are likely to be used in the course of a conversation. When we describe how humans find the words they want, we must show how people cope with this teeming mass of extra items.

The inadequacy of stepping-stones

Let us now consider what might be going on in a person's mind as they select a word. We shall do this by discussing in turn three possible models of the processes involved: a stepping-stone model, a waterfall model and an electricity model. Each of them envisages a somewhat different way of utilizing the basic components of words.

In a stepping-stone model, the speaker can be envisaged as someone crossing a stream, pausing at one stone before leaping to the next. Each stage is completed before the next one is started, and the various steps do not interact in any way. The two basic components of words – first, meaning and word class, then sounds – are the stepping-stones.

According to this model, a person picks a meaning and word class on the first stepping-stone – perhaps, for example, a smallish wild animal, which, though not yet clothed in sounds, is known to be the noun BEAVER. On the second stepping-stone the sound structure, *beaver*, is hooked on (figure 15.1).

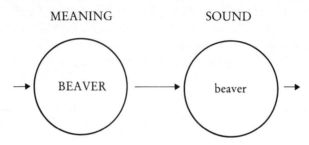

Figure 15.1   A basic stepping-stone model

Obviously this simple model needs to be elaborated. For a start, the first stepping-stone would have to be marked in some way to show speakers where to go next. So at the jumping-off point there would be a signpost saying where-abouts to go to in the next component. In the case of BEAVER there would be a sign pointing to a phonological 'area-code': a two-syllable word beginning in *b*- and ending in -*er* (figure 15.2).

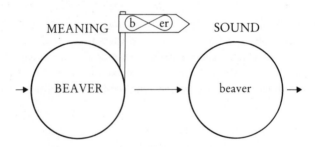

Figure 15.2   A stepping-stone model with signposting

But more refinements are needed. People activate a number of related words (as discussed earlier in this chapter), so the stepping-stones need to be broad at the entry end but progressively narrowed down as the target is approached. In the semantic component, OTTER, BEAVER, BADGER, RABBIT and other small wild animals might be activated at the early stage, then the choice narrowed down to BEAVER. Within the phonological component, numerous words with the same outline specification, *beaker, beaver, badger, bearer, beggar,*

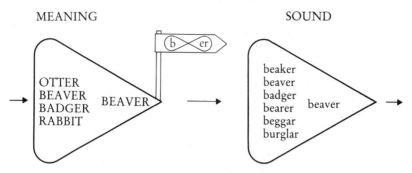

MEANING   SOUND

Figure 15.3   A stepping-stone model with narrowing down

burglar, will at first be under consideration, then the target will be narrowed down to *beaver* (figure 15.3).

This model can explain errors such as *otter* for 'beaver' on the assumption that the speaker accidentally eliminated the correct word as the choice was narrowed down within the semantics. Similarly, *beaker* for 'beaver' would be an erroneous narrowing-down within the phonology.

But there is one major flaw in the stepping-stone account: a large number of words picked in error or proposed in 'tip of the tongue' guesses have some meaning similarity and some sound similarity with the target – perhaps even the majority, according to some researchers (e.g. Browman, 1978). *Badger* is an actual error occurring instead of 'beaver' – both of them are smallish wild animals and neither of them very common, and both have the same beginning and ending and the same rhythmic pattern. Other errors with similar sound and meaning as the target were noted in chapter 2. Further examples are:

Don't contact lenses make your *ears* (eyes) sore?
I found it in the train *component* (compartment).
There's a *sparrow* (swallow): summer's arrived.
They picked up the language on trading *vehicles* (vessels).

The prevalence of this type of error is quite incomprehensible within a stepping-stone model because each stage is over and done with before the next is started. But these errors suggest that memory of related words activated in the semantic component is still present while the phonology is picked. The stepping-stone model therefore has to be abandoned, and another one which can cope with this phenomenon needs to be proposed.

Waterfalls can't flow backwards

We need a model which incorporates some of the features of the elaborated stepping-stone model, notably signposting and gradual narrowing down of possibilities. But we also need one which allows a person still to be thinking about the meaning as they select the sound. These characteristics are found in a waterfall or 'cascade' model (McClelland, 1979). Here, all the information activated at the first stage is still available at the next stage: it is, as it were, cascading down onto the next trough of water on the hillside. So, after a selection of word meanings have been activated, all of them remain available as a person deals with the sounds. They continue to be at hand until the required word has been pinpointed (figure 15.4).

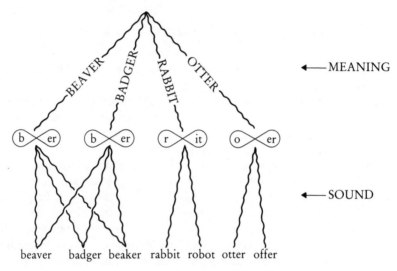

Figure 15.4   A waterfall model

In a waterfall model, therefore, the stages overlap. Once overlapping is possible, then a speaker can always jump ahead and start sorting out the next stage before completing the one before. The signposts to the phonology stage occur in the course of the meaning one, so that a person moves on to the sounds before the final choice is made between words such as OTTER, BEAVER, BADGER and RABBIT. Of course, this means that much more material is aroused than will eventually be required, since the outline phonology of several small animals will be triggered. But this overactivation fits in with the evidence we discussed previously.

This model, then, encapsulates the fact that 'down stream' processes still have access to earlier information. Furthermore, it suggests that word selection is not just a case of following one word through from beginning to end, like a dog chasing a particular rat, but is often a case of controlling and narrowing down a cascade of possible words which are pouring over one. The error *badger* for 'beaver' is explainable by assuming that the semantic information about small animals was cascading over one as the outline phonology was picked. As there were two which shared the same outline, the wrong one happened to get picked in the final selection.

The waterfall model, therefore, is a great improvement, because it shows how the various stages overlap. Furthermore, it explains why humans activate so many extra words: this is inevitable, once one allows overlapping stages. But such a model has a serious drawback. Waterfalls can't flow backwards. Just as making the phonology precise requires semantic evidence, so sometimes phonology may be needed to narrow down the semantics.

A possible example of information flowing backwards and forwards is when people are prompted. If you say to someone, 'Think up the names of some woodland animals', they might say, 'Rabbit, squirrel – I can't think of any more'. But if you prompt them 'Beginning with *b*', then *badger* or *beaver* might well spring to their lips. It's well known that this type of cueing helps both normal speakers and aphasics when they cannot think of words (Ellis, 1985). One way to account for this phenomenon is to assume that information can flow both ways: particular sounds can enable a speaker to activate meanings, just as meanings activate sounds. A waterfall or cascade model could account for this only if the animal had already been subconsciously aroused and was among the cascade of information reaching the phonology. In this case, a prompt 'B . . b . . b . .' could help them to narrow down the field to *badger*. But it could not deal with an animal which had not already been activated. Let us therefore go on to consider a model which allows information to flow both forwards and backwards.

Interactive circuitry

We require a model which is in many ways like the waterfall model but which allows information to flow backwards as well as forwards. An image of electricity might therefore be appropriate, with current flowing to and fro between various points in a complex electrical circuit.

In the production of speech the current is normally initiated in the semantic component, where a semantic field will be aroused, then narrowed down, perhaps to a clutch of woodland animals. Before a final choice has been made, the current flows to the phonological 'area code' of each, where a hoard of words will be triggered and those activated will feed back into the semantics, arousing more words there. All the links between the activated sections will metaphorically be lit up, with electric current rushing backwards and forwards. As it flows to and fro, it excites more and more related words. 'Spreading activation' or 'interactive activation' theories are the general name for models of this type, in which an initial impetus progressively fans out and activates more words as it spreads along the various connections (Dell and Reich, 1980; Stemberger, 1985; Ellis, 1985) (figure 15.5).

As the activated links are inspected, those that are relevant get more and

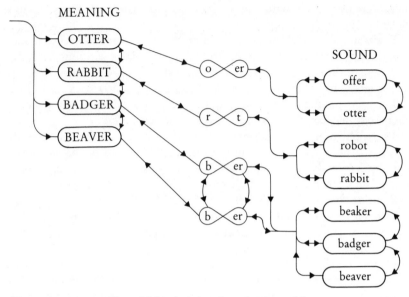

Figure 15.5   An interactive activation model

more excited while those that are unwanted fade away. The initial list of animals gets gradually pared down, with those which are semantically inappropriate disappearing, suppressed by the attention paid to the more likely candidates. Since the current is flowing to and fro, anything which is particularly strongly activated in the semantics will cause extra activation in the phonology, and vice versa. If the outline phonology fits more than one animal, then both animals will become more excited in the semantics. So *beaver* and *badger* will both become highly activated. If the speaker is not paying sufficient attention, the wrong one might get picked.

This combination of progressive activation of likely candidates and the corresponding suppression of unwanted links goes on until one overall word wins out. The winner pops up, perhaps as in a toaster when the toast is ready. It is unclear how to build this into the model – but we need to postulate some final point in selection at which one word emerges as the victor. Perhaps the electricity has to reach a required level, or perhaps one word has to get much more excited than the others. Some researchers have envisaged a device which collects up relevant information about the various aspects of a word: as soon as sufficient has been gathered, a response is triggered and the device 'gives birth to' a word (Morton, 1979). Different words require different levels of activation in order to be born: very frequently used words require relatively little to trigger them, while uncommon words are harder to arouse. Although the details are somewhat obscure, some such mechanism may be necessary.

A further requirement is possibly a 'monitoring device' – a double-check once the word has been chosen to confirm that the right one has been selected: people sometimes are able to catch themselves as they utter the wrong word (Laver, 1980).

Spreading activation models can account for all types of slip, including Freudian ones. Freudian slips occur because topics with which one is pre-occupied get subconsciously activated – and once a topic is activated then the whole range of related sound and meaning words get excited. Such slips are particularly likely to occur if there is some other link with the intended word, such as a sound link:

I'll give her a *prescription* (subscription) for a magazine.

said someone who was trying to keep a doctor's visit a secret. Furthermore it explains why we do not normally utter nonsense words – these do not exist, so cannot get excited.

A further advantage of spreading activation models is that they fit in with what we know about the brain. The human brain is known to contain billions of neurons, and many more billions of synapses connecting them. The excitation travelling along synapses in one area is likely to excite surrounding neurons in much the same way as the 'spreading activation' we have discussed. This model also suggests that the links between words are more important than their absolute location, and this also fits in with what we know about the human brain, where it seems to be impossible to locate particular brain areas with as much accuracy as we can a heart or a kidney.

We have therefore outlined a plausible way in which words are selected for utterance, and this has also given us some insight into how the various components in the mental lexicon might be linked. However, we now need to find out how people recognize words, and to see if a similar type of model is relevant.

Summary

In this chapter we have looked at how people produce words from their mental lexicon when they are speaking. We noted, first, that humans seem to activate many more words than they need as they plan speech, words which occasionally pop into one's utterance inconveniently. Any model of retrieval must recognize this fact.

We then looked at a number of possible models of the retrieval process. First, a stepping-stone model, in which the meaning of a word was picked before the sound was considered. This did not work because the various stages turned out to be interlinked, and partly simultaneous. Second, we examined a waterfall or cascade model, in which information from the meaning was still available while the sounds were being selected. This could not account for the fact that meaning and sound seem to mutually influence each other. We therefore concluded that a 'spreading activation' model was the most plausible. We likened the situation to complex electric circuitry, in which current flows backwards and forwards between particular points and in so doing excites numerous other points around. The relevant points and links get more and more excited and the irrelevant ones get suppressed, until finally one word wins out over the numerous ones activated.

We now need to consider whether word recognition works similarly. This will be the topic of the next chapter.

16

Organized Guesswork

— *Recognizing words* —

Some way ahead of them an awkward low shape was heaving itself
wretchedly along the ground . . . It was moving so slowly that before too
long they caught the creature up and could see that it was made of worn,
scarred and twisted metal . . .
'What is it?' whispered Fenchurch in alarm . . .
'He's a sort of an old friend', said Arthur. 'I . . .'
'Friend!' croaked the robot pathetically. The words died away in a kind
of crackle and flakes of dust fell out of his mouth. 'You'll have to excuse
me while I try and remember what the word means. My memory banks
are not what they were you know, and any word which falls into disuse for
a few zillion years has to get shifted down into auxiliary memory back-up.
Ah, here it comes.'
The robot's battered head snapped up a bit as if in thought.
'Hmmm', he said, 'what a curious concept.'

Douglas Adams, *So Long and Thanks for All the Fish*

To casual onlookers, word recognition might seem straightforward. As a first
guess, one might assume that hearers mentally record what they hear, then
'look up' the word in their mental lexicon, much as people find a word in a
printed dictionary by matching it segment by segment. On investigation,
however, this is a considerable oversimplification. Word recognition turns out
to be a complex procedure which requires considerably more skill than one
might expect. Let us therefore consider these complexities, and see whether
the same type of model which we hypothesized for word production is also
likely to work for word recognition.

There are a number of basic problems. First, in normal speech it is physically impossible to hear each phoneme – speech is just too fast. Twenty
segments a second is not unlikely, but the brain cannot distinguish even half
that number of separate sounds in that time (Liberman *et al.*, 1967). Second,
sounds are altered by their neighbours, sometimes quite radically. The 'same'

sound produced artificially was interpreted by listeners as [p], [t], or [k] depending on the vowel following it (Liberman *et al.*, 1957). Third, sound segments cannot be separated out, even in a laboratory. Each one merges into those on either side, like melting ice-cream. Although vowels can be sorted out, consonants cannot: 'If we take a piece of tape on which we have recorded the syllable [ba], and start cutting off pieces of tape from the consonant end, we eventually end up with . . . just the vowel [a]. But, if we cut the tape from the vowel end, we never get to a point where just the [b] sound is heard. As we cut pieces off, the syllable will get shorter and shorter until it suddenly turns into a sound like a chirp . . . a sound that doesn't even sound like speech, let alone a [b]' (Matthei and Roeper, 1983: 37). Finally, we live in a noisy world, and whole chunks of words can get masked by cars honking or people coughing. How, in the circumstances, does anybody understand anyone else at all?

The importance of guesswork

One of the best-known facts about word recognition is that a lot of it is guesswork. People recognize words by choosing the 'best fit': they match the portion they have heard with the word in their mental lexicon that appears to be the most likely candidate, and they fill in gaps, often without noticing they do so. One researcher played subjects sentences in which part of a key word such as *legislature* was hidden by a cough. Most people not only interpreted the word accurately but also hadn't noticed that part of it was missing. They admitted hearing a cough but thought it came somewhere else in the sentence (Warren, 1970).

The routine use of guesswork has been demonstrated in a number of other experiments. In the following sentences the last word was played indistinctly:

Paint the fence and the *?ate*.
Check the calendar and the *?ate*.
Here's the fishing gear and the *?ate*.

People reported hearing *gate* in the first, *date* in the second and *bait* in the third (Bond and Garnes, 1980; Garnes and Bond, 1980). In another experiment, a sound half-way between [k] and [g] was artificially constructed. This was interpreted as *kiss* when followed by -*iss* [ɪs], but as *gift* when followed by the sequence -*ift* [ɪft] (Ganong, 1980).

Furthermore, if the context is taken away, so hearers have nothing to guide them in their guesses, the result is often quite bizarre. Four people who were asked to listen to the somewhat unlikely utterance 'In mud eels are, in clay none are' came up with quite varied versions (Reddy, 1976, quoted in Cole, 1980: 137):

In muddies sar in clay nanar.
In my deals are in clainanar.

In my ders en clain.
In model sar in claynanar.

So since guesswork is so important, how are these guesses made?

Sorting out the sound waves

In word recognition, humans are faced with two different but interwoven problems: splitting up the stream of speech into words on the one hand, and identifying the words on the other. These two tasks proceed together, with people being perhaps slightly more efficient at the first than the second: 85 per cent of examples in a collection of 'slips of the ear' (cases in which people misheard what was said to them) involved a single word only, as in *Barcelona* for 'carcinoma', *simple* for 'sinful' (Browman, 1980).

Obviously, listeners have to start out by analysing the sound waves, though there is relatively little agreement as to how they do this. A few researchers have argued that the acoustic signals are assembled piecemeal and matched directly against items in the mental lexicon (e.g. Klatt, 1981). The majority, however, have proposed an intermediate stage, in which the information culled from the sound waves is translated into a sequence of phonemes (e.g. Cole and Jakimik, 1980) or syllables (e.g. Segui, 1984; Mehler, 1981), which are then fitted to words.

The reason behind the diverse viewpoints may be a simple one: perhaps there is no single way in which humans analyse the sound waves. Some procedures may be more common than others, and the frequency with which they are used may vary from language to language (Norris and Cutler, 1985; Frauenfelder, 1985). Also, the techniques may vary depending on the type of speech: somewhat different strategies might be needed for coping with, say, a clear television newsreader and a foreigner at a noisy party.

In spite of all this uncertainty, certain outline facts have been ascertained. Certain recurring factors aid the segmenting of speech into words. Sometimes, the beginning of a word is obvious because the previous one has already been recognized, since as we noted in chapter 1, words are often identified before the end (Marslen-Wilson and Tyler, 1980, 1981; Cole, 1980). At other times, various additional factors are taken into consideration. In English, the rhythmic pattern of the word is fairly easy to pick out, and this can help to indicate where words start and finish (Norris and Cutler, 1985; Bond and Garnes, 1980; Garnes and Bond, 1980). In addition, word beginnings and endings are sometimes signalled by phonetic clues (Lehiste, 1960, 1972; Frauenfelder, 1985): for example, [p], [t], [k] are often strongly aspirated (pronounced with a puff of breath) at the beginning of words, so this could signal the start of a word even if the exact consonant was not clearly identified.

Within words, vowels are perceived better than consonants (Browman, 1980). Stressed vowels are particularly easy to hear, and they tend to be retained in slips of the ear, as in *coffee* for 'hockey', *horrible* for 'tolerable' (Bond and Garnes, 1980; Garnes and Bond, 1980). Certain vowels vary less than others, notably [i], [u], [a]. If one of these is present, it can form a peg round which the rest of a word can be built (see Matthei and Roeper, 1983, for a summary of this work). Consonants can usually be assigned to the 'natural class' to which they belong: [s] sounds rather different from [b], for example, even though it might get confused with [ʃ] as in *shin*. (For a list of sounds which easily get confused, see Miller and Nicely, 1955; Wang and Bilger, 1973; Goldstein, 1980). All these factors can provide an outline framework.

But with regard to the finer details, there is 'a discouraging lack of acoustic invariance in the speech signal' (Matthei and Roeper, 1983: 43). There turns out to be more consistency in the way in which sounds are pronounced than in their acoustic image, so much so that some researchers have argued that people cannot recognize sounds adequately unless they have some notion of how they are pronounced. According to this view, 'the listener uses the inconstant sound as a basis for finding his way back to the articulatory gestures which produced it' (Liberman *et al.*, , 1967: 453; cf. Liberman and Mattingly, 1985). Many people feel that this view is somewhat exaggerated. Knowing how to produce a sound might aid perception but it is unlikely to be essential. This theory does, however, draw attention to one important aspect of human speech. In the course of evolution, humans have become particularly good at discriminating those sounds which they are capable of producing, just as frogs' eyes are tuned in to noticing the kinds of insects they normally eat (Lieberman, 1984).

Overall, then, the acoustic signal gives only a rough framework on which the hearer must work, and no portion of this can be relied upon, as a large sneeeze might have masked any part of it. There are probably a number of different words in the mental lexicon which are compatible with the rough framework. It seems unlikely that humans just flail around, wildly testing possible words at random. There must be some principled way in which they narrow down the various possibilities. Let us therefore consider how they might do this.

There are two main types of theory: some researchers argue that people test out probable words one after the other, a so-called 'serial' model of speech recognition. Others claim that all these candidates are considered simultaneously, and so argue for 'parallel' processing. Let us consider each of these.

'One after the other' theories

If you use a word often, it's easier to find it in your mental lexicon, and it's easier to remember it. On average, people find the word *cat* faster than *panther* or *cheetah*, and the word *nose* faster than *pelvis* or *spleen*, simply because they use them more often. This fits in with our everyday experience, and has been confirmed time and again by psycholinguists: common words are recognized as words faster than uncommon ones, a fact first pointed out over a quarter of a century ago (Solomon and Howes, 1951). In some cases, the common words are simply those which have been learnt earlier, so they have become ingrained in one's memory. However, in terms of the mental lexicon, what does 'ingrained in one's memory' mean? Are common words kept, as it were, on top of the heap of words, so they don't get buried or rubbed out? A number of psychologists have suggested just this. Perhaps words are organized within the sound system into heaps, or 'stacks', or 'bins', and within these bins perhaps the most frequently used words are kept on top (Forster, 1976).

Those who envisage the mental lexicon as organized in this way suggest that, when fitting a word to sounds one has heard, a person first goes to the relevant bin and then conducts an orderly search going from top to bottom of the heap, seeing if it matches. Bins, in the best-known model of this type (Forster, 1976), are based on word beginnings, so one might go past common words such as *hammer* and *hanger* before getting to one that truly matched, *hamper*. If the wrong word was accidentally picked, it would have to be replaced in the bin as soon as the mistake was discovered, and the search would continue as before.

In another serial model, frequent words have a separate section of the lexicon to themselves. According to this view they are stored twice, once in an easily available store and once in their proper place (Glanzer and Ehrenreich, 1979), just as one might keep an abridged pocket dictionary on one's desk for frequent fast consultation and a full-size lexicon the other side of the room on a bookshelf. On hearing a word, therefore, a person might check through the commonly used, readily available words first, and if it is not there, move on to the full mental lexicon. This 'double storage' hypothesis was put forward to account for the fact that frequent words are recognized faster in lexical decision tasks when they occur among other frequent words than when they occur among medium and low frequency words. The researchers suggested that this difference in access time for the same words might be due to the fact that hearers normally only had to zip through a relatively small store of frequent words; but that the slower access time when they were among the middle and low frequency words was because hearers had to seek them out from their proper place in the overall lexicon.

The word frequency effect, then, is the main reason why some researchers have argued for a serial model. They claim that faster processing of frequent words must mean that these are checked first, and the remainder later. But the frequency effect could have other explanations, and could be incorporated into a parallel processing model. Perhaps a group of candidate lexical items are looked at simultaneously, but activation takes place faster for frequent words, just as, if one opened the door of an aviary, some birds might rise from their perches faster than others. Or the word frequency effect might be due to extra strength in the stored representation (Morton, 1979). Perhaps frequent words are inked in more firmly, as it were, in one's mental notebook. Furthermore, we recognize words so fast that perhaps parallel access is inevitable. In addition, there is plenty of evidence to suggest that we think about several words at once. Let us go on to consider this.

Multiple meanings

'Look, no sooner had we got out there than the wind blew up . . .'
'And the house blew up. And your cruiser blew up. And Mrs Hutchmeyer blew up and this Mr Piper . . .'
Hutchmeyer blew up.

The comic effect of this passage from Tom Sharpe's novel *The Great Pursuit* is due to the different meanings of *blow up*. Studying how people cope with these multiple meanings can lead to useful insights into word recognition. The crucial question is this: do humans just latch on to the first plausible meaning that crosses their mind? Or do they, as in speech production, consider many more options than they actually use?

Psychologists have known for quite some time that, in cases where more than one meaning is plausible, subjects are likely to activate all of them, often without realizing it. In one experiment, subjects were asked to complete unfinished sentences as quickly as they could, some of which contained ambiguous words (Mackay, 1966):

After taking the *right* (= 'correct' or 'right-hand') turn at the intersection I . . .
After taking the *left* turn at the intersection I . . .

Subjects took longer to begin completing the ambiguous sentences, and in dealing with them they stuttered more, they sometimes repeated themselves and they tended to produce ungrammatical sequences. This happened even when they claimed not to have noticed the ambiguity.

In another experiment, listeners were asked to wear earphones and were instructed to pay attention to a sentence being played into their right ear, which they would have to paraphrase (Lackner and Garrett, 1972). This sentence was sometimes ambiguous, as in:

The spy *put out* (= 'extinguish' or 'display') the torch as our signal to attack.

Into the other, unattended ear the researchers played a sentence which could resolve the ambiguity:

The spy *extinguished* the torch in the window.
The spy *displayed* the torch in the window.

The subjects interpreted the attended sentence in accordance with the un-attended message, even though they were not consciously aware of having

Figure 16.1   Subconscious processing

heard it: they had no idea why they chose the particular reading of *put out* that they did (figure 16.1). Once again, this suggests that people may subconsciously consider more meanings than they are aware of.

A similar conclusion was reached in a phoneme monitoring experiment: 'Press a button if you come to a word starting with B' (Foss, 1970). Subjects monitored the required phoneme more slowly if the previous word was ambiguous, as in:

The seamen started to *drill* (drill holes or take part in a lifeboat drill?) before they were ordered to.

Once again, this happened even when those taking part claimed not to have noticed the ambiguity.

The overall conclusion to be drawn from these experiments is that when the same sequence of sounds has two meanings which fit equally well, people activate both and then select one, even if they are not aware of this process going on. But suppose a hearer is confronted with an ambiguous word in which one of the meanings is far less probable than the other. What happens then?

Take a sentence such as 'Aloysius was stuck in the jam for three hours'. Was Aloysius detained in congested and stationary traffic, or in a preserve containing fruit? And how might one decide? Either one could briefly consider both meanings of the word, then choose the most appropriate one. Alternatively, the likelihood of being stuck in traffic rather than fruit preserve is so strong that one would initially think of the traffic meaning only. In this case, fruit preserve would be considered only when prompted, perhaps if the speaker continued: 'The soles of his shoes were glued to the sticky mess.' The hearer would then realize that he had been led 'up the garden path', and he would then retrace his steps, abandoning his original interpretation of congested traffic. Which of these scenarios is the most likely?

This question was investigated in an ingenious experiment (Swinney, 1979). People were asked to listen to sentences such as the following:

For years the government building had been plagued with problems. The man was not surprised when he found several spiders, roaches and other bugs in the corner of his room.

While listening, the subjects were given a lexical decision task. Immediately after *bugs* – a word which is potentially ambiguous, though not in this context – three letters were flashed up onto a screen and subjects were asked, 'Is this a word?' People responded to the task faster if the original sentence included a word related in meaning to the lexical decision item. Therefore, if they had just heard the word *bugs*, subjects responded faster to ANT than they did to SEW. But there was one further finding. After hearing the sentence above, where *bugs* clearly relates to insects, people responded as fast to SPY as they did to ANT (figure 16.2). This result suggests that subjects briefly activate both meanings of a homonym, even in cases where one of them is inappropriate. These extra meanings are available very briefly, probably for less than a second. If the lexical decision task was moved more than two or three syllables away from the ambiguous word, the 'priming' effect disappeared, suggesting that one's mind wipes away extra words quite fast and does not leave them floating around indefinitely.

Figure 16.2   Activation of irrelevant meanings

Of course, one might argue that anything to do with governments was bound to elicit the spy sense of *bug*. But this experiment cannot be explained away so easily, because a number of other researchers have confirmed that people activate irrelevant meanings (e.g. Seidenberg *et al.*, 1982; Kinoshita, 1986). A further effect found in lexical decision tasks is that people respond faster to words with several meanings, an effect apparently unconnected with word frequency (Jastrzembski, 1981). This difference in the treatment of words with one and more than one meaning is a further piece of indirect evidence for the simultaneous activation of multiple meanings.

These findings indicate that in word recognition, as in word production, humans routinely contemplate many more words than they finally select. How, then, do they narrow down these numerous candidates? This is the topic of the next section.

Armies of words

'By-the-bye, what became of the baby?' said the Cat. 'I'd nearly forgotten to ask.'
'It turned into a pig', Alice answered . . .
'Did you say "pig" or "fig"?' said the Cat.

When the Cheshire Cat failed to hear Alice's answer as to what had happened to the baby, it is significant that it did not ask: 'Did you say "pig" or "big" or "fig"?' even though *big* is a possible misinterpretation of the sequence [pɪg]. It had used its common sense to eliminate unlikely words, and narrowed down the choice to two plausible candidates.

This is what appears to happen in speech recognition. Speakers flash up on their mental screen, as it were, any word that is consistent with what they hear, then make use of all available evidence – syntactic and semantic – to narrow down the possibilities. The more information they are able to bring to bear on the situation, the faster they can come to a decision. They recognize words more quickly in normal, plausible contexts than in strange, unacceptable ones (Marslen-Wilson and Tyler, 1980, 1981). Furthermore, people start doing this as soon as they hear any part of a word, and (as noted in chapter 1) they are often able to recognize a word before a speaker has finished saying it.

A whole army of words, it seems, marches up for consideration each time a word begins to be spoken. Some researchers have suggested that this army is specifically based on word beginnings (Marslen-Wilson and Tyler, 1980, 1981). According to this theory, a listener, on hearing the sequence *sta-*, immediately accesses the whole set of words beginning with *sta-* in the mental lexicon. This set is referred to as the 'word-initial cohort'. A cohort was originally a division of the Roman army, and one current dictionary definition is 'any band of warriors or associates'. So one must imagine metaphorically these serried ranks of words lined up ready for selection: *stab, stack, stag, stagger, stagnate, stalactite, stalagmite, stamina, stammer, stamp, stampede, stance, stand, standoffish, static* . . . and so on. (Although they are listed here for the sake of illustration in alphabetical order, there is no suggestion that this is their order in the cohort.)

The word initial cohort then gets narrowed down. Suppose one heard:

John was trying to get some bottles down from the top shelf. To reach them he had to *sta* . . .

The words immediately preceding *sta* . . . would enable a hearer to cut down the range of possibilities by restricting the choice to verbs: *stab, stack, stagger, stagnate, stammer, stamp, stampede, stand* . . . and so on. The topic of the preceding

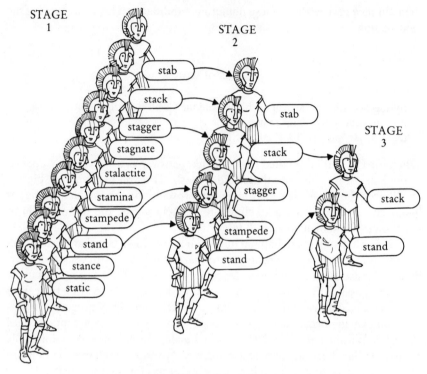

STAGE
1

STAGE
2

STAGE
3

stab

stack

stagger

stagnate

stalactite

stamina

stampede

stand

stance

static

stab

stack

stagger

stampede

stand

stack

stand

Figure 16.3   The cohort model

sentence, John getting down bottles, would then narrow the choice down to *stack* or *stand*. So with these two possibilities in mind, a hearer can very quickly reject *stack* and select *stand* as soon as [n] is heard (figure 16.3).

This cohort model incorporates a number of important facts about word recognition: first, many more words are activated than are needed; second, speakers utilize all kinds of information in order to reach their decision; third, they reach this decision fast, often while the word is still being spoken. There are, however, a number of problems associated with the theory, above all the fact that it requires undistorted acoustic signals at the beginning of the word. It could not cope with the *?ate* (*gate*, *bait*, *date*) situation discussed earlier in the chapter, where the first sound was indistinct: if a wrong decision was made the wrong cohort would be activated. A further problem is that it assumes that there are a fixed number of recognizable words in a person's mental lexicon: it does not make allowance for novelties, such as *fishling* (chapter 14), or compounds, as in *verandah table sprays* (Sparck-Jones, 1984).

In addition, the cohort model assumes that all words will be recognized at least by the end of the word: yet this is not the case. Short words are often identified one or two words after they have been spoken. Although a provisional decision may have been made before or around the end of the word, sure identification happens later (Grosjean, 1985). This is because one can often tell that a short word has ended only by the arrival of the next word. If you hear the sequence *bun*, then *bun*, *bundle*, *bunny*, *bunch* are all possibilities. One further problem with the cohort model is that it does not distinguish between a provisional identification and a sure one, so it does not explain how people change their preliminary guesses, which they sometimes do (Grosjean, 1985).

We therefore need a model which can cope with indistinct acoustic information at the beginning of the word, and also one which allows a person to continually update their opinions. Both these features occur in spreading activation models (e.g. Elman and McClelland, 1984; McClelland and Elman, 1986), as outlined in the last chapter for selecting words.

In a spreading activation model for word recognition, hearers start activating possible candidates as soon as a few segments of the word have been heard. Any sound identified will immediately form links with all those words which contain it in approximately the appropriate place. Any candidate is then linked up with its possible meanings: semantics influences the narrowing down of sounds, just as the sounds affect the meaning. As more information is added, some words will get an added boost, others will fade away. Take a word such as *bracelet*. Suppose this had initially been heard as *blace* . . . At first, words such as *blame*, *blade* will be activated to a level higher than *bracelet*, but when these fail to match the overall word, *bracelet* eventually turns out to be a better fit and the others are suppressed (McClelland and Elman, 1986). One's guesses as to the word being heard are continually updated, partly due to hearing more of it, partly due to integrating what has been heard with the context (figure 16.4).

The overall model, then, is very similar to that found in word production. Words which are likely to fit get more and more excited, until one finally pops up. Those that are unwanted will gradually be suppressed. The main difference is that the recognition process typically starts with sounds rather than meanings. Since words are spoken fast, and need to be interpreted fast, there may also be more attention to word beginnings than word endings, in the hope that the early sections of a word can lead to a decision.

Although many researchers are coming round to the notion that this represents a reasonable idea of how words are recognized, there are still a number of details which need to be specified. 'Spreading activation' models allow quite a lot of variation, just as 'internal combustion engines' can vary considerably from one to another. And the model described just now is in many ways somewhat vague, and has simply said that everything sets off everything else that is remotely connected with it. We need to know more about how all these excited words are controlled.

For example, as with word selection, some mechanism is required which specifies when firm identification occurs. We mentioned a possible device for word selection which collects up information for each word (chapter 15). A similar mechanism is probably needed for recognition. Each word might have

PERCEIVED SEQUENCE

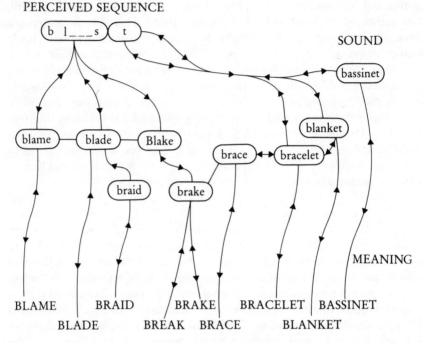

Figure 16.4   A spreading activation model

a level at which it 'pops up', with allowances for different types of information to counterbalance one another: a lot of phonetic information might involve somewhat less semantic information and vice versa (Morton, 1979). In addition, a 'score-board' might be needed which keeps track of the relative probability of different word candidates. One might envisage a device (figure 16.5)

	Stage I Likelihood rankings				Stage II Likelihood rankings		
	(order of probability)						
BLAME	1	2	2	→	–	–	–
BLADE	2	3	1		–	–	–
BREAK	3	1	4	→	–	–	–
BRACE	4	4	3		–	–	–
BRACELET	–	–	–		1	2	1
BLANKET	–	–	–	→	2	1	2
	Perceptual evidence	Frequency probability	Context		P	F	C

Figure 16.5   Possible score-board system

which from moment to moment assigned to every item a relative probability rating for each of three factors: perceptual evidence, frequency weighting and contextual evidence (Norris, 1986).

These requirements indicate that although spreading activation models present a plausible account of how the mind works in recognizing words, they are still in an early outline stage, and many details still need to be filled in.

Summary

This chapter has looked at word recognition. It noted that owing to the impossibility of mentally recording the sound of a word in full, hearers had to rely on informed guesswork to fill in the gaps.

As in speech production, it turned out that speakers consider many more words than they eventually select. A huge number are activated, then those that are not required are gradually suppressed. The same type of spreading activation model found in word production is also found in word recognition – even though many details are still obscure.

The processes involved in word production and word recognition have given us some clues as to how the various sections of the mental lexicon are organized in relation to one another. But a number of questions remain. These will be discussed in the next chapter.

17

Odd Arrangements and Funny Solutions
— *The organization of the mental lexicon* —

If God had designed a beautiful machine to reflect his wisdom and power, surely he would not have used a collection of parts generally fashioned for other purposes. Orchids were not made by an ideal engineer; they are jury-rigged from a limited set of available components ... Odd arrangements and funny solutions are the proof of evolution – paths that a sensible God would never tread but that a natural process, constrained by history, follows perforce.

Stephen Jay Gould, The Panda's Thumb

We are now in a position to start summarizing the conclusions reached in previous chapters. As we piece together the various findings we need to consider the nature of the human word-store. Is it a streamlined, well-designed device? Or is it a hotchpotch which has been cobbled together in the course of evolution, like orchids in the quotation above? According to one biologist, nature is an excellent tinkerer, not a divine artificer (Jacob, 1977). Parts of living organisms get modified for new purposes and compromises have to be made. The human mouth and throat is moderately useful for eating, speaking and breathing but is not ideal for any of them. More jagged teeth might be better for eating, but would interfere with the production of sounds. Our streamlined throat is useful for speech, but allows us to choke since the windpipe cannot be closed off. Language in general, according to one writer, is an evolutionary mishmash: 'Language has grown up like any big city: room by room ... house by house, street by street ... and all this is boxed together, tied together, smeared together' (Mauthner, quoted in Blackburn, 1984: 8). The mental lexicon is part of language. So do we find a similar collection of odd arrangements and funny solutions?

A mix-up

Words, we have said, are like coins, with meaning and word class on the one side and sounds on the other. The fragility of the links between the two sides of the coin provide one piece of evidence that the mental lexicon is an evolutionary mish-mash. This link is easily broken, as shown by the common but frustrating experience of knowing that a word exists, and being quite sure of its meaning, but being unable to clothe it in sounds, as when a professor said: 'Brain-half, but I can't think of its proper name.' Later she remembered *cerebral hemisphere*.

There is no intrinsic link between sound and meaning. The connection is arbitrary, apart from a small number of onomatopoeic words, such as *splash*, *bow-wow*, *quack-quack* – and even these differ from language to language: French ducks say *cancan*, and Danish ones go *rap-rap*. From time to time, individual languages may build up idiosyncratic associations between certain sound sequences and particular meanings (Chapman, 1984). For example, the sequence *-ump* in *bump, clump, dump, hump, lump, slump* and *thump* 'suggests a feeling of awkwardness or clumsy impact', according to a newspaper article (John Ayto, in *The Observer*, November 1985), and the writer George Orwell claimed that the words *plumb, plunge* and *plummet* indicate that 'the sound *plum-* or *plun-* has something to do with bottomless oceans' (quoted in Bolton, 1984: 34). But such links are of minor importance, and variable.

There may be 'a thread of sound symbolism in language, a thread conceivably universal' (Brown *et al.*, 1955: 389), in the sense that certain sounds are reliably judged to be more appropriate for certain meanings than others. In a famous experiment German subjects were presented with two line drawings, one composed of curves, the other of spikes and angles (Köhler, 1947). *Takete* and *maluma*, they were told, were the names to be applied to them, and they were asked which name was appropriate for which drawing. Overwhelmingly the rounded drawing was labelled *maluma* and the spiky one *takete*, and this finding was replicated both in America (Holland and Wertheimer, 1964) and in Tanganyika (Davis, 1961). But in spite of this result, no natural language links up [t], [k] with spikes, or [m], [l] with curves. This slender thread of sound symbolism, therefore, appears to exist only with respect to forced choices between nonsense words, and fades away in actual language use.

The sounds of words, therefore, seem to be easily unhooked from their meaning and word class. Why should this be? Why in the course of time do meaning and sound not join up, since each word requires both ingredients? One possibility is that the two parts are inherently detachable because the component dealing with the semantics and word class is arranged conveniently for production, whereas the phonology is organized primarily for speedy recognition. Let us explore this idea further.

Words seem to be organized in semantic fields (chapter 7), and within these fields there are strong bonds between co-ordinates which share the same word class. As far as producing speech is concerned, this is a useful arrangement. A speaker can then pick easily from a particular topic area, comparing several possible words which are linked closely together. 'Linked closely together', incidentally, is more likely to mean 'having a direct and strong connection' than literally 'located near one another'. The meaning side of a word, therefore, seems to be organized primarily in a way which helps speech planning. But this is quite inconvenient from the point of view of comprehension, for which it would be more useful to have all instances of the same sound sequence closely bound – *That was a good hit!*, *Felix hit the dog*, *a hit record*, and so on – as in a printed dictionary. This would enable a hearer to compare them fast. The semantic side of the coin, then, favours production in its organization.

Phonology, on the other hand, is quite inconveniently organized from the point of view of producing speech. It would be far better for production if the sound of each word was tightly bound to the meaning within its semantic field. Then nobody would ever have the embarrassing experience of accidentally saying *masturbate* instead of 'masticate' – a fairly common error. 'I always masturbate my food properly', said someone explaining why he never got indigestion. In a lexicon that was well organized for production, these two words would not be so inconveniently close. As it is, words which sound similar, particularly at their beginnings and ends, are those which are most closely linked. But from the point of view of word recognition it is useful to have similar sounding words together. Hearers can then examine several of them together, and find the best fit for what they have heard. The phonological component of the mental lexicon, therefore, appears to be organized primarily in accordance with the needs of recognition (Fay and Cutler, 1977).

Of course, the phonological representation in the mental lexicon is not exactly what a person hears. This is impossible, because different people have different pronunciations. The signals in the sound waves have to be converted into a form which can be matched against a person's internal representation. However, there are a couple of pieces of evidence which suggest that the internal form may be somewhat closer to its auditory image than its pronunciation.

First, in language learning situations people build up a passive vocabulary before they can actively use it. It can take a child months to discover how to say a particular word she knows quite well (chapter 12). This suggests that the sound structure of vocabulary is stored primarily in an auditory form.

Second, errors such as *moggy barsh* (boggy marsh), *reap of hubbish* (heap of rubbish), *leak wink* (weak link) suggest that words, after being retrieved from the mental lexicon, have to be assembled for production. The words are stored correctly, as shown by the fact that speakers often correct themselves after switching over sounds in this way. A possible explanation for this type of confusion is that, after being selected, words have to be put into a form in which they can be pronounced. A 'scan-copying' mechanism appears to come into play. The speaker scans the mental representation and copies it over into a form in which it can be articulated, checking off each segment as it is dealt with (Shattuck-Hufnagel, 1979). Occasionally this mechanism goes wrong. It muddles up the sounds involved, especially if they are similar. If each word was ready assembled in the form it which it was to be used, this type of error would be unlikely to occur. As far as the phonology is concerned, then, the lexicon is stored primarily in auditory terms, and production requires a complicated conversion of an auditory representation into a sequence which can be pronounced (figure 17.1).

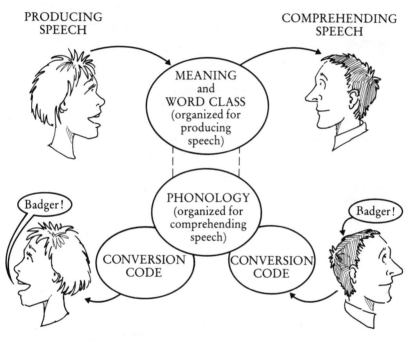

Figure 17.1   The fragility of the meaning–sound link

The mental lexicon, therefore, seems to be a mixed system which has found a workable compromise between the requirements of production and those of comprehension. The component that is required first in each case has imposed its demands on the organization. Production begins with the semantics and syntax, so these are arranged to suit production. Recognition begins with phonology, so this is organized to suit recognition. These differently organized components may be a hangover from a much earlier stage of evolution, when thoughts were not put into words and when listening for sounds was of major importance for survival. Now that meaning and sound are both required together, the links between them are relatively tenuous, and sometimes break down.

However, it may be an oversimplification to regard the mental lexicon as a simple tug-of-war between perception and production. There are signs that it has been further modified in order to take into account the needs of memory. Within each component, the set-up may have been modified not only to aid speedy retrieval but also to make words easier to remember. For example, the arrangement of words into word classes, and into clumps of co-ordinates, possibly occurs at least partly because the memory needs a more structured system in order to cope with the tens of thousands of words involved.

The mental lexicon, therefore, is a cobbled-together compromise in which the needs of production, perception and memory are all partially satisfied. Furthermore, on closer inspection it proves even messier, because of the way in which it overlaps with other aspects of cognition and language. Let us go on to consider this.

A rough map

In outline, then, the mental lexicon can be regarded as consisting of two major components: semantic–syntactic and phonological. Perhaps these components should be viewed as towns on a map: first, Semtown which contains both meaning and word class specifications, and second Phontown, containing the sounds. Both of these are linked to Novtown, which deals with the creation of new words (figure 17.2).

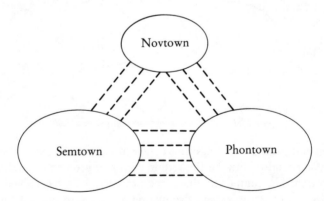

Figure 17.2   Components of the mental lexicon

To continue the map analogy, each town has only a small portion on the surface but consists to a large extent of a vast underground network. On the surface, outline addresses are marked: the semantic fields in Semtown, the phonological 'area codes' in Phontown. These constitute the entrance-points to the underground network. Then one can descend ever deeper, like Alice going down the rabbit-hole, until one finds the detailed information required. The further one travels in these subterranean tunnels, the more one can retrieve. Some of the tunnels are well worked and well lit, others have to be created afresh.

However, the underground tunnels stretch not only downwards but also sideways, linking up with tunnels from other 'towns'. The Semtown tunnels join up with tunnels from a person's general cognitive ability, allowing someone to link up an enormous amount of general knowledge and memory. Because the tunnels join, a tunnel starting in Semtown might be the same tunnel as one starting in a general memory section. It is therefore impossible to say where the 'meaning' of a word ends and general knowledge begins. Other tunnels from Semtown link up with the syntax of a language, with verbs in particular being intermingled with general syntactic rules. And all areas have links with the 'back-up' store, showing how words can be split up into morphemes, and via this, with the lexical tool-kit, which contains procedures for making new words (figures 17.3 and 17.4).

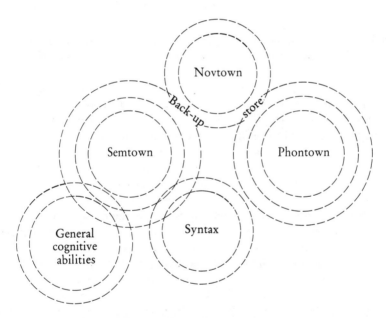

Figure 17.3   'Aerial' view of links with other components

Finding a word in the mental lexicon can be envisaged as following a path through this complex network, with some network links being stronger than others. For well-known, common words the paths are well worn, and it is easy to travel fast. But for words used only occasionally the paths are narrow and dimly lit. Meanwhile, new tunnels are perpetually being dug. Furthermore, the

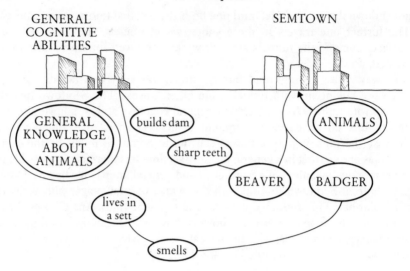

Figure 17.4   'Subterranean' view of some Semtown links

word itself cannot ultimately be regarded as a finite package. Since each word has links with so many others, and with general memory information, all these connections are in a sense part of the sum total of what we mean by a 'word'.

The analogy of 'towns' and 'tunnels' is helpful, in that it emphasizes the multidimensional nature of the links. It also suggests that, as with real towns, it is hard to see exactly where one town ends and another begins: it is easier to identify them by their centres than by their boundaries. But it is flawed, in that it suggests that the buildings and tunnels are fixed structures, with locations that can be pinpointed. This may be misleading because the quality of the links in each case is probably more important than the exact location of the various pieces of information. The situation is somewhat like a life support system in a hospital: what matters is the effectiveness of the pumps and tubes carrying blood and oxygen to the patient. The exact location of the equipment from which the tubes emerge is not of primary importance.

An alternative way of looking at the connections between these 'lexical towns', therefore, is one which focuses on the inhabitants rather than on fixed architecture. Any town in real life is likely to contain 'social networks', groups of people who know one another and interact fairly often (Milroy, 1987). Sometimes these networks are dense and multiplex, in that the same group of people live, work and play together. However, even in dense networks, some of these people are likely to have links outside their particular social group, though not such close ones. This analogy can be transferred to the mental lexicon. Each 'lexical town' will contain numerous clumps of words with strong ties to one another – though each clump will also have bonds, though weaker ones, with other groups. In addition, there will be connections, weaker

still, between individuals in different towns. Like social ties, these connections will fluctuate. Perhaps the most important difference between lexical
networks and people networks is that the links between words are likely to be
much more numerous than the social bonds any one individual can contract
(figure 17.5).

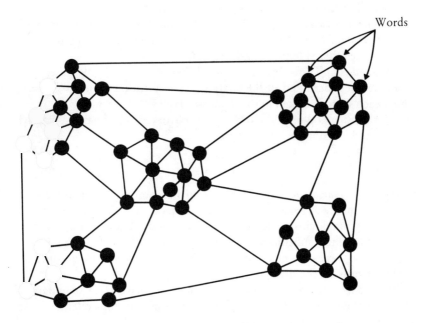

Words

Figure 17.5   Clumps of words

Overall, the links are numerous and interwoven. They are carried by
millions of miles of nerve fibres within the brain. According to one writer, 'If
the cells and fibre in one human brain were all stretched out end to end, they
would certainly reach to the moon and back. Yet the fact that they are not
arranged end to end enabled man to go there himself. The astonishing tangle
within our heads makes us what we are' (Blakemore, 1977: 85). The mental
lexicon, and the links from it to other portions of the brain, account for a largish
portion of this astonishing tangle.

Basic specifications for Dumbella

Let us now return to Dumbella, the robot we talked about earlier (chapter 3).
Our overall aim, we said, was to provide outline specifications for program-
ming her so that she would behave like a human being as far as her word-store
is concerned. The overall layout for this was illustrated in figure 17.3 (above).

But, just to be clear that the robot-manufacturer has understood the main points made in this book, let us provide a summary list of the requirements, split into four sections: units, layout, processing, novelty.

A UNITS

1 *Words*. The lexicon is to contain whole words.

2 *Meaning versus sound.* These whole words should be viewed as coins, in which one side is detachable from the other. On one side is the meaning and word class, on the other side the sound structure.

3 *Word analysis.* The sides of the word-coin are to be analysable, and the characteristics identified in the analysis are to form the basis of the ways in which each word is linked to the other words.

4 *Types of analysis.* Words are to be analysable in terms of meaning, word class, sounds, and morphological structure.

B LAYOUT

5 *Modular organization.* The lexicon is to be composed of two main components or modules: semantic–syntactic which contains the meaning and word class, and phonological which contains the sounds. These components are to be linked to a third subsidiary component, 'the lexical tool-kit', which contains procedures for creating new words. The link is to be via a back-up store showing how words can be divided into morphemes.

6 *Overlapping modules.* The modules should not have rigid boundaries but should overlap with each other and with adjoining modules relating to syntax and general cognitive abilities.

7 *Network.* Each module is to be a complex network, with relatively tight links to other items within the module and somewhat looser links to items outside the module. Within each module there should be clusters of dense, multiplex mini-networks.

8 *Fluid structure.* The network must not be a fixed structure, although some links should be fairly durable. New links must be able to be added easily, and old ones must be alterable.

9 *Mixed organization.* The semantic–syntactic module is to be arranged conveniently for production, with words from the same semantic field linked closely. The phonological module is to be organized for fast identification of sounds in speech comprehension, with words which sound similar tightly bonded together.

C PROCESSING

10 *Entry points.* There should be entry points into the network, which activate it: via a semantic field in word production, and via acoustic signals in speech comprehension. Within each of the two main components there should be

'signposts' to entry points in the other component for words which have been partially processed.

11 *Parallel processing.* Numerous links must be activated simultaneously while the network is being used. This will involve links for many more words than will eventually be required.

12 *Interactive activation.* Any point or node in the network which has been activated must automatically activate those points with which it is most closely connected. Information must flow down the links in both directions.

13 *Excitation and inhibition.* Perpetual alteration and adjustment of the activated parts must be possible while the network is in use, with continuous arousal of new sections and damping down of previously aroused ones as processing proceeds. This excitation and inhibition must go on until a suitable word is found.

14 *Narrowing down.* A search for a word should involve first a broad sweep through a general area, in which numerous words which fulfil certain outline specifications are to be activated. The extra ones are to be gradually filtered out as the word required is selected. Narrowing down within each component should happen simultaneously, though the one which initiated the search should be in the lead.

D NOVELTY

15 *Endless exploration.* The links which can be activated, both within the mental lexicon and in adjacent components, such as syntax and memory, must be potentially limitless. This is to allow full exploration to continue until sufficient has been activated to cope with the word being sought, or until an alternative is found.

16 *Additional segmentation.* A word must optionally be able to be analysed into its component morphemes. This is primarily to aid comprehension of unfamiliar words, or as a preliminary to creating new words.

17 *New word creation.* It must be possible to create a potentially infinite number of new words with the aid of the back-up information used in segmentation, and the 'lexical tool-kit'.

These outline specifications, at least, must be fulfilled if Dumbella is to behave at all like a human in her ability to cope with words.

Can Dumbella be programmed?

'Hal (for Heuristically programmed Algorithmic computer, no less) was a masterwork of the third computer breakthrough . . . Most of his communication with his shipmates was by means of the spoken word. Poole and Bowman could talk to Hal as if he were a human being, and he would reply in the perfect idiomatic English he had learned during the fleeting weeks of his electronic childhood.'

This optimistic account of a talking computer occurs in Arthur Clarke's space fiction novel *2001: A Space Odyssey*. In real life, however, we are nowhere near being able to create robots like Hal. At the moment, it is simply impossible to program Dumbella with anything like the flexibility and power of the human mental lexicon. The most powerful device we have for producing models, the computer, is quite inadequate: 'It is a striking fact that computers are virtually incapable of handling the routine mental feats of perception, language comprehension and memory retrieval that we humans take so much for granted' (Elman and McClelland, 1984: 337). The most elaborate computer models of the lexicon so far are those which have attempted to simulate speech perception (e.g. Elman and McClelland, 1984; McClelland and Elman, 1986; Marcus, 1984; Klatt, 1980). Yet not one of them has come near the overall requirements of human word recognition.

Furthermore, we may be fundamentally wrong in assuming that the mind works like a computer. Two foremost researchers argue that 'attempts to model this area of human behavior have been seriously hampered by the lack of an adequate computational framework ... There is a fundamental flaw in the assumption that speech perception is carried out in a processor that looks at all like a digital computer' (Elman and McClelland, 1984: 369–70).

Perhaps, therefore, a true breakthrough cannot occur until there is a new 'technological revolution'. A leap forward in understanding is often due to the drawing of an analogy between the ill-understood phenomenon and a technological artefact (chapter 3): the heart is a pump, the lungs are bellows. As one medical writer notes: 'Once man succeeded in making equipment which performed – looms, furnaces, forges, kilns, bellows, whistles and irrigation ditches – he was confronted by mechanisms ... which were intelligibly systematic and systematically intelligible. By mechanising his practical world, man inadvertently paved the way to the mechanisation of his theoretical world. The success of modern biology is not altogether due to the technology with which we pursue it; the number of technical images we have for thinking about it play an almost equally important part' (Miller, 1978: 182).

It is possible, therefore, that we have not yet invented the technology which enables us to think usefully about the detailed working of the mental lexicon. As one researcher comments: 'There are some human abilities that appear to me to defeat our present understanding. We sense that there is something difficult to explain, but it seems almost impossible to state clearly what the difficulty is. This suggests that our entire way of thinking about such problems may be incorrect' (Crick, 1979: 219).

Summary

This chapter has looked at the overall organization of the mental lexicon. We have suggested that it is an evolutionary mishmash, in which the various parts have developed over the ages into a somewhat strange amalgam: the two main components are organized in different ways, one for easy production, the other for easy comprehension. And they both overlap and interact with other aspects of language and cognition.

18
Last Word
— Final comments and future questions —

Words, words, words, in songs and stories . . .
If I only understood them. . . .
Would not this world be changed?
Pete Seeger, 'Words, Words, Words'

'In the beginning was the word. But by the time the second word was added to it, there was trouble. For with it came syntax, the thing that tripped up so many people' (Simon, 1981: 111). This quotation represents the standard linguistic viewpoint over the past quarter century – that syntactic structures are the most complex aspect of language, and consequently the area which merits the greatest attention. Words, in contrast, have been regarded as a collection of bric-à-brac, a jumble of miscellanea which speakers learn 'item by item, in a more or less rote fashion' (Katz and Fodor, 1963: 183). They were treated as superficial trivia, 'brittle pieces of crystalline structure that may be picked up but not absorbed' (Bolinger, 1965: 571).

This book, on the other hand, has taken the opposite viewpoint, which has been expressed clearly by a neurologist: 'I must confess that I have always been more impressed with the capacity of the human brain to discriminate, characterize and store in memory the thirty thousand plus arbitrary words in active use than with the complexity claimed to be involved in learning a few dozen syntactic algorithmic rules' (Marin, 1982: 64). As we noted in chapter 1, the large number of words stored and the speed with which they are retrieved suggests that the mental lexicon is a far more complex matter than most people have supposed – and this has been borne out in the course of the book.

The complexity of the mental lexicon and the relative ease with which children learn to cope with words indicate that humans are probably innately equipped with a knowlege of how to acquire and handle a huge vocabulary: 'The only way to begin to account for the child's wizardry as a word learner, given the sheer weight of how much there is to be learned, is to grant that the child brings a great deal to the "original word game"' (Carey, 1978: 265).

In this chapter we shall suggest how humans have evolved this complex word-store, and show why it gives them such an advantage over other animals. We shall also point out a number of unsolved questions concerning the mental lexicon.

Coins for communication

Many living organisms – humans included – are endowed with complex and specialized communication systems. Humans, together with cows, grass-hoppers, frogs, monkeys, owls and numerous other species, are genetically programmed to use sound signals as their main means of conveying messages to one another. These signals, like words, can be viewed as coins, with meaning on one side and sound on the other. The human sound–meaning coin, the word, is more sophisticated than that of most animals because of one crucial factor: humans have an apparently innate realization that the coins are not just indivisible wholes. Instead, they can be analysed. Various characteristics can be identified on each side, and some of these will be more prominent than others. This single factor is the foundation-stone on which the complexities of the mental lexicon have been built.

The ability to analyse each 'side' of a word into a set of characteristics and the capacity to rank these in order of importance has several consequences. First, it provides an efficient storage method: words which share characteristics can be linked together in clumps. This allows many more words to be stored than if each one had to be memorized entirely separately. Second, it enables words to be retrieved fast, since the speaker/hearer can first locate a word by means of an 'area code', a selection of prominent characteristics, before filling in the details.

A further, major benefit of the capacity to dissect words is that they do not have to be exact, either in sound or meaning: something may be regarded as the same word if it shares sufficient characteristics: a bird with one leg and pink and blue stripes might still be classified as a parrot, though a somewhat un-typical one. The word *butter* can be recognized, whether pronounced as *butter*, *budder*, or *bu'er*.

In the animal world, flexible systems are far superior to fixed ones. In a rigid system, a creature is often forced into a disadvantageous yes/no decision based on rule-of-thumb criteria. Take the case of the blue-footed booby, a type of bird resident in the Galapagos Islands. If a baby booby falls out of the nest, its parents don't recognize it: they have a simple rule of thumb: 'In the nest ours, out of the nest nothing to do with us' (Gould, 1984). Similarly, reed warblers feed baby cuckoos purely on the basis of the orange colour of the inside of the mouth: this is the only method they have of identifying their own offspring. This type of mistake is typical of communication systems with a fixed set of signals. A more complex fixed system might use more numerous criteria, but this puts a greater strain on the memory and still allows the baby cuckoo syndrome to occur. A fluid system, combined with a computational ability to make decisions, is enormously powerful and useful. Its flexibility in day-to-day usage and its potential for responding to altered circumstances, make its owners far more likely to adapt and survive over the ages. Such systems inevitably change continually. In view of this, it is quite suprising how often educated humans mistakenly deplore the fluidity of words as 'sloppy' or 'slipshod', making repeated pleas for language to remain unaltered, as if it were a statue to be preserved and admired rather than a tool for communication (Aitchison, 1981).

Another advantage of a human-type word system is that the 'coins' can be disassembled and then the pieces reassembled to create new words. Furthermore, the system allows for reorganization: as more words are acquired the items can be shuffled about or reanalysed in order to allow more efficient storage or easy retrieval – as indeed seems to happen throughout life.

The characteristics into which meaning and sound are analysed are likely to be similar – though not identical – the world over. The human eye, ear and mind are predisposed to pay attention to certain phenomena, as shown by the fact that children and adults select the same type of characteristics when they analyse words. However, as we have seen, their priorities differ: characteristics which are important for children are less salient for adults and vice versa. Children, therefore, appear to be pre-programmed with an instinctive knowledge of how to deal with words. But an understanding of how best to organize and rank the characteristics which they have identified develops slowly, partly as a result of maturation and partly through discovering the nature of the particular language to which they are exposed. The fact that different languages may require different organizations of the mental lexicon leads to a number of questions for the future.

Questions for the future

This book has concentrated on the lexicon underlying the spoken language of native English speakers. Other languages have been mentioned only intermittently, and then only if they supported the findings based on English. But English is just one of the several thousand languages spoken in the world. There is no reason to believe that it is superior, or inferior, to the others. It happens to have been studied in more depth than most other languages, so more information about it is available. But is it representative of all languages? Are our conclusions about the mental lexicon likely to be true of other languages also?

So far, the answer appears to be both 'yes' and 'no'. Certain areas of other languages have been studied, and these suggest that there are both similarities and differences in the ways in which the mental lexicon is organized in languages unlike our own. To take random examples, a study of child language acquisition in Telegu, a Dravidian language spoken in south India, showed that the semantic errors of children acquiring Telegu are very like those found among English-speaking children (Nirmala, 1981). And in a miscellaneous collection of Indian languages, many of the word formation processes found have strong similarities to English ones (Krishnamurti and Mukherjee, 1984).

On the other hand, studies of Welsh slips of the tongue indicate that phonological storage might be somewhat different from that for English words, especially as the initial consonant of Welsh words 'mutates' systematically, depending on the preceding word (Meara and Ellis, 1982). Polish speakers are reported to respond somewhat differently from English speakers in word association experiments (Grover Stripp and Bellin, 1985). Serbo-Croatian speakers probably deal with morphologically related words in a way that is not found in English: one inflected form seems to be at the hub of an array of related forms (Lukatela *et al.*, 1980). The treatment of morphology is possibly also different from English in Dutch (Jarvella and Meijers, 1983) and German (Mackay, 1979). French speakers perhaps pay more attention to syllables than English speakers when they recognize words (Mehler, 1981).

These various papers suggest that it is important to compare and contrast findings obtained from English with those from other languages. Only in this way will we be able to confidently distinguish universal features of the mental lexicon from those which are due to the structure of an individual language.

Furthermore, the conclusions reached here about English need to be checked against other English-type languages. The evidence on which this book is based – mainly the speech of British and Americans – may be untypical in two ways. First, a large proportion of English speakers are literate. This may have affected lexical storage. Many English adults report that they are unable to remember a word unless they see it written down. And spelling can play a role in lexical decision tasks involving spoken words (Jakimik *et al.*, 1985). This suggests that the spoken form of a word can be affected by its written representation. And the reverse is true: whether or not someone can read a word may depend on features of its spoken form, such as the rhythm (Black and Byng, 1986). There is now a large and informative body of work on reading and spelling (for a useful summary see Ellis, 1984). But the interrelationship between the spoken and written forms is not well understood (for a useful discussion see Allport and Funnell, 1981).

A second biasing factor is that many English speakers are monolingual, a situation somewhat unusual in the world at large, where it is common for humans to use more than one language. There is no general agreement as to how the various lexicons are organized in the minds of bilingual and multilingual speakers (for a useful bibliography on vocabulary in a second language see Meara, 1983) – though there is increasing evidence in favour of a single integrated network (Green, 1986; Kirsner *et al.*, 1984). If a person knows two languages reasonably well, words are possibly subconsciously activated in both languages and then the language which is not wanted is suppressed (Green, 1986). The fact that words from both languages are activated is shown by the occurrence of blends, such as *Springling* (a blend of the English word *spring* and the equivalent German word *Frühling*). It is further shown by the fact that if two speakers who both know the same set of languages are in conversation, then they often switch from one to the other, inserting lexical items from one language into the syntax of the other. The process of selecting one word and inhibiting the others when two languages are involved seems to be fairly similar to the process of choosing the most relevant word from a range of stylistic options. However, considerably more work is needed in order to fully understand how the various languages known by a single speaker are interwoven.

A further general problem which needs attention is the interrelationship between the lexicon and general syntactic rules, those which do not depend on the choice of any particular lexical item. Recently a number of linguists have come round to the view that the lexicon is the central component of a person's internal grammar, and that the syntax is subsidiary (e.g. Hudson, 1984a). If this viewpoint becomes general, then indeed 'the time of the lexicon has set in' (Hakulinen, quoted in Bauer, 1983: 1).

Much desire to learn ...

'Where there is much desire to learn, there of necessity will be much arguing, much writing, many opinions; for opinion in good men is but knowledge in the making.' These words of the seventeenth-century poet John Milton (in his treatise *Areopagitica*) are entirely applicable to the research going on around the mental lexicon today. This book has attempted to summarize a number of important findings, and tried to provide an overall picture of how people store and find words. Hopefully, it is on the right track – though undoubtedly some sections of it will be controversial, and others might be proved wrong by future research.

However, as a wise elderly monk William said in Umberto Eco's novel *The Name of the Rose*: 'Books are not made to be believed, but to be subjected to enquiry.' My overall hope is that this book will act as a jumping-off point – that many people will, like me, be captivated by the importance and mystery of words, and will work to fill in the gaps in our knowledge. Perhaps in the foreseeable future we shall solve the secrets of the human word-store, much as our ancestors solved the mystery of the circulation of the blood:

> On a huge hill,
> Cragged and steep, Truth stands, and he that will
> Reach her, about must, and about must goe;
> And what the hills suddennes resists, win so.
>
> John Donne, 'Satyre III'

Abbreviations and Symbols

The following abbreviations are mostly used for standard dictionaries after their first mention in the text, where they are referred to by their full title:

CCED = *Collins Concise English Dictionary* (1982)
COD = *Concise Oxford Dictionary* (1982)
LCED = *Longman Concise English Dictionary* (1982)

In order to make the text easier to read, spoken words have been mostly represented by their conventional written form. Where the use of phonetic symbols is unavoidable, these are put into square brackets [ ], regardless of their linguistic status (i.e. phones or phonemes, on which see Aitchison, in press). Most of the phonetic symbols are obvious, as with [d] as in *did*. The following non-obvious IPA (International Phonetic Alphabet) symbols occur in the text:

[θ] as at the beginning of *thin*
[ʃ] as at the beginning of *shin*
[ŋ] as at the end of *sing*

An asterisk * is intermittently used to denote an impossible word, phrase, or sentence, as in *kbad*, which is not a possible English word.

References

Where two dates appear together, e.g. Freud, S. (1901/1975), the first is the date of the original publication of the work, the second the date of the edition listed in the references.

Adams, V. (1973). *An introduction to modern English word-formation*. London: Longman.
Aitchison, J. (1972). 'Mini-malapropisms'. *British Journal of Disorders of Communication* 7, 38–43.
Aitchison, J. (1981). *Language change: Progress or decay?* London: Fontana; New York: Universe.
Aitchison, J. (1981a). 'Mad, bad and dangerous to know'. *Literary Review*, July, 81–2.
Aitchison, J. (1983). *The articulate mammal: An introduction to psycholinguistics*. 2nd edn. London: Hutchinson; New York: Universe.
Aitchison, J. (1983–4). 'The mental representation of prefixes'. *Osmania Papers in Linguistics* 9–10 (Nirmala Memorial Volume), 61–72.
Aitchison, J. (1985). 'Cognitive clouds and semantic shadows'. *Language and Communication* 5, 69–93.
Aitchison, J. (in press). *Linguistics*. 3rd edn. Teach Yourself Books. Sevenoaks, Kent: Hodder and Stoughton.
Aitchison, J. (in press). 'Reproductive furniture and extinguished professors'.
Aitchison, J. and Chiat, S. (1981). 'Natural phonology or natural memory? The interaction between phonological processes and recall mechanisms'. *Language and Speech* 24, 311–26.
Aitchison, J. and Straf, M. (1982). 'Lexical storage and retrieval: a developing skill'. In Cutler (1982).
Allport, D. A. and Funnell, E. (1981). 'Components of the mental lexicon'. *Philosophical Transactions of the Royal Society of London* B 295, 397–410. (Also published as *Psychological mechanisms of language*. London: The Royal Society and the British Academy.)
Anderson, R. C. and Freebody, P. (1981). 'Reading comprehension and the assessment and acquisition of word knowledge'. In J. T. Guthrie (ed.), *Comprehension and teaching*. Newark, Del.: International Reading Association.
Anglin, J. M. (1970). *The growth of word meaning*. Cambridge, Mass.: MIT Press.

Arbib, M. A., Caplan, D. and Marshall, J. C. (1982). *Neural models of language processes*. New York: Academic Press.

Armstrong, S. L., Gleitman, L. R. and Gleitman, H. (1983). 'What some concepts might not be'. *Cognition* 13, 263–308.

Aronoff, M. (1976). *Word formation in generative grammar*. Linguistic Inquiry Monograph 1. Cambridge, Mass.: MIT Press.

Asch, S. E. and Nerlove, H. (1960). 'The development of double-function terms in children: An exploratory investigation'. In B. Kaplan and S. Wapner (eds), *Perspectives in psychological theory*. New York: International Universities Press. Also in De Cecco (1967).

Ayto, J, (1980). 'When is a meaning not a meaning?'. *Times Educational Supplement*, 25 April, 45.

Ayto, J. (1984). 'The vocabulary of definition'. In D. Goetz and T. Herbst (eds), *Theoretische und praktische Probleme der Lexicographie*. Munich: Max Hueber Verlag, 50–62.

Baars, B. J. (1980). 'The competing plans hypothesis: An heuristic viewpoint on the causes of errors in speech'. In H. W. Dechert and M. Raupach (eds), *Temporal variables in speech*. The Hague: Mouton.

Baddeley, A. (1976). *The psychology of memory*. New York: Basic Books.

Baddeley, A. (1983). *Your memory: A user's guide*. Harmondsworth: Penguin.

Balota, D. A. and Chumbley, J. I (1984). 'Are lexical decisions a good measure of lexical access? The role of word-frequency in the neglected decision stage'. *Journal of Experimental Psychology: Human Perception and Performance* 10, 340–57.

Bar-Adon, A. and Leopold, W. F. (1971). *Child language: A book of readings*. Englewood Cliffs, NJ: Prentice-Hall.

Barrett, M. (1983). 'Scripts, prototypes and the early acquisition of word meaning'. *Working Papers of the London Psycholinguistics Research Group* 5, 17–26.

Barton, M. (1971). 'Recall of generic properties of words in aphasic patients'. *Cortex* 7, 73–82.

Bates, E., Benigni, R., Bretherton, L., Camioni, R. and Volterra, V. (1979). *The emergence of symbols: Communication and cognition in infancy*. New York: Academic Press.

Bauer, L. (1983). *English word-formation*. Cambridge: Cambridge University Press.

Benson, D. F. (1979). 'Neurologic correlates of anomia'. In H. Whitaker and H. A. Whitaker (eds), *Studies in neurolinguistics* 4. New York: Academic Press.

Berko, J. and Brown, R. (1960). 'Psycholinguistic research methods'. In P. H. Mussen (ed.), *Handboook of research methods in child development*. New York: Wiley.

Berlin, B. and Kay, P. (1969). *Basic color terms: Their universality and evolution*. Berkeley, Calif. and Los Angeles: University of California Press.

Bever, T. G., Carroll, J. M. and Miller, L. A. (1984). *Talking minds*. Cambridge, Mass.: MIT Press.

Bickerton, K. (1981). 'Jargon aphasia: A headache in aphasiology'. *Working Papers of the London Psycholinguistics Research Group* 3, 13–24.

Bierwisch, M. (1967). 'Some semantic universals of German adjectivals'. *Foundations of Language* 3, 1–36.

Bierwisch, M. (1970). 'Semantics'. In J. Lyons (ed.), *New horizons in linguistics*. Harmondsworth: Penguin Books.

Black, M. and Byng, S. (1986). 'Prosodic constraints on access in reading'. *Cognitive Neuropsychology* 3, 369–409.

Blackburn, S. (1984). *Spreading the word: Groundings in the philosophy of language*. Oxford: Clarendon Press.

Blakemore, C. (1977). *Mechanics of the mind*. Cambridge: Cambridge University Press.

Blasdell, R. and Jensen, P. (1970). 'Stress and word position as determinants of imitation in first language learners'. *Journal of Speech and Hearing Research* 12, 193–202.

Bloomfield, L. (1933). *Language*. New York: Holt.

Bolinger, D. (1965). 'The atomization of meaning'. *Language* 41, 555–73.

Bolton, W. F. (1984). *The language of 1984*. Oxford: Basil Blackwell.

Bond, Z. S. and Garnes, S. (1980). 'Misperceptions of fluent speech'. In Cole (1980).

Bouma, H. and Bouwhuis, D. G. (1984). *Attention and performance X: Control of language processes*. Hillsdale, NJ: Erlbaum.

Bowerman, M. (1978). 'Systematizing semantic knowledge: Changes over time in the child's organization of meaning'. *Child Development* 49, 977–87.

Bowerman, M. (1980). 'The structure and origin of semantic categories in the language learning child'. In D. Foster and S. Brandes (eds), *Symbol as sense: New approaches to the analysis of meaning*. New York: Academic Press.

Bowerman, M. (1982). 'Reorganizational processes in lexical and syntactic development'. In E. Wanner and L. R. Gleitman, (eds), *Language acquisition: The state of the art*. Cambridge: Cambridge University Press.

Bradley, D. C. (1983). *Computational distinctions of vocabulary type*. Bloomington, Ind.: Indiana University Linguistics Club.

Bradley, D. C., Garrett, M. F. and Zurif, E. B. (1980). 'Syntactic deficits in Broca's aphasia'. In Caplan (1980).

Braine, M. D. S. (1974). 'On what might constitute learnable phonology'. *Language* 50, 270–99.

Bresler, F. (1983). *The mystery of Georges Simenon*. London: Heinemann.

Browman, C. P. (1978). *Tip of the tongue and slip of the ear: Implications for language processing*. *UCLA Working Papers in Phonetics* 42.

Browman, C. P. (1980). 'Perceptual processing: Evidence from slips of the ear'. In Fromkin (1980).

Brown, E. K. (1984). *Linguistics today*. London: Fontana.

Brown, G. and Yule, G. (1983). *Discourse analysis*. Cambridge: Cambridge University Press.

Brown, R. (1958). *Words and things*. New York: The Free Press.

Brown, R. (1970). *Psycholinguistics: Selected papers*. New York: The Free Press.

Brown, R. and Berko, J. (1960). 'Word association and the acquisition of grammar'. *Child Development* 31, 1–14. Also in De Cecco (1967).

Brown, R., Black, A. H. and Horowitz, A. E. (1955). 'Phonetic symbolism in natural languages'. *Journal of Abnormal Social Psychology* 50, 388–93. Also in Brown (1970).

Brown, R. and McNeill, D. (1966). 'The "tip of the tongue" phenomenon'. *Journal of Verbal Learning and Verbal Behaviour* 5, 325–37. Also in Brown (1970).

Brownell, H. H., Potter, H. H. and Michelow, D. (1984). 'Sensitivity to lexical denotation and connotation: a double dissociation?' *Brain and Language* 22, 253–65.

Bulmer, R. (1967). 'Why is the cassowary not a bird?' *Man* (new series) 2, 5–25. Also in M. Douglas (ed.), *Rules and meanings*. Harmondsworth: Penguin, 1973.

Butterworth, B. (1979). 'Hesitation and the production of neologisms in jargon aphasia'. *Brain and Language* 8, 133–61.

Butterworth, B. (1980). *Speech production*, vol. 1. New York: Academic Press.

Butterworth, B. (1980a). 'Evidence from pauses in speech'. In Butterworth (1980).

Butterworth, B. (1983). *Language production*, vol. 2. New York: Academic Press.

Butterworth, B. (1983a). 'Lexical representation'. In Butterworth (1983).

Butterworth, B., Howard, D. and McLoughlin, P. (1984). 'The semantic deficit in aphasia: The relationship between semantic errors in auditory comprehension and picture naming'. *Neuropsychologia* 22, 409–26.

Caplan, D. (1980). *Biological studies of mental processes*. Cambridge, Mass.: MIT Press.

Carey, S. (1978). 'The child as word learner'. In M. Halle, J. Bresnan and G. A. Miller (eds), *Linguistic theory and psychological reality*. Cambridge, Mass.: MIT Press.

Carroll, L. (1876/1967). *The annotated snark*, ed. M. Gardner. Harmondsworth: Penguin.

Chaika, E. O. (1974). 'A linguist looks at "schizophrenic" language'. *Brain and Language* 1, 257–76.

Chand, N. (n.d.). *Improve your vocabulary*. New Delhi: New Light Publications.

Chapman, R. (1984). *The treatment of sounds in language and literature*. Oxford: Basil Blackwell.

Cheshire, J. (1982). *Variation in an English dialect: A sociolinguistic study*. Cambridge: Cambridge University Press.

Chiat, S. (1979). 'The role of the word in phonological development'. *Linguistics* 17, 591–610.

Chiat, S. (1983). 'Why Mikey's right and my key's wrong: The significance of stress and word boundaries in learning to output language'. *Cognition* 14, 275–300.

Chomsky, N. (1965). *Aspects of the theory of syntax*. Cambridge, Mass.: MIT Press.

Chomsky, N. (1970). 'Remarks on nominalization'. In R. A. Jacobs and P. Rosenbaum (eds), *Readings in English transformational grammar*. Waltham, Mass.: Ginn.

Chomsky, N. (1978). 'On the biological basis of langue capacities'. In G. A. Miller and E. Lenneberg (eds), *Psychology and biology of language and thought*. New York: Academic Press. Also in Chomsky (1980).

Chomsky, N. (1980). *Rules and representations*. Oxford: Basil Blackwell.

Chomsky, N. and Halle, M. (1968). *The sound pattern of English*. New York: Harper and Row.

Clark, E. V. (1973). 'What's in a word? On the child's acquisition of semantics in his first language'. In T. E. Moore (ed.). *Cognitive development and the acquisition of language*. New York: Academic Press.

Clark, E. V. (1981). 'Lexical innovations: how young children learn to create new words'. In W. Deutsch (ed.), *The child's construction of language*. London: Academic Press.

Clark, E. V. (1982). 'The young word maker: A case study of innovation in the child's lexicon'. In E. Wanner and L. R. Gleitman (eds), *Language acquisition: The state of the art*. Cambridge: Cambridge University Press.

Clark, E. V. and Clark, H. (1979). 'When nouns surface as verbs'. *Language* 55, 767–811.

Clark, E. V., Hecht, B. F. and Mulford, R. C. (1986). 'Coining complex compounds in English: affixes and word order acquisition'. *Linguistics* 24, 7–30.

Clark, H. H. and Gerrig, R. J. (1983). 'Understanding old words with new meanings'. *Journal of Verbal Learning and Verbal Behavior* 22, 591–608.

Clark, R. (1974). 'Performing without competence'. *Journal of Child Language* 1, 1–10.

Cohen, J. M. and Cohen, M. J. (1980). *Dictionary of modern quotations*. 2nd edn. Harmondsworth: Penguin.

212   *References*

Cole, R. A. (1980). *Perception and production of fluent speech*. Hillsdale, NJ: Erlbaum.
Cole, R. A. and Jakimik, J. (1980). 'A model of speech perception'. In Cole (1980).
Coleman, E. B. (1964). 'Supplementary report: On the combination of associative probabilities in linguistic contexts'. *Journal of Psychology* 57, 95–9.
Coleman, L. and Kay, P. (1981). 'Prototype semantics: The English word *lie*'. *Language* 57, 26–44.
Collingwood, R. G. (1938). *The principles of art*. Oxford: Oxford University Press.
Collins, A. M. and Quillian, M. R. (1969). 'Retrieval time from semantic memory'. *Journal of Verbal Learning and Verbal Behavior* 8, 240–47.
Conan Doyle, A. (1930/1981). *The complete Sherlock Holmes*. Harmondsworth: Penguin.
Cooper, W. and Walker, E. C. T. (1979). *Sentence processsing*. Hillsdale, NJ: Erlbaum.
Crick, F. H. C. (1979). 'Thinking about the brain'. *Scientific American* 241 (3), 219–30.
Critchley, M. (1970/1973). 'Articulatory defects in aphasia: The problem of Broca's aphasia'. In Goodglass and Blumstein (1973).
Cutler, A. (1980). 'Productivity in word formation'. *Papers from the Sixteenth Regional Meeting, Chicago Linguistic Society*, 45–51.
Cutler, A. (1981). 'Degrees of transparency in word formation'. *Canadian Journal of Linguistics* 26, 73–7.
Cutler, A. (1982). *Slips of the tongue and language production*. Berlin: Mouton. (Also published as *Linguistics* 19 (1982).)
Cutler, A. (1982a). 'The reliability of speech error data'. In Cutler (1982).
Cutler, A. (1983). 'Lexical complexity and sentence processing'. In Flores d'Arcais and Jarvella (1983).
Cutler, A., Hawkins, J. A. and Gilligan, G. (1985). 'The suffixing preference: A processing explanation'. *Linguistics* 23, 723–58.
Cutler, A. and Norris, D. (1979). 'Monitoring sentence comprehension'. In Cooper and Walker (1979).
Davis, R. (1961). 'The fitness of names to drawings. A cross-cultural study in Tanganyika'. *British Journal of Psychology* 52, 259–68.
De Cecco, J. P. (1967). *The psychology of thought, language and instruction*. New York: Holt, Rinehart & Winston.
Deese, J. (1965). *The structure of associations in language and thought*. Baltimore, Md.: The Johns Hopkins University Press.
Dell, G. S. and Reich, P. A. (1980). 'Toward a unified model of slips of the tongue'. In Fromkin (1980).
Diack, H. (1975). *Standard literacy tests*. St Albans: Hart-Davis.
Diller, K. C. (1978). *The language teaching controversy*. Rowley, Mass.: Newbury House.
Downing, P. (1977). 'On the creation and use of English compound nouns'. *Language* 53, 810–42.
Drachman, G. (1973). 'Some strategies in the acquisition of phonology'. In M. J. Kenstowicz and C. W. Kisseberth (eds), *Issues in phonological theory*. The Hague: Mouton.
Dressler, W. (1985). *Morphophonology: The dynamics of derivation*. Ann Arbor, Mich.: Karoma.
Dupré, J. (1981). 'Natural kinds and biological taxa'. *Philological Review* 40, 66–90.
Dupreez, P. (1974). 'Units of information in the acquisition of language'. *Language and Speech* 17, 369–76.
Eimas, P. D. (1985). 'The perception of speech in early infancy'. *Scientific American* 252 (1), 34–40.

Eimas, P., Siqueland, E., Jusczyk, P. and Vigorito, J. (1971). 'Speech perception in infants'. *Science* 171, 303–6.

Ellis, A. W. (1980). 'On the Freudian theory of speech errors'. In Fromkin (1980).

Ellis, A. W. (1984). *Reading, writing and dyslexia: A cognitive analysis*. London: Lawrence Erlbaum Associates.

Ellis, A. W. (1985). 'The production of spoken words: A cognitive neuropsychological perspective'. In A. W. Ellis (ed.), *Progress in the psychology of language*, vol. 2. London: Lawrence Erlbaum Associates.

Elman, J. and McClelland, J. L. (1984). 'Speech perception as a cognitive process: The interactive activation model'. In N. Lass (ed.), *Speech and language: Advances in basic research and practice*, vol. 10. New York: Academic Press.

Entwisle, D. R. (1966). *Word-associations of young children*. Baltimore, Md.: The Johns Hopkins University Press.

Farrar, F. W. (1865). *Chapters on language*. London: Longmans Green.

Fay, D. (1977). 'Prefix errors'. Paper presented at the 4th Salzburg International Linguistics Meeting, August 1977.

Fay, D. and Cutler, A. (1977). 'Malapropisms and the structure of the mental lexicon'. *Linguistic Inquiry* 8, 505–20.

Ferguson, C. A. and Farwell, C. B. (1975). 'Words and sounds in early language acquisition'. *Language* 51, 439–91.

Fillmore, C. J. (1971). 'Types of lexical information'. In Steinberg and Jakobovits (1971).

Fillmore, C. J. (1975). 'An alternative to check-list views of meaning'. *Proceedings of the 1st Annual Meeting, Berkeley Linguistics Society*, 123–31.

Fletcher, P. and Garman, M. (1986). *Language acquisition*. 2nd edn. Cambridge: Cambridge University Press.

Flores d'Arcais, G. B. and Jarvella, R. J. (1983). *The process of language understanding*. New York: Wiley.

Fodor, J. A. (1981). *Representations: Philosophical essays on the foundations of cognitive science*. Cambridge, Mass.: MIT Press.

Fodor, J. A. (1983). *The modularity of mind*. Cambridge, Mass.: MIT Press.

Fodor, J. A., Garrett, M. F., Walker, E. C. T. and Parkes, C. H. (1980). 'Against definitions'. *Cognition* 8, 263–367.

Fodor, J. D., Fodor, J. A. and Garrett, M. F. (1975). 'The psychological unreality of semantic representations'. *Linguistic Inquiry* 6, 515–31.

Forster, K. (1976). 'Accessing the mental lexicon'. In Wales and Walker (1976).

Foss, D. (1970). 'Some effects of ambiguity upon sentence comprehension'. *Journal of Verbal Learning and Verbal Behavior* 9, 699–706.

Fourcin, A. J. (1978). 'Acoustic patterns and speech acquisition'. In N. Waterson and C. Snow (eds), *The development of communication*. Chichester: Wiley.

Fowler, C. A., Napps, S. E. and Feldman, L. (1985). 'Relations among regular and irregular morphologically related words in the lexicon as revealed by repetition priming'. *Memory and Cognition* 13, 241–55.

Frauenfelder, U. H. (1985). 'Cross-linguistic approaches to lexical segmentation'. *Linguistics* 23, 669–88.

Freud, S. (1901/1975). *The psychopathology of everyday life*. Transl. A. Tyson. Harmondsworth: Penguin.

Friederici, A. (1982). 'Syntactic and semantic processes in aphasic deficits: The availability of prepositions'. *Brain and Language* 15, 249–58.

References

Friederici, A. (1985). 'Levels of processing and vocabulary types: Evidence from on-line comprehension in normals and agrammatics'. *Cognition* 19, 133–66.

Fromkin, V. A. (1971). 'The non-anomalous nature of anomalous utterances'. *Language* 47, 27–52. Also in Fromkin (1973).

Fromkin, V. A. (1973). *Speech errors as linguistic evidence*. The Hague: Mouton.

Fromkin, V. A. (1980). *Errors in linguistic performance: Slips of the tongue, ear, pen, and hand*. New York: Academic Press.

Galton, F. (1883). *Inquiries into human faculty and its development*. London: Dent.

Ganong, W. F. (1980). 'Phonetic categorization in auditory word perception'. *Journal of Experimental Psychology: Human Perception and Performance* 6, 110–25.

Gardner, H. (1974). *The shattered mind*. New York: Random House.

Garnes, S. and Bond, Z. (1980). 'A slip of the ear: a snip of the ear? A slip of the year?'. In Fromkin (1980).

Garrett, M. F. (1976). 'Syntactic processes in sentence production'. In Wales and Walker (1976).

Garrett, M. F. (1980). 'Levels of processing in sentence production'. In Butterworth (1980).

Gibbs, R. W. and Gonzales, G. P. (1985). 'Syntactic frozenness in processing and remembering idioms'. *Cognition* 20, 243–59.

Glanzer, M. and Ehrenreich, S. L. (1979). 'Structure and search of the internal lexicon'. *Journal of Verbal Learning and Verbal Behavior* 18, 381–98.

Gleitman, H. and Gleitman, L. (1979). 'Language use and language judgement'. In C. J. Fillmore, D. Kempler and W. S.-Y. Wang (eds), *Individual differences in language ability and language behavior*. New York: Academic Press.

Gleitman, L. R. and Gleitman, H. (1970). *Phrase and paraphrase: Some innovative uses of language*. New York: Norton.

Goldstein, L. (1980). 'Bias and asymmetry in speech perception'. In Fromkin (1980).

Goodglass, H. (1978). *Selected papers in neurolinguistics*. Munich: Wilhelm Fink Verlag.

Goodglass, H. and Baker, E. (1976). 'Semantic field, naming and auditory comprehension in aphasia'. *Brain and Language* 3, 359–74. Also in Goodglass (1978).

Goodglass, H. and Blumstein, S. (1973). *Psycholinguistics and aphasia*. Baltimore, Md.: The Johns Hopkins University Press.

Goodglass, H., Kaplan, E., Weintraub, S. and Ackerman, N. (1976). 'The "tip-of-the-tongue" phenomenon in aphasia'. *Cortex* 12, 145–53.

Goodglass, H., Klein, B., Carey, P. and James, K. J. (1966). 'Specific semantic word categories in aphasia'. *Cortex* 2, 74–89.

Goodglass, H. and Menn, L. (1985). 'Is agrammatism a unitary phenomenon?'. In M. -L. Kean (ed.), *Agrammatism*. Orlando, Fla.: Academic Press.

Goodglass, H., Theurkauff, J. C. and Wingfield, A. (1984). 'Naming latencies as evidence for two modes of lexical retrieval'. *Applied Psycholinguistics* 5, 135–46.

Gordon, B. (1983). 'Lexical access and lexical decision: mechanisms of frequency sensitivity'. *Journal of Verbal Learning and Verbal Behaviour* 22, 22–44.

Gordon, B. and Caramazza, A. (1982). 'Lexical decision for open and closed class items: Failure to replicate differential frequency sensitivity'. *Brain and Language* 15, 143–80.

Gould, S. J. (1983). *The panda's thumb*. Harmondsworth: Penguin.

Gould, S. J. (1984). *Hen's teeth and horse's toes*. Harmondsworth: Penguin.

Gowers, E. (1986). *The complete plain words*. 3rd edn. London: HMSO.

Green, D. (1986). 'Control, activation and resource: A framework and a model for the control of speech in bilinguals'. *Brain and Language* 27, 210–23.

Green, J. (1982). *A dictionary of contemporary quotations*. London: Pan Books.

Greenberg, J. H. and Jenkins, J. J. (1964). 'Studies in the psychological correlates of the sound system of American English'. *Word* 20, 157–77.

Gregg, V. H. (1986). *Introduction to human memory*. London: Routledge & Kegan Paul.

Grice, H. P. (1975). 'Logic and conversation'. In P. Cole and J. Morgan (eds), *Syntax and semantics 3: Speech acts*. New York: Academic Press.

Grosjean, F. (1985). 'The recognition of words after their acoustic offset: Evidence and implications'. *Perception and Psychophysics* 38, 299–310.

Grover Stripp, M. and Bellin, W. (1985). 'Bilingual linguistic systems revisited'. *Linguistics* 23, 123–36.

Halle, M. and Clements, G. N. (1983). *Problem book in phonology*. Cambridge, Mass.: MIT Press.

Halle, M. and Vergnaud, J. R. (1980). 'Three-dimensional phonology'. *Journal of Linguistic Research* 1, 83–105.

Hand, C. R., Tonkovich, J. D. and Aitchison, J. (1979). 'Some idiosyncratic strategies utilized by a chronic Broca's aphasic'. *Linguistics* 17, 729–59.

Hart, J., Berndt, R. S. and Caramazza, A. (1985). 'Category-specific naming deficit following cerebral infarction'. *Nature* 316, 439–40.

Hayes, B. (1983). 'A grid-based theory of English meter'. *Linguistic Inquiry* 14, 357–93.

Hayes, B. (1984). 'The phonology of rhythm in English'. *Linguistic Inquiry* 15, 33–74.

Herbert, A. P. (1935). *What a word!* London: Methuen.

Holland, M. K. and Wertheimer, M. (1964). 'Some physiognomic aspects of naming, or *maluma* and *takete* revisited.' *Perception and Motor Skills* 19, 111–17.

Hopper, P. J. and Thompson, S. A. (1984). 'The discourse basis for lexical categories in universal grammar'. *Language* 60, 703–52.

Hotopf, W. H. N. (1980). 'Semantic similarity as a factor in whole-word slips of the tongue'. In Fromkin (1980).

Householder, F. W. (1966). 'Phonological theory: A brief comment'. *Journal of Linguistics* 2, 99–100.

Howard, D. V., McAndrews, M. P. and Lasaga, M. I. (1981). 'Semantic priming of lexical decisions in young and old adults'. *Journal of Gerontology* 36, 707–14.

Hudson, R. (1984). *Invitation to linguistics*. London: Martin Robertson.

Hudson, R. (1984a). *Word grammar*. Oxford: Basil Blackwell.

Hurford, J. (1981). 'Malapropisms, left-to-right listing, and lexicalism'. *Linguistic Inquiry* 12, 419–23.

Ingram, D. (1986). 'Phonological patterns in the speech of young children'. In Fletcher and Garman (1986).

Inhelder, B. and Piaget, J. (1964). *The early growth of logic in the child*. London: Routledge & Kegan Paul.

Jackendoff, R. (1983). *Semantics and cognition*. Cambridge, Mass.: MIT Press.

Jacob, F. (1977). 'Evolution and tinkering'. *Science* 196, 1161–6.

Jakimik, J., Cole, R. A. and Rudnicky, A. I. (1985). 'Sound and spelling in spoken word recognition'. *Journal of Memory and Language* 24, 165–78.

Jakobson, R. (1956). 'Two aspects of language and two types of aphasic disturbance'. In R. Jakobson and M. Halle, *Fundamentals of anguage*. The Hague: Mouton.

Jakobson, R. (1941/1968). *Child language, aphasia and phonological universals*. The Hague: Mouton.

Jakobson, R., Fant, G. and Halle, M. (1952). *Preliminaries to speech analysis: The distinctive features and their correlates*. Cambridge, Mass.: MIT Press.

James, W. (1981). *The principles of psychology*, vol. 1. Cambridge, Mass.: Harvard University Press.

Jarvella, R. J. and Meijers, G. (1983). 'Recognizing morphemes in spoken words: Some evidence for a stem-organized mental lexicon'. In Flores d'Arcais and Jarvella (1983).

Jastrzembski, J. E. (1981). 'Multiple meanings, number of related meanings, frequency of occurrence, and the lexicon'. *Cognitive psychology* 13, 278–305.

Jenkins, J. J. (1970). 'The 1952 Minnesota word association norms'. In Postman and Keppel (1970).

Johnson-Laird, P. N. (1983). *Mental models*. Cambridge: Cambridge University Press.

Katz, J. J. (1975). 'Logic and language: An examination of recent criticisms of intensionalism'. In K. Gunderson and G. Maxwell (eds), *Minnesota studies in philosophy of science*, vol. 6. Minneapolis, Minn.: University of Minnesota Press.

Katz, J. J. (1985). *The philosophy of linguistics*. Oxford: Oxford University Press.

Katz, J. J. and Fodor, J. A. (1963). 'The structure of a semantic theory'. *Language* 39, 170–210. Also in J. A. Fodor and J. J. Katz (eds), *The structure of language*. Englewood Cliffs, NJ: Prentice-Hall, 1964.

Kean, M. -L. (1977). 'The linguistic interpretation of aphasic syndromes: Agrammatism in Broca's aphasia, an example'. *Cognition* 5, 9–46.

Keil, F. C. and Batterman, N. (1984). 'A characteristic-to-defining shift in the development of word meaning'. *Journal of Verbal Learning and Verbal Behavior* 23, 221–36.

Kempson, R. (1977). *Semantic theory*. Cambridge: Cambridge University Press.

Kinoshita, S. (1986). 'Sentence context effect on lexically ambiguous words: Evidence for a postaccess inhibition process'. *Memory and Cognition* 13, 579–95.

Kintsch, W. (1974). *The representation of meaning in memory*. Hillsdale, NJ: Erlbaum.

Kintsch, W. (1984). 'Approaches to the study of the psychology of language'. In Bever, Carroll and Miller (1984).

Kirsner, K., Smith, M. C., Lockhart, R. S., King, M. L. and Jain, M. (1984). 'The bilingual lexicon: language-specific units in an integrated network'. *Journal of Verbal Learning and Verbal Behavior* 23, 519–39.

Klatt, D. (1980). 'Speech perception: a model of acoustic-phonetic analysis and lexical access'. In Cole (1980).

Klatt, D. H. (1981). 'Lexical representations for speech production and perception'. In Myers, Laver and Anderson (1981).

Köhler, W. (1947). *Gestalt psychology*. New York: Liveright.

Koriat, A. and Lieblich, I. (1974). 'What does a person in a "TOT" state know that a person in a "don't know" state doesn't know'. *Memory and Cognition* 2, 647–55.

Krishnamurti, B. H. and Mukherjee, A. (1984). *Modernization of Indian languages in news media*. Osmania Publications in Linguistics 2. Hyderabad, India: Osmania University.

Kuhl, P. and Miller, J. D. (1974). 'Discrimination of speech sounds by the chinchilla: /t/ vs /d/ in CV syllables'. *Journal of the Acoustical Society of America* 56, series 42 (abstract).

Kuhl, P. and Miller, J. D. (1975). 'Speech perception by the chinchilla: phonetic boundaries for synthetic VOT stimuli'. *Journal of the Acoustical Society of America* 57, series 49 (abstract).

Labov, W. (1973). 'The boundaries of words and their meanings'. In C.-J. N. Bailey and R. W. Shuy (eds), *New ways of analyzing variation in English*. Washington, DC: Georgetown University Press.

Lackner, J. R. and Garrett, M. F. (1972). 'Resolving ambiguity: Effects of biasing context in the unattended ear'. *Cognition* 1, 359–72.

Ladefoged, P. (1982). *A course in phonetics*. 2nd edn. New York: Harcourt Brace Jovanovich.

Lakoff, G. (1972). 'Hedges: A study in meaning criteria and the logic of fuzzy concepts'. *Papers of the Eighth Regional Meeting, Chicago Linguistic Society*, 183–228.

Lakoff, G. and Johnson, M. (1980). *Metaphors we live by*. Chicago: University of Chicago Press.

Laver, J. (1980). 'Monitoring systems in the neurolinguistic control of speech production'. In Fromkin (1980).

Lehiste, I. (1960). *An acoustic-phonetic study of internal open juncture. Phonetica*, Supplement 5.

Lehiste, I. (1972). 'The timing and utterances of linguistic boundaries'. *Journal of the Acoustical Society of America* 51, 2018–24.

Lehnert, M. (1971). *Rückläufiges Wörterbuch der englischen Gegenwartssprache*. Leipzig: VEB.

Lehrer, A. (1983). *Wine and conversation*. Bloomington, Ind.: Indiana University Press.

Lenneberg, E. (1967). *Biological foundations of language*. New York: Wiley.

Leopold, W. F. (1947). *Speech development of a bilingual child*, vol. 2: *Sound-learning in the first two years*. Evanston, Ill.: Northwestern University Press.

Liberman, A. M., Cooper, F., Shankweiler, D. and Studdert-Kennedy, M. (1967). 'Perception of the speech code'. *Psychological Review* 74, 431–61.

Liberman, A. M., Harris, K. S., Hoffman, H. S. and Griffith, B. C. (1957). 'The discrimination of speech sounds within and across phoneme boundaries'. *Journal of Experimental Psychology* 54, 358–68.

Liberman, A. M. and Mattingly, I. G. (1985). 'The motor theory of speech perception revised'. *Cognition* 21, 1–36.

Liberman, M. and Prince, A. (1977). 'On stress and linguistic rhythm'. *Linguistic Inquiry* 8, 249–336.

Lieberman, P. (1984). *The biology and evolution of language*. Cambridge, Mass.: Harvard University Press.

Lukatela, G., Gligorijevic, B., Kostic, A. and Turvey, M. T. (1980). 'Representation of inflected nouns in the internal lexicon'. *Memory and Cognition* 8, 415–23.

Lyons, J. (1968). *Introduction to theoretical linguistics*. Cambridge: Cambridge University Press.

Mackay, D. (1966). 'To end ambiguous sentences'. *Perception and Psychophysics* 1, 426–36.

Mackay, D. (1979). 'Lexical insertion, inflection, and derivation: creative processes in word production'. *Journal of Psycholinguistic Research* 8, 477–98.

Macken, M. A. (1980). 'The acquisition of stop systems: a cross-linguistic perspective'. In G. Yeni-Komshian, J. Kavanagh and C. A. Ferguson (eds), *Child phonology* I: *Perception and production*. New York: Academic Press.

Macnamara, J. (1982). *Names for things*. Cambridge, Mass.: MIT Press.

Manelis, L. and Tharp, D. A. (1977). 'The processing of affixed words'. *Memory and Cognition* 5, 690–5.

Maratsos, M. P. (1973). 'Decrease in the understanding of the word "big" in preschool children'. *Child Development* 44, 747–52.

Marchand, H. (1969). *The categories and types of present-day English word-formation*. 2nd edn. Munich: Bech.

Marcus, S. M. (1984). 'Recognizing speech: On the mapping from sound to word'. In Bouma and Bouwhuis (1984).

Marin, O. S. M. (1982). 'Brain and language: The rules of the game'. In Arbib, Caplan and Marshall (1982).

Marshall, J. C. (1977). 'Minds, machines and metaphors'. *Social Studies of Science* 7, 475–88.

Marslen-Wilson, W. D. and Tyler, L. K. (1980). 'The temporal structure of spoken language understanding'. *Cognition* 8, 1–71.

Marslen-Wilson, W. D. and Tyler, L. K. (1981). 'Central processes in speech understanding'. *Philosophical Transactions of the Royal Society of London* B 295, 317–32. (Also published as *Psychological mechanisms of language*. London: The Royal Society and the British Academy.)

Matthei, E. and Roeper, T. (1983). *Understanding and producing speech*. London: Fontana.

McCawley, J. D. (1983). 'The syntax of some English adverbs'. *Papers of the Nineteenth Regional Meeting, Chicago Linguistic Society*, 263–82.

McClelland, J. L. (1979). 'On the time relations of mental processes: An examination of systems of processes in cascade'. *Psychological Review* 86, 287–330.

McClelland, J. L. and Elman, J. E. (1986). 'The TRACE model of speech perception'. *Cognitive Psychology* 18, 1–86.

McShane, J. (1979). 'The development of naming'. *Linguistics* 17, 879–905.

McShane, J. (1980). *Learning to talk*. Cambridge: Cambridge University Press.

Meara, P. (1983). *Vocabulary in second language*. Specialised Bibliography 3. London: Centre for Information on Language Teaching and Research.

Meara, P. and Ellis, A. W. (1982). 'The psychological reality of deep and surface phonological representations: Evidence from speech errors in Welsh'. In Cutler (1982).

Mehler, J. (1981). 'The role of syllables in speech processing: Infant and adult data'. *Philosophical Transactions of the Royal Society of London* B 295, 333–52. (Also published as *Psychological mechanisms of language*. London: The Royal Society and the British Academy.)

Menn, L. (1978). 'Phonological units in beginning speech'. In A. Bell and J. B. Hooper (eds), *Syllables and segments*. Amsterdam: North-Holland.

Menn, L. and MacWhinney, B. (1984). 'The repeated morph constraint'. *Language* 60, 519–41.

Menyuk, P. and Menn, L. (1979). 'Early strategies for the perception and production of words and sounds'. In Fletcher and Garman (1979).

Meringer, R. and Mayer, K. (1895/1978). *Versprechen und Verlesen: Eine Psychologisch-Linguistische Studien*. Amsterdam: John Benjamins.

Miller, G. and Nicely, P. (1955). 'An analysis of perceptual confusions among English consonants'. *Journal of the Acoustical Society of America* 27, 338–52.

Miller, G. A. and Johnson-Laird, P. N. (1976). *Perception and language*. Cambridge: Cambridge University Press.

Miller, J. (1978). *The body in question*. New York: Random House.

Milroy, L. (1987). *Language and social networks*. 2nd edn. Oxford: Basil Blackwell.

Minsky, M. (1975). 'A framework for representing knowledge'. In P. H. Winston (ed.), *The psychology of computer vision*. New York: McGraw-Hill.

Morse, P. A. (1976). 'Speech perception in the human infant and rhesus monkey'. In S. Harnad, H. Steklis and J. Lancaster (eds), *Origins and evolution of language and speech. Annals of the New York Academy of Sciences*, vol. 280.

Morton, J. (1979). 'Word recognition'. In Morton and Marshall (1979).

Morton, J. and Marshall, J. C. (1979). *Psycholinguistics 2: Structure and processes*. London: Elek.

Motley, M. T. (1985). 'Slips of the tongue'. *Scientific American* 253 (3), 114–19.

Murrell, G. A. and Morton, J. (1974). 'Word recognition and morphemic structure'. *Journal of Experimental Psychology* 102, 963–8.

Myers, T. Laver, J. and Anderson, J. (1981). *The cognitive representation of speech* . Amsterdam: North-Holland.

Nelson, K. (1973). *Structure and strategy in learning to talk. Monographs of the Society for Research in Child Development* 38.

Nelson, K., Rescorla, L., Gruendel, J. and Benedict, H. (1978). 'Early lexicons: What do they mean?' *Child Development* 49, 960–8.

Nirmala, C. (1981). *First language (Telegu) development in children: A short descriptive study*. Unpublished doctoral diss., Osmania University, Hyderabad.

Norris, D. (1986). 'Word recognition: Context effects without priming'. *Cognition* 22, 93–136.

Norris, D. and Cutler, A. (1985). 'Juncture detection'. *Linguistics* 23, 689–706.

Ohala, J. J. (1981). 'Articulatory constraints on the cognitive representation of speech'. In Myers, Laver and Anderson (1981).

Osherson, D. N. and Smith, E. E. (1981). 'On the inadequacy of prototype theory as a theory of concepts'. *Cognition* 9, 35–58.

Palmer, F. (1984). *Grammar*. Harmondsworth: Penguin.

Parlett, D. (1981). *Botticelli and beyond: 100 of the world's best word games*. New York: Pantheon Books.

Peters, A. (1983). *The units of language acquisition*. Cambridge: Cambridge University Press.

Pollio, H. R., Barlow, J. M., Fine, H. J. and Pollio, M. (1977). *Psychology and the poetics of growth: Figurative language in psychology, psychotherapy and education*. Hillsdale, NJ: Erlbaum.

Postman, L. and Keppel, G. (1970). *Norms of word associations*. New York: Academic Press.

Priestley, T. M. S. (1977). 'One idiosyncratic strategy in the acquisition of phonology'. *Journal of Child Language* 4, 45–66.

Pulman, S. G. (1983). *Word meaning and belief*. London: Croom Helm.

Putnam, H. (1975). 'The meaning of "meaning"'. In K. Gunderson (ed.), *Language, mind and knowledge. Minnesota Studies in the Philosophy of Science*, vol. 7. Minneapolis, Minn.: University of Minnesota Press.

Quine, W. V. (1971). 'The inscrutability of reference'. In Steinberg and Jakobovits (1971).

Quine, W. V. (1961/1985). 'The problem of meaning in linguistics'. In Katz (1985).

Randall, J. H. (1980). '*-ity*: a study in word formation restrictions'. *Journal of Psycholinguistic Research* 9, 523–33.

Richards, M. M. (1979). 'Sorting out what's in a word from what's not: Evaluating

Clark's semantic features acquisition theory'. *Journal of Experimental Child Psychology* 27, 1–47.

Romaine, S. (1983). 'On the productivity of word formation: Rules and limits of variability in the lexicon'. *Australian Journal of Linguistics* 3, 177–200.

Room, A. (1979). *Room's dictionary of confusibles*. London: Routledge & Kegan Paul.

Rosch, E. (1975). 'Cognitive representations of semantic categories'. *Journal of Experimental Psychology: General* 104, 192–233.

Rubin, D. C. (1975). 'Within word structure in the tip-of-the-tongue phenomenon'. *Journal of Verbal Learning and Verbal Behavior* 14, 392–397.

Rubin, G. S., Becker, C. A. and Freeman, R. H. (1979). 'Morphological structure and its effect on visual word recognition'. *Journal of Verbal Learning and Verbal Behavior* 18, 757–67.

Saporta, S. (1961). *Psycholinguistics: A book of readings*. New York: Holt Rinehart & Winston.

Schank, R. C. (1972). 'Conceptual dependency: A theory of natural language understanding'. *Cognitive Psychology* 3, 552–631.

Seashore, R. H. and Eckerson, L. D. (1940). 'The measurement of individual differences in general English vocabularies'. *Journal of Educational Psychology* 31, 14–38.

Segui, J. (1984). 'The syllable: A basic perceptual unit in speech processing?'. In Bouma and Bouwhuis (1984).

Seidenberg, M. S., Tanenhaus, M. K., Leiman, J. M. and Bienkowski, M. (1982). 'Automatic access of meanings of ambiguous words in context: Some limitations of knowledge based processing'. *Cognitive Psychology* 14, 489–537.

Selkirk, E. O. (1980). 'The role of prosodic categories in English word stress'. *Linguistic Inquiry* 11, 563–605.

Selkirk, E. O. (1982). *The syntax of words*. Linguistic Inquiry Monograph 7. Cambridge, Mass.: MIT Press.

Selkirk, E. O. (1984). *Phonology and syntax: the relation between sound and structure*. Cambridge, Mass.: MIT Press.

Shattuck-Hufnagel, S. (1979). 'Speech errors as evidence for a serial-ordering mechanism in sentence production'. In Cooper and Walker (1979).

Shattuck-Hufnagel, S. and Klatt, D. H. (1979). 'The limited use of distinctive features and markedness in speech production: Evidence from speech error data'. *Journal of Verbal Learning and Verbal Behavior* 18, 41–55.

Simon, J. (1981). *Paradigms lost*. London: Chatto & Windus.

Slobin, D. I. (1973). 'Cognitive prerequisites for the development of grammar'. In C. A. Ferguson and D. I. Slobin (eds), *Studies of child language development*. New York: Holt.

Smith, E. and Medlin, D. (1981). *Categories and concepts*. Cambridge, Mass.: Harvard University Press.

Smith, M. K. and Montgomery, M. B. (1982). 'The semantics of winning and losing'. Paper presented at the Southeastern Conference on Linguistics, March 1982.

Smith, M. K., Pollio, H. R. and Pitts, M. K. (1981). 'Metaphor as intellectual history: Conceptual categories underlying figurative usage in American English from 1675–1975'. *Linguistics* 19, 911–35.

Smith, N. V. S. (1973). *The acquisition of phonology*. Cambridge: Cambridge University Press.

Solomon, R. L. and Howes, D. H. (1951). 'Word frequency, personal values and visual duration threshholds'. *Psychological Review* 58, 256–70.

Sparck-Jones, K. (1984). 'Compound noun interpretation problems'. In F. Fallside and W. A. Woods, *Computer speech processing*. Englewood Cliffs, NJ: Prentice-Hall.

Sperber, D. and Wilson, D. (1985/6). 'Loose talk'. *Proceedings of the Aristotelian Society* (new series) 86, 153–71.

Sperber, D. and Wilson, D. (1986). *Relevance: Communication and cognition*. Oxford: Basil Blackwell.

Sperber, H. (1930). *Einführung in die Bedeutungslehre*. 2nd edn. Leipzig: K. Schroeder Verlag.

Stampe, D. (1969). 'The acquisition of phonemic representation'. *Proceedings of the Fifth Regional Meeting, Chicago Linguistic Society*, 433–44.

Stampe, D. (1979). *A dissertation on natural phonology*. New York: Garland Press.

Stanners, R. F., Neiser, J. J. and Painton, S. (1979). 'Memory representation for prefixed words'. *Journal of Verbal Learning and Verbal Behavior* 18, 733–43.

Steinberg, D. D. and Jakobovits, L. A. (1971). *Semantics: An interdisciplinary reader in philosophy, linguistics and psychology*. Cambridge: Cambridge University Press.

Stemberger, N. (1985). *The lexicon in a model of speech production*. New York: Garland.

Swinney, D. (1979). 'Lexical access during sentence comprehension: (Re)consideration of context effects'. *Journal of Verbal Learning and Verbal Behavior* 18, 645–59.

Swinney, D. A. and Cutler, A. (1979). 'The access and processing of idiomatic expressions'. *Journal of Verbal Learning and Verbal Behavior* 18, 523–34.

Taft, M. (1981). 'Prefix stripping revisited'. *Journal of Verbal Learning and Verbal Behavior* 20, 289–97.

Taft, M. and Forster, K. I. (1975). 'Lexical storage and retrieval of prefixed words'. *Journal of Verbal Learning and Verbal Behavior* 15, 607–20.

Taylor, S. H. (1978). 'On the acquisition and completion of lexical items'. *Parasession on the lexicon*. Chicago: Chicago Linguistic Society.

Tourangeau, R. and Sternberg, R. J. (1982). 'Understanding and appreciating metaphors'. *Cognition* 11, 203–44.

Tulving, E. (1972). 'Episodic and semantic memory'. In E. Tulving and W. Donaldson (eds), *Organization of memory*. New York: Academic Press.

Tweney, R., Tkacz, S. and Zaruba, S. (1975). 'Slips of the tongue and lexical storage'. *Language and Speech* 18, 388–96.

Van den Broecke, M. P. R. and Goldstein, L. (1980). 'Consonant features in speech errors'. In Fromkin (1980).

Velten, H. V. (1943). 'The growth of phonemic and lexical patterns in infant language'. *Language* 19, 281–292. Also in Bar-Adon and Leopold (1971).

Vihmann, M. M. (1978). 'Consonant harmony: Its scope and function in child language'. In J. H. Greenberg (ed.), *Universals of human language*. Stanford, Calif.: Stanford University Press.

Vihmann, M. M. (1981). 'Phonology and the development of the lexicon: Evidence from children's errors'. *Journal of Child Language* 8, 239–64.

Vygotsky, L. S. (1934/1962). *Thought and language*. Trans. E. Hanfmann and G. Vakar. Cambridge, Mass.: MIT Press.

Wales, R. J. and Walker, E. (1976). *New approaches to language mechanisms*. Amsterdam: North-Holland.

Wang, M. D. and Bilger, R. C. (1973). 'Consonant confusions in noise: A study of perceptual features'. *Journal of the Acoustical Society of America* 54, 1248–66.

Warren, R. M. (1970). 'Perceptual restoration of missing speech sounds'. *Science* 167, 393–5.

Warrington, E. K. (1981). 'Neuropsychological studies of verbal semantic systems'. *Philosophical Transactions of the Royal Society of London* B 295, 411–23. (Also published as *Psychological mechanisms of language*. London: The Royal Society and the British Academy.)

Wason, P. (1965). 'The contexts of plausible denial'. *Journal of Verbal Learning and Verbal Behavior* 4, 7–11.

Waterson, N. (1970). 'Some speech forms of an English child: A phonological study'. *Transactions of the Philological Society*, 1–24.

Weinreich, U. (1966). 'On the semantic structure of language'. In J. H. Greenberg (ed.), *Universals of Language*, 2nd edn. Cambridge, Mass.: MIT Press.

Weizenbaum, J. (1976/1984). *Computer power and human reason: From judgement to calculation*. Harmondsworth: Penguin.

Werner, H. and Kaplan, E. (1950). 'Development of word meaning through verbal context: An experimental study'. *Journal of Psychology* 29, 251–7. Also in De Cecco (1967).

Whaley, C. P. (1978). 'Word-nonword classification time'. *Journal of Verbal Learning and Verbal Behavior* 17, 143–54.

White, T. G. (1982). 'Naming practices, typicality, and underextension in child language'. *Journal of Experimental Child Psychology* 33, 324–46.

Wiegel-Crump, C. A. and Dennis, M. (1986). 'Development of word finding'. *Brain and Language* 27, 1–23.

Wittgenstein, L. (1958). *Philosophical investigations*. Trans. G. E. M. Anscombe. 2nd edn. Oxford: Basil Blackwell.

Zwicky, A. (1982). 'Classical malapropisms and the creation of a mental lexicon'. In L. K. Obler and L. Menn (eds), *Exceptional language and linguistics*. New York: Academic Press.

Index